# Case Management for Healthcare Professionals

**Rufus S. Howe, RN, MN, FNP**
**Editor**

**Precept Press, Chicago**
***Division of Bonus Books, Inc.***

98 97 96 95 5 4 3 2

Library of Congress Catalog Card Number: 93-83247

International Standard Book Number: 0-944496-37-7

Precept Press
*Division of Bonus Books, Inc.*
160 East Illinois Street
Chicago, Illinois 60611

To Ruth, my loving wife, on whom I depend far more than she knows . . .
and to my sons Christopher and Gregory, who let me relive my childhood.

# Contents

# Acknowledgments

I would like to thank the authors for taking the time to write these chapters. Case managers are extremely committed professionals, and there is little time for extra projects. I would also like to thank my professional mentor friends, Tim Williams, Martha Bell, Barry Wolcott, Cathie Burns, Kathie Errico, and Bill Griffon.

# About the Editor

Rufus S. Howe, RN, MN, FNP, is a family nurse practitioner in the United States Army Nurse Corps, serving at the United States Military Academy, West Point, New York. A noted national speaker on quality improvement and case management in the managed care environment, he is also the author of numerous publications relating to quality improvement and case management. In addition to clinically based articles, he is coauthor of *Applying Total Quality Management: A Nursing Guide*, and *Deming's 14 Points, a Nursing Interpretation*. He is a consultant for several quality improvement project teams and is developing an assessment and intervention tool for organizations that wish to implement a quality improvement program.

# Contributors

MARIE BERGER, RN, PhD, is a partner in the Creative Resources Group, a management development company, 400 S.W. Second Street, Box 2, Lake Oswego, Oregon 97034. The company conducts in-house training programs in case management.

CECELIA CAPUZZI, RN, PhD, is an associate professor at the Oregon Health Sciences University School of Nursing, 3181 Southwest Sam Jackson Park Road, Portland, Oregon 97201. Dr. Capuzzi teaches courses in health planning and health policy in the school's community health care systems department. She also is director of the Community Home Visiting Service, a faculty practice providing home visiting and case management services to maternity patients.

JOYCE CARDINAL, RN, BS, CCRN, is a case manager at Emanuel Hospital and Health Center, 2801 North Gantenbein Avenue, Portland, Oregon 97227. She also has been a critical care staff nurse, a trauma resuscitation nurse, and a critical care nurse manager.

VIRGINIA DEL TOGNO-ARMANASCO, RN, MN, is coordinator of nursing case management at Tucson Medical Center, 5301 East Grant Road, PO Box 42195, Tucson, Arizona 85733.

RUFUS S. HOWE, RNC, MN, FNP, is a family practice nurse practitioner on the staff of the Family Practice Clinic of Keller Army Hospital, West Point, New York 10996.

VICKY KNECHT KRAUSHAR, RN, MS, is a case manager at Emanuel Hospital and Health Center, 2801 North Gantenbein Avenue, Portland, Oregon 97227. Holder of a master of science degree in medical/surgical nursing from the University of Arizona, she has worked as an oncology clinical nurse specialist, as a director of staff development, and as an IV/transfusion nurse manager.

COLLEEN M. LUCAS, RN, MN, CNS, is a medical / surgical clinical nurse specialist and project manager for case management integration at Good Samaritan Hospital and Medical Center, 1015 Northwest 22nd Avenue, Portland, Oregon 97210.

JOHN C. McDONALD, RN, MS, CPQA, is director of quality review services, Baptist Memorial Hospital, 899 Madison Avenue, Memphis, Tennessee 38146. He holds a master of science degree in community health. He is nationally recognized as a lecturer and writer on health care quality and resource management.

JUDY McGEE, RN, BS, is director of nursing, Good Samaritan Hospital and Medical Center, 1015 Northwest 22nd Avenue, Portland, Oregon 97210.

KATHLEEN C. MILNE, RN, BSN, is the director of Resource Connectors, Ltd., a brokered care case management company at 5520 Southwest Macadam Avenue, Suite 270, Portland, Oregon.

BECKY MUNGAI, RN, BA, whose background includes teaching and psychology, is an independent nurse consultant in Lake Oswego, Oregon (PO Box 977, ZIP 97034), who has been an advice nurse for several years. Her specialties include pediatrics, women's health, and employment-related injuries.

KAREN PUGSLEY, RN, MSN, a lieutenant colonel in the U.S. Army Nurse Corps, is presently assigned to the Office of the Surgeon General as a consultant in community nursing services and health risk appraisal. (Mail address: 15129 Stillfield Place, Centreville, Virginia 22020)

ELLEN RADAKOVICH, RN, MN, CNS, a geriatric clinical nurse specialist, is a care manager on the staff of Resource Connectors, Ltd., 5520 Southwest Macadam Avenue, Suite 270, Portland, Oregon.

SUSAN N. RIDDICK, RN, is president of Riddick & Associates, 1903 Grove Avenue, Richmond, Virginia 23220, a medical-legal consulting firm specializing in life care planning for catastrophically injured persons. She also lectures and conducts educational programs on traumatic injury and offers consultation services in this and related areas to other health care professionals.

SOPHIA CHU RODGERS, RN, MSN, is a professional nurse case manager at Lovelace Medical Center, 5400 Gibson Boulevard, Albuquerque, New Mexico 87108. The developer of the nursing case management program at Lovelace, she also functions as an orthopedic case manager.

ROBIN THOMAS, RN, MN, FNP, is a family practice nurse practitioner on the staff of the Multnomah County Health Department, Portland, Oregon. (Mail address: 2724 Northeast Dunckley Street, Portland, Oregon 97212)

VIVIAN TILLMAN, RN, CIRS, has been a case manager for 23 years, currently specializing in workers compensation matters for a large insurance carrier. She is secretary of the Oregon Head Injury Foundation and a member of the advisory board of the Portland (Oregon) Family Head Injury Support Group and of the Portland Community College Professional Skills Program. (Mail address: c/o Industrial Indemnity, 101 Southwest Main Street, Suite 1300, Portland, Oregon 97204)

DANA UNDERDAHL, RN, BSN, is nursing quality and standards coordinator at Good Samaritan Hospital and Medical Center, 1015 Northwest 22nd Avenue, Portland, Oregon 97210.

TERESA WAGIE, RN, MS, is a case manager at Emanuel Hospital and Health Center, 2801 North Gantenbein Avenue, Portland, Oregon 97227. Holder of a master of science degree in oncology nursing from Rush University, Chicago, she has worked as a coordinator on a medical/surgical unit and as an oncology nurse manager.

SUSAN L. WELLONS, RN, BSN, PO Box 2369, Lake Grove, Oregon 97035, is a self-employed independent nurse consultant. She is the founder and chairperson of the Oregon Medical Case Management Group, a member of the National Task Force for Case Management Steering Committee for Reorganization, and a local and national board member of the Association of Rehabilitation Nurses.

LYNN D. WHEELER, RN, MSN, WHCNP, 3730 Southeast 63rd Avenue, Portland, Oregon 97206, has an extensive background in perinatal and women's health nursing. In addition to staff nursing, her experience includes childbirth education, clinical nurse specialist roles, and obstetric and gynecologic nurse practitioner care.

Editor's note: At the time they prepared their chapters, two of the contributors to this book—Rufus S. Howe and Karen Pugsley—were active duty officers in the U.S. Army Nurse Corps. The views expressed in their contributions are those of the authors and do not reflect official policy or the position of the Department of the Army, Department of Defense, or the U.S. government.

# Introduction

There are only two objectives for this book:

To organize case management into a beginning framework from which to operate.

To provide current, practical information from frontline case managers to those who are case managers, or are interested in learning more about case management.

# How to Use this Book

*Case Management For Health Care Professionals* is not meant as a comprehensive guide to case management, nor is it strictly a "how to" book. If we knew the "how to's" for everybody in every situation, putting this book together would have been a lot easier! The fact is that case management does not replicate well across organizations. Are we left with a broad concept description and not a lot of detail? I think not. Although some of the chapters are more abstract than others, we have attempted to provide as much detail as possible. It is understood that different situations will command different solutions, but try to seek out the kind of detail in each chapter you think is necessary for your situation. It may be that the finer details are best left to you because only you know what will work in your setting. All of the authors are more than willing to be contacted—I know them all and can attest to their expertise and friendliness. You will find the authors listed along with their affiliations and mailing address in the Contributors section beginning on page xv. This book then is meant to organize your thoughts and provide direction to your case management program. It is based on a case management model designed especially for this book. This model describes four dimensions of case management (described a little later) that are a first effort to discriminate between the way a case manager "operates" and the client receives health care.

The first section of this book outlines the philosophy, framework, and tools on which the rest of the book is based.

The second section describes self-care case management as we know it today. Unfortunately, very few health care providers actively recognize the power of self-care—though it lies at the very foundations of any health care intervention.

The third section describes the primary care case manager. In this model, the physician or advanced practice nurse is considered a primary care provider, and thus a candidate for primary care case management. The primary care provider as case manager is a concept in evolution. Few people are willing to write about it.

The fourth section, episodic care case management, is the fastest-developing form of case management today, mostly due to the rising costs of health care and lower reimbursement rates, which have mandated a system for cost containment.

The fifth section, brokered care case management, is the oldest form of case management. Florence Nightingale was a proponent of public health who understood that health care services must reach beyond the hospital walls. Because of the upward shift in the aging population and the move toward fewer hospital days (per DRGs), health service coordination will grow at an astounding rate and will probably dominate as a method of case management.

# Definitions of Case Management

Defining case management is not an easy task, considering the wide range of possibilities. Careful examination of the following definitions illustrates this point.

Case management is:

- Both a model and a technology for restructuring the **clinical production process** and roles that facilitate quality outcomes (Putney, Hauner, Hall, & Kobb, 1989).
- A multidisciplinary care process method that aims, by case type, to achieve a **purposeful and controlled connection between the quality of care and the costs of that care** (Olivas, Del Togno, Erikson, & Harter, 1990).
- **A process of service coordination** that links the client with formal and informal service providers to ensure the needs are met (Oleson, Thomas, & King, 1990).
- **A set of logical steps** and a process of interaction with service networks which assures that a patient receives needed services in a supportive, efficient, and cost-effective manner (McKenzie, Torkelson, & Holt, 1989).
- **A collaborative process** that assesses, plans, implements, coordinates, monitors, and evaluates services necessary to meet an individual's needs with the use of communication and available resources to promote high quality, cost-effective outcomes.

# Central Qualities

Whatever and wherever case management happens, there appear to be common threads. The following are major factors to consider in your case management program; they are gleaned from the above definitions and current literature.

## Client-Focused

Focusing on the client is sometimes not easy, but successful programs do it well. The primary care provider considers a client's perception of his or her disease in the plan of care; the staff nurse hands the critical path to the client and the family upon admission for their input; the community health nurse seeks the family's opinion on placement of an elderly client. All are examples self-care in action.

## Role Identification

The nursing profession is still undergoing rapid role transformation. One of the hidden agendas of case management is to establish once and for all the role of the nurse—and for that matter, the role of the entire health team—while delivering care. The act of case management, as we will see, necessitates increased levels of expertise. The case manager will be expected to fulfill an expanded role—one that perhaps either the person or organization may not be ready for. Many a case manager has felt the wrath of another discipline while introducing the "new role." Department boundaries are very high, and some of us (including nurses) are territorial and need to leave our scent wherever we go.

## Collaborative Practice

True collaborative practice is a beauty to behold. The health care team consists of the traditional members; doctors, nurses, therapists, and some nontraditional members—clients, family, and ancillary staff. Case management defines collaborative practice. When someone tells me they are a case manager and have critical paths up and running, I ask, "Do you have a line on the critical path for medications?" If the answer is no, the medical staff is not truly bought into collaborative practice, and the incomplete critical path is a reflection of that.

## Tracking System

The health care profession is much better at tracking money than health care practices or standards. Case management's basic premise is one of tracking and accounting for activities, timing and events that surround the client's care. Practice guidelines, critical paths, data bases, and algorithms are all mechanisms for tracking. The question becomes, "What do we track?" The short answer is that you start by tracking what "is." Establishing current practice patterns and tracking key events provides a sound basis for quality improvement of the health care delivery process.

## Mechanism for Variance Analysis

Charting variances or deviations from the usual practice patterns can be painful. A list of variations can be too revealing for anyone responsible for providing health care. The initial hurdle is to realize that deviations can be opportunities to improve service. Some variations, such as client and family variations, occur by chance. The client's response to treatment varies, and this variation may fall out of the expected range. This is an example of a variation that may be impossible to control. Case managers who are involved with catastrophic illness, for instance, can attest to the unpredictable path clients follow during care. Because of the painfulness of variance charting, many organizations put it low on the priority list. A well-balanced case management program uses variance analysis to continuously build and improve the program. The Joint Commission on Accreditation of Healthcare Organizations (JCAHO) is rapidly moving toward this ideal of "continuous quality improvement" (CQI). Each organization will be required to address what it is doing to improve its service come JCAHO survey time, and at the heart of CQI is variance analysis.

# Let's Get Started

You no doubt would like to jump to the section of the book that interests you, but please read the next two chapters first ("Framework for Case Management" and "Quality Improvement and Case Management"). Case management does not happen in a vacuum, and an understanding of the background information upon which this book is based will accelerate your learning.

Finally, let me tell you about how this book was conceived. I am a family nurse practitioner who considers himself a primary care case manager and who has a nagging feeling that there must be a better way. My research revealed that the current case management literature does not speak to the ambulatory world, and a growing frustration propelled me to explore other forms of case management. The journey was fraught with twists and turns, confusion and disarray. My challenge was to make some sense out of case management as a whole. I started to read all the case management literature I could find (well over 400 references) and spoke to as many "case managers" as possible from all over the country. Soon it was clear that I wasn't the only confused person. In a desperate attempt for organization, I developed the framework for case management. Once developed, I then sought out case managers who were recognized leaders and who were involved in successful case management programs. Not all of these case managers were nationally known, nor did they have long publishing experience. You will notice that all the authors are nurses. Case management is not limited to nursing, but most case managers are nurses.

The authors of this book met the following criteria. They were:

— case managers in their respective fields.
— committed to the concept of case management.
— involved with the design and implementation of their program.
— have made a significant local impact on the health care delivery system.
— willing and able to put down their thoughts and actions on paper for all to see.
— willing to share their expertise with others through personal contact.

I am excited about this book not because I am the editor, but because of the potential impact case management has and can make on health care. Please enjoy this book, contact the authors if you desire, and send me your comments and suggestions for the next edition.

—RUFUS S. HOWE, RN, MN, FNP

# I

# AN OVERVIEW OF CASE MANAGEMENT

# 1

# A Framework for Case Management

Rufus S. Howe, RN, MN, FNP

## Some Definitions

As is true in many fields of endeavor, the field of case management has developed a language all its own. And as in any other developing field, the words—and sometimes their meanings—tend to change. For example, *total quality management* has been variously known as *total quality management, quality management, continuous quality improvement, and quality management.* An understanding of the following terms, defined as they are currently being used in the case management field, is essential to benefiting fully from materials presented in this volume.

**Self-Care Case Management**—Any health preventive or promotive action carried out as a direct result of a person's decision to care for himself/herself.

**Primary Care Case Management**—Preventive or promotive care by a health care provider credentialed and privileged to diagnose and treat.

**Episodic Care Case Management**—Health care provided by one or more caregivers as a result of an episodic illness, injury, or condition.

**Brokered Care Case Management**—Coordinated health care provided with the intention of organizing care in an appropriate, timely, and cost-effective manner. The brokered care case manager is the least likely to engage in direct patient care.

**Critical Path**—Strictly speaking, the longest route taken to accomplish a task. "Mature" critical paths feature a time, activity, and event dimension. *Time* can be measured in minutes to years. *Activities* are specific tasks performed to arrive at the expected outcome. Activities are something one *does. Events* are those observable milestones that reflect progress toward the expected outcome. Events are something that one *sees*.

**Multidisciplinary Action Plan**—Similar to the critical path in design, but lists only time and event dimensions. Some institutions use documentation categories as defined by the Joint Commission on Accreditation of Healthcare Organizations to organize events. Examples of categories are physical, social, discharge planning, and knowledge.

**Collaborative Practice**—The sharing of practice patterns among the health care delivery team. Critical paths and multidisciplinary action plans are evidence of collaborative practice.

**Practice Guidelines**—There are several versions of practice guidelines. Practice guidelines are a consensus statement that contains diagnosis-specific information relating to etiology, history, physical assessment, decision-making mechanisms, and therapies.

**Customer and Supplier Relationships**—The recognition of both internal and external customer/supplier relationships during the clinical production process. For example, the radiology department supplies a valuable service to the health care provider. Patients are customers of physicians as well.

**Mission Statement**—A statement that serves to translate a strategic principle into a tactical framework. Strategic principles are delineated in the organizational vision statement. An example mission statement would be "To study the admission process."

**Vision Statement**—A group of statements that together sum up the organization's purpose and principles. As opposed to a mission statement, vision statements are worded in such a way that it would be impossible to attain the goal described. An example of a vision statement might be: "Millvale General Hospital will provide state-of-the-art patient education service that has no peer in the health care industry."

## Case Study

Before proceeding to a detailed discussion of the four broad categories of care named above that are provided under model case management programs—self-care, primary care, episodic care, and brokered care—it may be helpful to describe elements of these types of care by means of a case study that traces the progress of a patient through the continuum represented:

### Self-Care

Mary B. is an 82-year-old widow who lives alone in her own apartment. Mary has been able to care for herself and do the routine chores around the apartment. Shopping for food is becoming difficult because Mary can no longer drive after she failed the examination for a driver's license. Mary's circle of friends is dwindling due to deaths and relocation.

In September, Mary developed a cough that wouldn't go away. The cough was keeping her up at night, and she would occasionally have blood in her sputum. She tried over-the-counter cough medicine, but that didn't stop the cough. Her home remedy book told her to try a steam vaporizer and menthol rub, but these didn't work either. Mary's sister Edith visited her about two weeks after the cough had started. She did not like the way Mary looked, so she called her own physician and made an appointment.

### Primary Care

When Mary saw the physician, she was very sick and was exhausted due to lost sleep and poor appetite. A chest X ray showed lobar pneumonia. Based on the physician's algorithm and practice guidelines, Mary would need to be admitted to the hospital for treatment of pneumonia and for rehydration.

### Episodic Care

Mary was admitted that afternoon under diagnosis-related group (DRG) no. 89—simple pneumonia with pleurisy. Mary's health care team implemented care based on the critical path written especially for that DRG. Mary responded well to the treatments and was to be discharged on time, but her sister voiced strong concerns that Mary would need "some help" at home. An optional social service consultation was initiated and a nursing case management organization was contacted.

### Brokered Care

In concert with the hospital staff, the admitting physician, and Mary's sister, a plan of care was developed. Mary was to have a home health aide visit her three times a week for cleaning, cooking, and shopping. A nurse case manager would visit Mary as needed and report her status to the family and physician.

# Models of Case Management

## Overview

What does a case manager do? A health care worker in a hospital might assume that this person coordinates the care of patients with catastrophic illness. A public health practitioner probably would associate this person with social work or mental health. Case management as a concept is well established among certain health care specialists but not well established in the health care field as a whole. The model shown as Figure 1 proposes to unravel the mystery of what a case manager is and does.

It would be helpful for the reader to refer to Figure 1 while examining the descriptions of each case management component. Each component is mutually exclusive, yet interdependent of the others by design. Self-care case management, for example, is not anything like primary care case management, but the two may coexist in the plan of care of the primary health care adviser. Consider the following plan of care for a streptococcal throat infection:

**Diagnostic**—Throat culture.

**Therapeutic**—Penn VK 250 mg 1 four times a day for 10 days; Tylenol 325 mg 2 every 4 hours for fever and pain; warm saltwater gargle as needed to soothe throat.

**Education**—Strict handwashing. Take all Penn VK even if symptoms disappear.

**Return if**—Symptoms worsen or fever not controlled with Tylenol.

The diagnostic and medication portion of this plan of care could be initiated only by a primary care practitioner with prescriptive privileges. The rest of the instructions either direct or enhance already established self-care capacity.

| Model | Customers | Suppliers | Objective | Tools |
|---|---|---|---|---|
| **Self-Care** | Self | Professional community, media, family, friends, etc. | Maintain optimal level of health and well-being within natural boundaries and capabilities<br><br>The objective of self-care case management is to maintain an optimal level of health and well-being within natural boundaries and capabilities | Written, audio, or video media<br><br>Log books, reminder systems |
| **Primary Care** | Client | Physician<br><br>Advanced practice nurse | Provide diagnostic and intervention services that are health promotive and beyond the client's capacity for self-care | Data bases<br><br>Alert and reminder systems<br><br>Algorithms and decision trees<br><br>Critical paths |
| **Episodic Care** | Client<br><br>Primary care case manager | Physician<br><br>Advanced practice nurse (NP, CNS)<br><br>Hospital staff | During periods of stress, to provide specialized diagnostic and intervention services which are beyond the client's and primary care provider's capabilities | Data bases<br><br>Critical paths<br><br>Multidisciplinary action plans<br><br>Flow sheets<br><br>Collaborative agreements<br><br>Contractual agreements |
| **Brokered Care** | Client<br><br>Primary care case manager<br><br>Episodic care case manager | Federal and community agencies<br><br>Private, legal or trust services | To match the target population with appropriate services based on predefined agreements and standards of practice | Data bases<br><br>Customer and supplier agreements<br><br>Flow sheets |

**Figure 1.** *Models of case management*

Episodic care case management, according to this model, occurs only when called for by providers in any of the other three models of case management. A lay person can contact a podiatrist directly for an ingrown toenail, but so can a primary care provider. A brokered care manager can also assess the need and refer the person to the podiatrist. The key feature of the episodic model is that it can only be reactionary—that is, it can only be in reaction to the admission, consultation, or phone call. The episodic care manager has no way of knowing who in the population has ingrown toenails, heart disease, or an impending stroke. This episodic model "lies in waiting" until called upon.

The brokered care case manager is compared by many to an orchestra conductor: He or she may not play instruments as well as the musicians, but does know the best combinations for beautiful music. This type of case manager is in sharp contrast to any of the other models, in that a brokered care manager does not normally give direct care.

## Self-Care

The objective of self-care case management is to maintain an optimal level of health and well-being within natural boundaries and capabilities.

### Customer/Supplier

In self-care case management, the person seeking health care advice is the customer. For the most part, the suppliers of health information are friends, family, and the media. It is up to the customer to determine the reliability and validity of the information gleaned from these sources. In a research study conducted at the U.S. Military Academy, West Point, New York, the beneficiaries of the local hospital were asked what they wanted most from the health care system. An overwhelming number (89%) desired an easy source of expert opinion. Advice nurses fill this gap in some communities.

Caring for ourselves is a fundamental skill that we all possess. Like any other skill, there is a normal distribution of capabilities within a given population. Presumably, health care providers have more self-care capability than those who are not in the health field, and children, for instance, have very little self-care ability.

Caring for oneself, however, goes beyond hygiene, aspirin, and first-aid kits. Everyone should know the how, when, and where of seeking help. Moving to a strange town, losing a loved one, or becoming sick can drastically affect self-care capacities. Knowing an individual's capacity for self-care or that of a self-care agency is crucial to the understanding of why it is important to recognize self-care as a distinct form of case management. The most successful health care providers account for the capacity of their clients while developing the plan of care. Understanding this variability is important for many reasons. We know, for instance, that diabetics need to limit their intake of sweets and fats, get plenty of exercise, monitor their blood glucose, and take their medicine (if prescribed). We also know that not all diabetics are capable, either physically and emotionally, of carrying out these tasks, but even if they are, many do not. Helping to facilitate self-care for these patients becomes very important in terms of patient outcomes.

### Tools

The instruments of self-care case management center around media. Home health books, pamphlets, videos, and health-related advertisements abound. Log books for headaches, contractions, fetal movement, blood glucose, and ashthma attacks are but a few of the tools health care providers can use to facilitate self-care. Medication reminder systems such as timers and pillboxes are other examples.

### Evaluation

Evaluation in self-care case management is problematic. Research has demonstrated a wide range of "acceptable" self-care for something as simple as a cold. Most research in this area depends on self-reporting or observation, both of which have serious limitations in terms of accurate data collection. The most promising avenue for self-care evaluation remains in objective patient outcomes. There is, for example, a saliva test to determine whether a person is smoking or is exposed to tobacco smoke. Objective measures such as this can be used to evaluate the impact of a smoking cessation program or the effects of passive smoking on others.

Illustrating the difficulties in self-care evaluation is a client I once had, an elderly male with a long list of risk factors for cardiovascular disease. At every visit, I plainly outlined his risks and attempted to work out a plan with him to stop smoking, drinking, and eating foods high in fat or sodium. I made sure to document this teaching and even had the client sign his name to the chart stating that he understood each recommendation. I confronted him with the choices he was making—he was choosing to live a risky existence. You can guess the end of this story. He was admitted to our ICU with a massive stroke and died shortly thereafter. His wife became very angry because she thought we should have "saved him" by preventing the stroke in the first place. The physician showed her my documentation (complete with the client's signature) detailing my admonitions to modify his risky behavior. One can imagine the thoughts that were going through her head. The traditional "health care team to the rescue" that some expect of us turned into a striking case for self-care case management.

## Primary Care

The objective of primary care case management is to provide diagnostic and intervention services that are health promotive and beyond the client's capacity for self-care.

### Customer/Supplier

The client is the "customer" of services provided by the "supplier," either a physician, advanced practice nurse, or physician's assistant. The primary care case manager is responsible and accountable for the routine care of that person. In this model, the office staff (including the office nurse) are not considered primary care case managers because the ultimate responsibility for diagnosis and treatment rests with the primary provider.

### Setting

Primary care case management takes place in ambulatory settings such as outpatient clinics or in the client's home if the provider makes home visits. Like self-care, primary care isn't limited to a specific location.

### Tools

Tools for the primary health provider include data bases, alert and reminder systems, practice guidelines, algorithms or decision trees, and critical paths. Data base development for the ambulatory setting is now evolving into a science of its own. Early versions of these data bases tracked only enough demographic information for billing purposes. In fact, many current ambulatory data bases emphasize administrative rather than health care issues. A data base has one major advantage: It doesn't forget or overlook important information.

Alert and reminder systems include flow sheets generated by the primary provider to track specific health care parameters that need addressing at regular intervals. Flow sheets are an excellent way to quickly document and refer to health care milestone information; also, they can easily be individualized.

Practice guidelines, standard orders, or standard operating procedures are time-tested methods of describing practice patterns. Practice guidelines are useful in that they form a basis for development of algorithms and critical paths. Furthermore, practice guidelines can become a statement of unity between providers and disciplines that can support a collaborative practice base.

Algorithms, or decision trees, represent an exciting avenue in health care. Algorithms are designed to reflect current standards of practice and aid in the decision-making process. Unfortunately, many providers shy away from algorithms, stating they are "cookbook" or "robot" medicine. There are many arguments for and against the regular use of algorithms. More mature algorithms include the art and the science of health care and are not overly restrictive.

Critical paths are not generally used in ambulatory care for many reasons. Among the major ones:

- Critical paths are designed for a specific DRG, and little has been done so far in this regard for ambulatory care
- Critical paths follow time frames that are usually measured in days or hours
- Ambulatory critical paths would measure time in weeks, months, or years
- Most of the time, only one provider is involved with health care. The current design for critical paths lends itself more to multifunctional care, but use of critical paths in the ambulatory setting warrants further investigation.

### Evaluations

No matter what system or combination of systems of case management are in place, effective evaluation cannot occur without a concurrent system of tracking practice patterns. The data base method is the top candidate for effective concurrent tracking. Algorithms can act as a "criteria map" for auditing charts for key events. Analysis of provider, system, and client variances is possible through combined use of data base and algorithm or critical paths.

## Episodic Care

The objective of episodic case management is to provide, during periods of stress, specialized diagnostic and intervention services that are beyond the capabilities of the client and the primary care provider.

### Customer/Supplier

The customer in the episodic care model is the person who, by the nature of some extraordinary circumstances, cannot be cared for by the primary health care provider. The supplier may be a hospital; day surgery center; birthing center; specialized treatment center, such as substance abuse or weight loss; or a specialist, such as a podiatrist or physical therapist.

### Setting

Examples of physical settings have been listed, but the setting in this case refers to timing. In other words, when does this kind of case management occur? Episodic care management is episodic. That means there must be a starting and ending point to the care. Put another way, episodic care concerns itself with deviations in health and attempts to bring the client back to prior levels of health. Following is an example:

Start of the episode: Mr. A. is a 50-year-old blue-collar worker who injured an arm on the job. Mr. A. was admitted through the emergency room to the orthopedic service for reduction and casting of a fractured femur and spent several days in the hospital. He was cared by the orthopedic health care team using a critical path designed for fracture of the femur. Mr. A. received all relevant services per the critical path.

End of episode: After several months of rehabilitation, the orthopedic team cleared Mr. A. for returning to work. Mr. A. no longer saw the orthopedist, but resumed regular medical care with his primary health provider.

### Tools

The critical path is the cornerstone of episodic case management — many words in this book are devoted to its creation and implementation. The critical path is far more than a "visible card file in new clothes"; it is the result of thoughtful analysis and prioritization of the needs of the organization, provider, and client. Once in place, the critical path serves as proof of collaborative practice and managed care. The multidisciplinary action plan (MAP) is another key document that complements the critical path. The MAP is designed to track measurable outcomes or events that should occur as a result of the interventions listed in the critical path.

### Evaluation

Most episodic care facilities are bogged down with evaluation. This evaluation takes the form of externally mandated requirements from funding sources—traditional "quality assurance." Evaluating case management services is accomplished using quality improvement style problem-solving and data analysis.

## Brokered Care

The objective of brokered care case management is to match the target population with appropriate services based on predefined agreements and standards of practice.

### Customer/Supplier

Brokered care case managers are sometimes confused about who their customer (or supplier) is. Is it the client or the family? The insurance company or the trust officer? The long-term nursing facility or its staff? The physician or the attorney? Sometimes it is hard to tell who the customer is, and that creates problems. Most of the confusion surrounding this form of case management centers on this issue alone. In reality, the brokered care case manager interacts with a tangled web of customers and suppliers that often includes both customers and suppliers.

The case managers in this brokered model are constantly breaking new ground. Most of them are nurses who have, by necessity, turned into nurse entrepreneurs. But this expanded role calls for expertise in marketing, advertising, sales, and accounting—skills not likely to have been developed in a typical nursing school curriculum.

### Setting

Brokered case management occurs anywhere and any time. These case managers are a flexible lot who can perform under almost any circumstances. They are often required to negotiate with high-powered attorneys for small concessions, and with home health aides for major factors that directly affect the client.

### Tools

The tools of the brokered care case manager center around time-activated events and routine activities. Most interventions are tracked using daily planning calendars and alert and reminder flow sheets. Routine information is kept on specially designed data bases that can generate demographic information on clients. Like primary care, brokered care does not use critical paths per se. Some organizations have developed a "care matrix" that lists physical, psychological, social, and environmental factors specific to the age of the client. From this matrix, a plan of care can be customized.

### Evaluation

Evaluating brokered care is best accomplished using criteria mapping and customer survey techniques. Criteria mapping (examining salient features of care) is the same thing as checking to see if the provider did what he/she promised. Brokered care is heavily laden with small details. Knowing how much and what "falls through the cracks" can directly affect both client care and satisfaction. Because it is extremely important to the brokered care organization to know its customer, regular feedback is essential. Surveys—either telephone follow-up or written instruments—are the most cost-effective for this purpose.

## Summary

This beginning framework for case management strives to explain the verb "to case manage." Note that each model flows logically from the other and is based on capacities of the provider and not the client. In the self-care model, the provider (self) is overwhelmed, so the primary care model is approached. If the primary care provider needs help, the episodic care providers come to the rescue. When the needs extend beyond what any of the models can provide, the brokered care case manager takes over to coordinate care.

Even though the objectives and settings are different for each model of case management, the tools are basically the same. This is important because establishing links between models is paramount. Establishing the links, however, may be the hardest step in the evolution of this model. Because providers' responsibilities to clients extend past their own services, providers must construct algorithms and critical paths containing "links" to the other models. Many of these links already exist, but many are neglected. Prenatal care providers in one clinic should coordinate their care (and paperwork) with that of the labor and delivery department of the local hospital. Surprisingly, many clinics and hospitals do not do this. Gaining access to primary health care providers for expert advice is a common problem; primary care providers do not always communicate well with referral sources or episodic care facilities, a fact that in turn disturbs the continuity of care and post-hospitalization follow-up. Finally, both episodic and primary care case managers may be unsure of the role of the brokered care case manager's role, leading to underutilization.

The hope, then, is that through the understanding of case management in its various manifestations, clients will be better served with the right care at the right time, and for the right cost.

# 2

# Quality Improvement and Case Management

Rufus S. Howe, RN, MN, FNP

The literature is replete with analysis and discussion of quality improvement (QI) and case management as separate concepts, but little has been written on the combination of the two. The objectives for this chapter, therefore, are to briefly describe the nature, history, and direction of QI, list names and contributions of persons credited with laying the foundation for QI, and describe the three aspects of QI and how case management applies to each.

## The Nature of Quality

To begin a discussion of quality, a few questions need to be posed. What is quality? Is your perception of quality the same as mine? Does improving quality increase the cost of a product or service? And how can quality be improved? There are answers to these difficult questions—too many answers.

Most experts define quality as "satisfying or delighting" the customer in some way. Satisfaction with the product or service promotes the concept of the competitive edge—satisfied customers will stay. In manufacturing circles, quality can mean conformance to specifications, fitness for use, or zero defects. In the service industry, of which health care is one sector, some balk at the thought of defining quality as an absence of defects. "The human response to our interventions is too unpredictable to expect zero defects," they say. Others maintain that in the spirit of QI, zero defects is a worthwhile and attainable goal. No one organization will be free from defects all the time, but the closer one comes to this lofty goal, the higher quality the service must be.

The key to defining quality lies within one's own setting. An organizational definition and plan for quality is an important first step. One way to define quality is to use a vision statement setting forth the purpose and principles of the organization. Developed by the leadership, the statement is then distributed for all to see and adopt. This allows the entire staff to come to a full understanding of what is meant by the word *quality* as defined by the organization.

Everyone has a different perception of quality. In health care organizations, the doctors, nurses, and administrators assume that they know what is best for the clients, and that is how decisions are made. Unfortunately, the only time a customer-driven desire is adopted is when that customer becomes the "squeaking wheel." *Know your customer* is an old adage in the QI literature, and it is an important one. Knowing your customer, both internally and externally, will help to "delight and satisfy."

It has been shown over and over again that as quality increases, costs decrease. Many of us can identify with the cost of quality—it might be called the "planned ineptitude" of the system. A doctor orders his lab work "STAT", because if he doesn't, the results won't get back to him in a reasonable amount of time. The supply clerk orders more of a particular product than is needed because "there are always 10% that are not usable." And finally, a committee is formed with more members than necessary because only half of them will attend meetings. A list of planned ineptitudes could be endless.

And how can quality be improved? To reduce the cost of quality, the process in question must consistently produce to right results at the right time, with the least complexity possible. Typically, the blame for wrong acts falls on people. But QI experts have demonstrated that in any given situation, people are *not* the problem 85% of the time.

# History of Quality Improvement

It is beyond the scope of this book to provide a detailed chronology of the development of the quality movement, but a short explanation will help to put this "steamroller" of a movement in perspective.

During the post-World War II period, American industry could do no wrong. Much of Europe and all of Japan were in ruin. America could well afford to produce second-rate goods because we were for all intents and purposes the only show in town. Because of Japan's almost complete devastation, the Japanese leadership made some very significant decisions. First, they decided to spend no more money on defense, resolving to fight no more. Second, the manufacturing companies decided to start from scratch. They built new factories and new philosophy with the help of persons qualified to teach them how to build quality into their products. Prior to the war, "Made in Japan" was synonymous with "cheap" or "poorly made." The top leaders understood this and were determined to turn this perception around.

The transition to high-quality goods and services did not take place overnight. For example, the first Honda automobile sold in this country was not of top quality. The company spent years after that adopting new philosophies and learning new methods for QI. It was inevitable, however, that with such diligence, the Japanese eventually would produce a very high-quality product at very competitive prices. The Honda line of cars is now one of the most highly regarded in its class today.

Where was America during this time? It would be unfair to say that we ignored Japan's rise as a world-class manufacturing force. But the truth is that we ignored *why* Japan rose to the top. Incredibly, for most American companies it was business as usual until manufacturing plants began closing down after losing market share. The Japanese simply outdid us. They could deliver a high-quality product—one that we were "delighted" with—at a lower price than its American counterpart.

Soon, major American companies such as Ford, General Electric and Harley-Davidson made the move to "total quality management," a "new" concept to us that was decades old in Japan. The results have been positive. As in Japan, the move to quality improvement has not been fast, but the pace is sure.

In the early days, most QI applications were in the manufacturing area. Service industries, such as health care, have not had the benefit of years of trial and error. The truth is that the health care field is in the trial-and-error phase now. The health care QI literature, once nonexistent, is plentiful. Most of the early literature concentrated on QI philosophy and principles and attempted to sell the concept to the reader. Today, one can find papers describing full implementations of QI programs in small and large health care organizations.

## Key Figures in Quality Improvement

A detailed history of the movement to improve quality of goods and services in America would contain the names of many individuals and organizations whose innovations contributed to increasingly sophisticated philosophies and methodologies. In the brief summary presented here, it will be possible to mention only a few individuals whose contributions are of special importance.

Dr. Walter Shewhart, a statistician, is widely credited with developing statistical process control and describing the presence of variation within a process. This method of analyzing the performances of a process remains central to QI today. Dr. Shewhart also developed the "plan-do-check-act" paradigm, which remains an important tool for problem-solving in QI.

Dr. W. Edwards Deming, another statistician, is probably best known for his pivotal role in Japan's rise as a world industrial power and as the author of the now-famous "14-point transition to quality improvement." Now in his nineties, Dr. Deming has finally developed a strong following in the United States. It is ironic to note that the Japanese emperor awarded Dr. Deming Japan's most prestigious medal over 20 years ago when he was virtually unknown in this country.

Dr. Joseph Juran, yet another statistician, has had a significant impact on our understanding of the meaning of quality. His quality of design and performance models have helped us to understand and measure another of his contributions—the cost of quality.

Hitoshi Kume is an expert in statistical methods for quality improvement. He is a specialist in quality control and has published widely on this subject.

# Philosophy of Quality Improvement

Of the three distinct dimensions of quality improvement—as a philosophy, as a management platform, and as a set of methodologies—the underlying philosophy undergirding the entire effort is of fundamental importance. This philosophy is best described as a set of principles that support QI. The following principles are derived from the literature and are generally thought of as "core" principles. These principles are self-evident, but as a group they are difficult to adopt. The prospective case manager will do well to keep these principles in mind while designing, selling, and implementing a case management program.

1. **Top Management's Accountability**—Without top management's full commitment, the program is doomed. A program of education through seminars and real life examples of successful small case management programs in your institution will help to gain this commitment. The organization as a whole has to embrace the meaning of quality and desire to become "world class." This is why top management must adopt the philosophy and insist on quality service. Case management is ideally suited for QI because of its systems of tracking and accountability.
2. **Customer-Driven Organization**—As was stated earlier, knowing who your customers are and what they want is of critical importance. Case managers should always include their customers in the design and evaluation aspects of the program.
3. **Service-Oriented Strategy**—The concept of service and support must pervade the organization. Support staff should not lose sight of the end customer. The critical path is a handy "menu" to educate and inform the client during the episode of illness, for example. Another aspect of service is production or service line delivery. The "servers" or suppliers of care are actors in a production process that directly affects a given patient outcome. Case managers, then, become designers and implementers of this service line production process.
4. **New Management Style**—In the move to quality, managers become more responsive to the needs of their customers. Middle managers act as liaisons between top management and case managers. Managers in a QI organization "walk the talk" and are aware of the frustrations of their subordinates, listening attentively to their suggestions for improvement. Top management must take the lead in accepting, then adopting suggestions from service line workers. Many case management programs include a mechanism for variance reporting. These variances often act as proof-positive events that are used for QI initiatives.
5. **Work Force Empowerment**—Employee involvement is the cornerstone of a successful QI program. Case managers are often in a unique position to suggest, then implement changes. These suggestions are generated during multidisciplinary team meetings whose sole purpose is to design the most efficient care plan for a given patient population.
6. **Influence without Authority**—There are many processes within any organization. Each of these processes has steps that are monitored by people who can be considered process owners. In a QI organization, process owners have authority over their processes. Case managers have a set of processes they own and can change as needed without fear of retribution.
7. **Performance Systems**—Performance appraisal is based solely on the contribution of each employee to QI. The hallmark of a QI performance appraisal is the absence of numerical quotas or number ranking. Employees should not be rated on factors over which they have no true control and are system-dependent. Case managers can, through before-and-after evaluation, measure patient outcomes, costs, length of stay, etc., to demonstrate the efficiency of case management services.
8. **Prevention-Oriented**—Employees realize that solving problems early is less costly

than solving them late. Case managers do this very well because a large percentage of their time is spent in the planning phase before the actual implementation.

9. **Team Approach**—Every case management model uses a team approach. Multidisciplinary teams are used to formulate and revise the program. Consensus is difficult for some Americans, but necessary in a QI organization.
10. **Statistical Thinking**—Thinking statistically is not an innate characteristic for most of us. The statistics used in QI are basic and simple to learn, but they aren't the only consideration. Many QI experts extol the virtues of management by facts—not hunches or experience. In a QI organization, experience is balanced with data to support implementation of improvement initiatives. (See Figure 1) Case managers examine practice patterns, tally survey results, and operate from data bases, critical paths, and algorithms.

| Data Characteristics | Data Source | Comments |
|---|---|---|
| Most subjective | Single opinion | Desk theory (educated guess) |
| | Brainstorming | Expert (?) panel |
| | Storyboarding | Organized hunches |
| | Nominal group technique | Opinions without fear |
| | Survey | Compares hunches of a few with a larger population |
| | Interview | Increases clarity of survey questions |
| | Observation | Field study, defines characteristics of phenomena |
| | Indirect measurement | Done when direct measurement is not practical (Blood Pressure) |
| Most objective | Direct measurement | As reliable as measuring tool |

**Figure 1.** *Data Reliability Continuum*

11. **Ongoing Education and Training**—The thought transformation is not accomplished without a lot of reading, listening, and discussion. Ample opportunity must be given to all to learn and to implement QI. The case managers must also be supported professionally and educationally in order to refine their skills. The staff or organization also will need to be educated in the ways of case management. In many settings, this could mean one-on-one education.

# Management Platform

The second dimension of QI is as that of a management platform. A management platform can be defined as an organization's manifestation of its management philosophy. Notice that QI is not included in the definition. It is entirely possible to have a management platform without a QI philosophy. More will be said on that topic later in this chapter, but let us first turn our attention to the major health care management platform issue—managed care.

Managed care is care that is *managed*. It differs from what we are already doing because much of health care is *not* managed. We do not, for the most part, have shared practice patterns. Examine the following examples, then think of some others on your own:

- The way one doctor treats a cold may be completely different from the way the next one does.
- The way one surgeon wants his operating sets always differs from the next one's.
- The length of stay for a given diagnosis varies widely among doctors and hospitals.
- There are many instances of persons using unnecessary diagnostic services.

These costly inconsistencies are a part of unmanaged care. Case management, in any of its forms, aims to manage care on several levels. First, a shared practice pattern is developed, tested, and refined. This practice pattern can take the form of an alert and reminder system, practice guideline, or a critical path. Second, the cost of that care is reviewed through multidisciplinary teams that discuss acceptable alternative treatment options. Finally, variances are tracked on a concurrent basis for the purpose of correcting special problems and controlling common ones. These variances are usually divided into patient, provider, and system variances. Each of these variances is further divided into common cause and special cause.

# Quality Improvement Methodology

The above discussion of variances, process development, and improvement afforded by case management leads logically into the last dimension of quality improvement—the statistical thinking of QI methodology.

There are as many problem-solving strategies as there are problems. To address this problem, QI pioneers developed a series of basic tools that could be used no matter what the situation. These are collectively known as the "basic tools of quality improvement." None of them are hard to learn and use. It is not necessary to use all of them for every problem.

Brainstorming and storyboarding are among several approaches that can be used by groups charged with problem solving (see Figure 2). Brainstorming is useful in generating a creative, free-flowing exchange of ideas. Be careful not to criticize anyone during this process because it might hamper creativity. Normally, ideas are jotted down for all to see and discuss.

Storyboarding is similar to brainstorming, but features a more organized approach. Ideas are jotted down separately on cards to be categorized by the group under major headings. If the group is stalled on a fine point and is trying to discover a root cause, it might try asking Why? four or five times. With this technique, in order to stay on the subject its important to "nest" the whys. Each question should be a logical subset of the preceding "why" question.

There are times when the team needs to prioritize its information in order to function more efficiently and achieve greater impact. One of the tools of prioritization is the nominal group technique, which is especially helpful when there is a need to vote secretly on sensitive issues. A secret ballot is used to record ranking by individuals of the top five or ten issues. The cards

| Activity | Advantages | Disadvantages |
|---|---|---|
| **Brainstorming**<br><br>**Members suggest thoughts at random** | Free flow of ideas, spontaneous, most creative | Only works when team members are comfortable with each other, are nonjudgemental, and are dealing with politically safe issues |
| **Storyboarding**<br><br>**Members write thoughts on index cards, then put into major heading piles** | Excellent tool for organizing many different thoughts. Major headings can be transferred into a fishbone diagram | May stifle creativity because group interaction is limited in the early phases of the exercise |
| **Nominal group technique**<br><br>**Members secretly submit their thoughts on index cards, then a secret ballot sets the priority of each idea** | Excellent method to prioritize sensitive issues. Allows members to honestly contribute ideas without fear of retribution | Rigid process that disallows group synergy and creativity |
| **5 why's**<br><br>**To look for a root cause, why? is asked 4-5 times** | Excellent method of finding root causes, looking upstream | Sometimes difficult to "nest" why's. Easy to get off track. |

**Figure 2.** *Group Think Methods*

are then collected by a disinterested body and ranked as indicated by the vote. The group can agree to whittle the new list down and vote repeatedly until the top five, four, three, or two issues are selected.

Another prioritization tool is the Pareto chart (Figure 3). The Pareto chart was developed as a result of the Pareto principle, or 80/20 rule, which states that 80% of problems come from 20% of items. Put another way, the Pareto chart separates the vital few from the trivial many. This chart is used to display the relative frequency of items.

The storyboarding technique described above is especially useful when the group attempts to describe a process or to construct a top-down flow chart showing the steps and substeps in a given process. A critical path is a very mature form of a top-down flow chart. Sometimes a detailed flow chart needs to be developed. This is especially true when there are a fair number of decision points in a process and there is confusion among team members about the placement of these points. It should be remembered that constructing a detailed flow chart is a time-consuming task and that too much or too little detail will defeat its purpose. The detailed flow chart is the second hardest of all the tools to use.

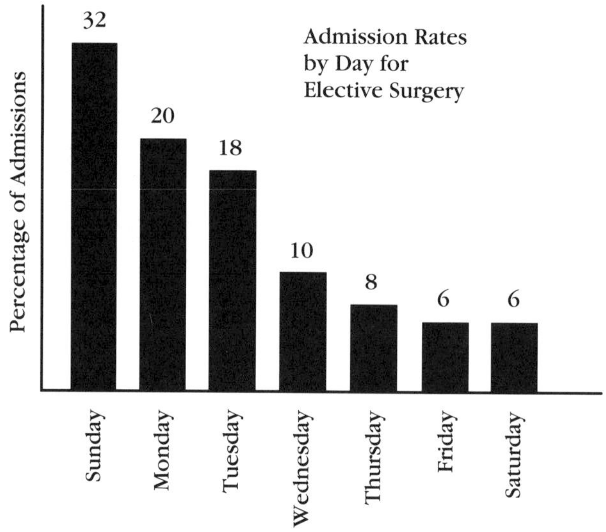


**Figure 3.** *Pareto Chart*

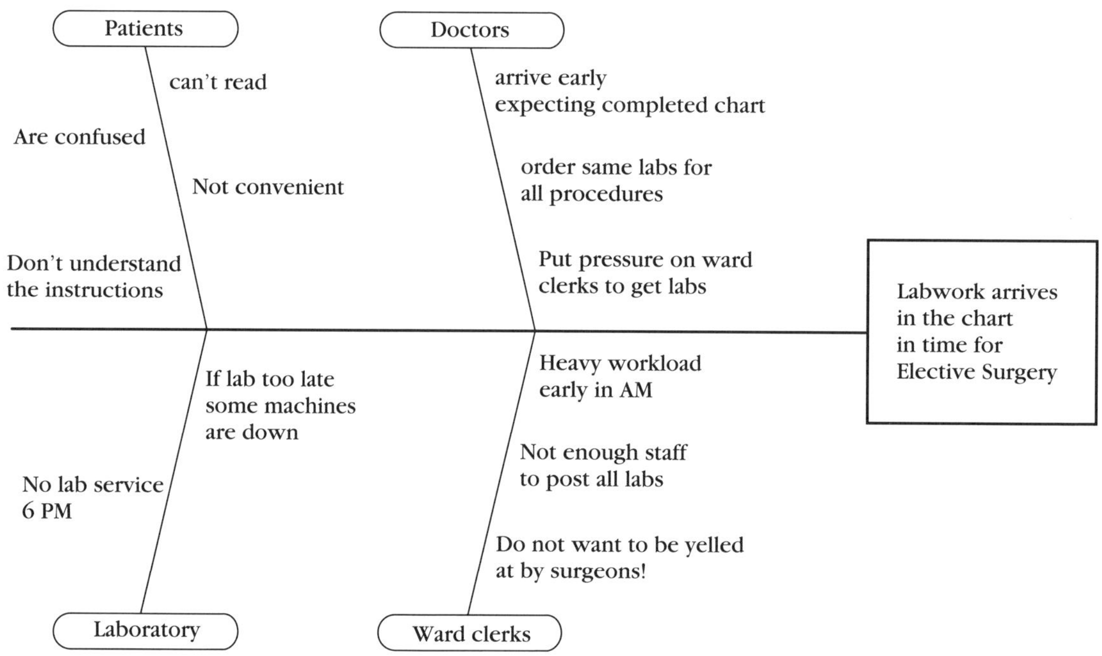


**Figure 4.** *Fishbone Diagram*

The hardest tool for most teams is the cause-and-effect diagram. This tool is also called a fishbone diagram or the Ishikawa diagram (after its inventor, Kaoru Ishikawa) (see Figure 4). The quality characteristic is the spine, while primary, secondary, and tertiary subcharacteristics form the ribs. Developing this diagram requires patience. Beginner teams sometimes spend several hours developing a workable cause-and-effect diagram, but the effort is worthwhile because the information gathered is essential for understanding the process.

## Tools of Data Collection

Tools of data collection include run sheets, tally sheets, histograms, and survey instruments. All of these tools are difficult to apply properly. Careful analysis must precede a decision to use them in actual data collection. The best advice is to consult research texts or a qualified researcher before proceeding. A run sheet tracks continuous data. Nurses use run sheets to track vital signs such as temperature, pulse, and respiration. Case managers might construct a run sheet to track the number of patients admitted with a particular diagnosis over the previous year in order to uncover temporal variances. A tally sheet is used to record raw data by category. Care should be taken to collect data in a meaningful way. A good tally sheet will automatically stratify data and display its distribution.

A histogram is a bar graph that displays a pattern (see Figure 5). The case manager may want to track the number of patients admitted under a certain disease by day of the week. The raw data are collected with a tally sheet, then transferred onto a histogram. Care should be taken in categorizing data; each category should be mutually exclusive and include an equal interval.

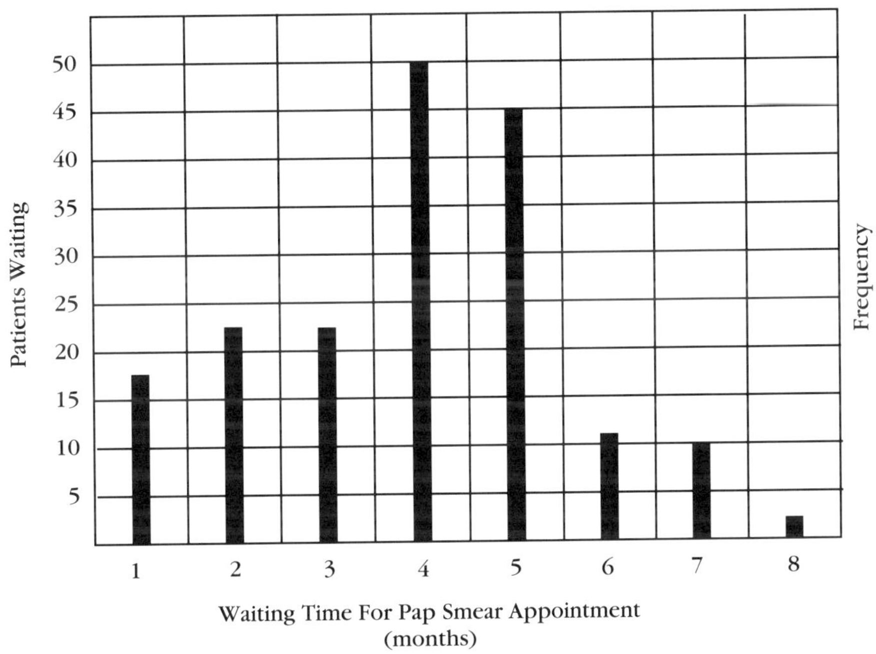


**Figure 5.** *Histogram*

Surveys come in many forms. The basic principles are as follows:

- Write down what you want to accomplish with the survey
- Assure the respondent of confidentiality
- Ask demographic questions last
- Plan for maximum return
- Once developed, have an expert panel review the survey for face and content validity
- Pilot the instrument with a small sample first

- Attempt to code the answers and perform the intended statistical analysis
- Refine the instrument based on pilot testing

The tool for quality control is the statistical process control chart (Figure 6). This chart, which has several applications, is based on the concept of variation within the system. The middle line represents the mathematical average or mean, while the upper and lower lines represent limits of reasonable variation. The usual reasonable variation is defined as three standard deviations above and below the mean. Data points falling within these lines are the result of a common cause variation; data points outside of the upper and lower control limits are due to a special cause variation. (The best explanation of this chart is found in Hitoshi Kume's book, *Statistical Methods for Quality Improvement*, AOTS (ISBN 4-906224-34-2 C0034).

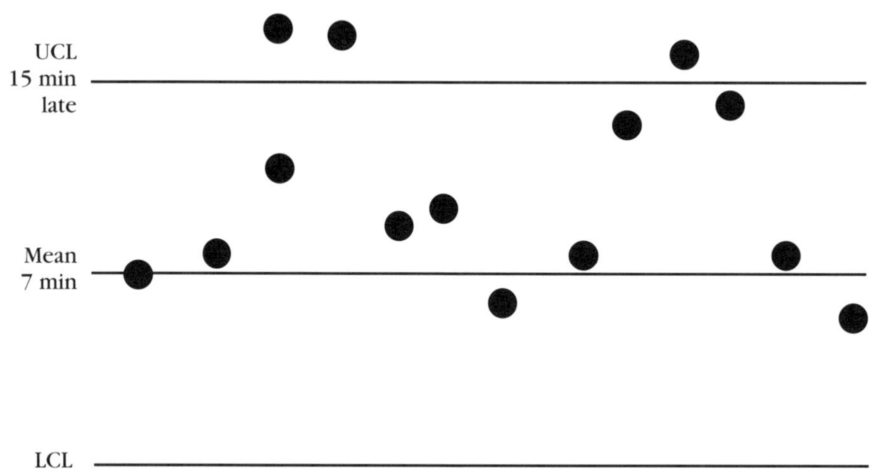


**Figure 6.** *Statistical Process Control Chart*

## Summary

Some hospitals in the United States have focused on the first two dimensions of quality improvement—that of a philosophy and that of a management platform. Several organizations have incorporated variance sheets in their case management programs, and many quality improvement teams have been initiated as a direct result of information gleaned from case management tracking. Most of this is the result of knowing the customer *and* the process. These teams are using the aforementioned tools to discover root causes, prioritize findings, collect data, and then to develop or refine the process. This process results in the development of the critical path, practice guideline, or algorithm.

Some organizations, eager to jump on the case management bandwagon, have instituted a case management program without adopting a QI philosophy. Others have adopted a QI philosophy without initiating a case management program. Both groups should reevaluate their approach to health care delivery, for the reason that in developing a case management program, one needs to combine a balanced approach to quality improvement with a mechanism for improving the program. Maintaining a competitive edge by following QI principles, managing health care delivery wisely, and providing for continuous improvement will place almost any case management program on the road to success.

# 3

# Traits and Skills of the Nursing Case Management Team

Marie Berger, RN, PhD

With the competitive environment in health care, hospitals have been struggling to find ways to maximize their financial and human resources while maintaining the quality of patient care. One of the strategies used to accomplish this goal has been to look for different ways of managing the patient care process. Nursing case management, a professional practice model that focuses on managed care in acute care settings, is one of the most prominent systems for patient care that has emerged. Case management moves nurses from planned care to managed care by organizing the work process within a specified time frame for a patient's episode of illness. Nurses, along with other health professionals involved with care of the patient during a specific episode of illness, identify desired patient outcomes for each day of the hospital stay. Nurse case managers assume responsibility for mobilizing and coordinating appropriate resources to achieve these outcomes. The goals of a case management program are to facilitate successful patient outcomes, to promote collaboration between health professionals, to coordinate care so that duplication and/or delay of service is avoided, and to facilitate the earliest possible discharge of the patient.

Even though it can be seen as a new strategy, case management is not new to nursing practice. The expert nurse in the acute care setting has always known what treatment, tests, medications, etc., certain physicians typically order on a specific day. The difference is that with the case management model, the expert nurse's knowledge is conveyed to other nurses through a written, detailed daily plan of care in a format similar to the PERT charts used by managers and administrators to list various tasks that make up a program or project and to indicate the time frames for their completion. Every nurse caring for the patient has access to this written plan of care. Even when the expert nurse is not available, the nurse who is a novice practitioner or an expert nurse unfamiliar with the care of a particular patient can provide efficient quality patient care. For this reason, development and implementation of nursing case management programs is proliferating.

For a case management program to be successful, the right people have to be selected to design and implement it. Whether the person is the hospital-wide coordinator of the program, the head nurse, or the nursing case manager, the skills and personality characteristics of these key team members play an important role in the success of the program and thus deserve attention. This chapter will describe some of the important skills and characteristics needed by these individuals and the potential effects of personality type on program development and implementation.

# Brainstorming

One way to identify the skills and personality characteristics of the team members is to use a brainstorming technique. When my partner and I present the roles component in our workshops on the development and implementation of a nursing case management program, we ask participants to pretend that they are in the process of interviewing candidates for three positions: the hospital-wide case management coordinator, the nurse manager on the unit where the case management program is to begin, and the nurse case manager. We ask participants to think about what characteristics and skills they believe are important for each of these key individuals to have. As you might suspect, groups develop a detailed and varied list, ranging from "good communication skills" to "having a life outside of work." We have found, however, that there is remarkable consistency across groups in identifying what can be called the human relations skills. All groups identify excellent communication skills such as: active listening, ability to answer questions, and sensitivity to nonverbal messages as important skills for individuals in all three roles. Good interpersonal skills, i.e., "people skills," are also commonly identified as important for individuals regardless of the role they have on the team. These skills include the ability to help others develop and grow and the ability to facilitate group cohesion and staff morale. Psychological characteristics commonly identified as important for people in all three roles are self-confidence, high self-esteem, and a low level of need for control.

Characteristics and skills that are typically identified as important for the hospital-wide coordinator include: understand the research process, be goal-directed, a self-starter, be a good time manager, charismatic, trustworthy, have the ability to see the "big picture" as well as the details, and have the ability to function independently.

Important differences in the identified skills and characteristics begin to emerge around the level of clinical knowledge and skills people think each person should have. They want the hospital-wide coordinator to have broad clinical knowledge with some recent clinical application. They expect the person to have some "system savvy" and to be able to function as a broker and innovator. The innovator skills include knowing how to "manage, live with, and love" change, and to think creatively. Brokering skills include the ability to build and maintain a power base in the system, to negotiate agreement between and across many different groups, and to sell new ideas. Brokering skills also encompass the ability to respond to the external environment and to interpret the case management program to stakeholders and interested parties outside the institution.

Some of these same brokering skills are identified for the nurse manager but are not emphasized as much. Rather, groups typically identify facilitation and mentoring skills more often for the nurse manager than they do for either the hospital-wide coordinator or the nurse case manager. More specific clinical skills are expected for the nurse manager than for the hospital-wide coordinator. Groups frequently state that it is critical that staff nurses and physicians respect the clinical abilities of the nurse manager. They also emphasize that she must also have a high level of legitimacy for these skills. She must be a cheerleader with an ability to recognize the staff's talents and abilities, to be fair in assignments, and to feel good about seeing staff develop. Other skills most often mentioned specifically for the nurse manager fall within what can be called the director and producer role competencies, such as: taking initiative, goal setting, delegating, personal productivity, and motivating others.

The case manager must have the respect of staff and physicians for her clinical skills and knowledge. She must be able to work well autonomously, be committed to the program, be knowledgeable about the system, be a good problem solver, and be able to work well with the nursing staff and members of the support services.

The clinical skills required of the nursing case manager are more specific than those of either the hospital-wide coordinator or the nurse manager. The relationship between the physician(s) on the case management team and the nurse case manager is very important to the success of the program. Groups always mention that this relationship has to be based on mutual respect and collegiality. Other skills most commonly identified for the nurse case manager fall within the coordinator and monitor roles. They include such things as attention to detail and accurate documentation, tracking activity and performance, planning, organizing, and maintaining work flow, trouble shooting, and establishing and enforcing compliance to standards.

Although these lists are helpful in a general way, it is very difficult to gather such broad information about a person during an interview. In addition, it is unrealistic to think that one person could possibly fill the expectations these lists imply. The second way to look at the characteristics of the people involved in the case management program is to use a more objective measure. The remainder of this chapter will examine one such measure, the Myers-Briggs Temperament Indicator.

# Myers-Briggs Temperament Indicator

The Myers-Briggs Temperament Indicator (MBTI) can be used to match peoples' preferences with the requirements of the job they are expected to perform. Doing this provides a positive environment for both personal success and the success of the project. The MBTI is more objective than lists generated by brainstorming and can help maximize the potential success of the program by reducing the unproductive interpersonal and intra-organizational conflict that results from placing individuals in positions that are not compatible with their personalities. Individuals applying for positions in the case management team or those already in the positions would find the MTBI helpful in assessing their strengths and their blindspots in a nonthreatening and nonjudgmental way.

Since its publication by Consulting Psychologists Press, Inc., in 1975, over one million people have taken the MBTI. It has become one of the most widely used psychological instruments in groups and organizations. The instrument focuses on four pairs of preferences that address how we get energized, how we take in information, how we make our decisions, and whether we prefer to have closure and structure or openness and flexibility. It helps people identify their own preferences and how these preferences affect their working relationships, their communication, and their decision making.

We will begin our discussion by looking at how we value diversity in the workplace. Nearly all of us say that we accept and respect differences between ourselves and others. But in reality, truly accepting and understanding such differences is not a simple matter for even the most open-minded person. One way we deal with differences is by "all in fun" teasing through name-calling. "She's such a motor-mouth"; "He's such an eager beaver"; or "She's so uptight." Name-calling is a convenient and often accepted way to label and catalog another person's differences. Often it seems the natural thing to do. The person who insists on reading over every word of a document three times is called a "nitpicker" (or worse); the one who comes into your office talking continuously even though you are obviously busy is called a "chatterbox"; the boss who never gives praise is labeled a "cold fish"; the one who wants to do everything his own way or is always asking questions is called either a "rebel," a "troublemaker," or a "royal pain."

The fact is that each of us has our own way of relating to situations and people and of meeting the challenges we face in our lives. One person's style may be perceived by another as annoying, distracting, or aggressive. These differences in style can cause a great deal of misunderstanding and miscommunication in the work place. In the process, feelings get hurt and productivity, morale, and quality suffer. The ability to get a program such as case management off the ground successfully is directly linked to the degree to which key players in the program communicate effectively with one another. This does not imply that everyone has to be best friends or that there even has to be a frank and open exchange of views. What it does mean is that there has to be a way for all of our good intentions about respecting differences to be put into play. One way to do this is to understand how to use "type" in the workplace, a process that has been called "typewatching" by Krueger & Theusen (1991). As these writers point out in their book, ***Type Talk At Work***, "typewatching" is a good way to celebrate our differences without making judgments. It also helps us to use these differences constructively rather than allowing them to create strife. Typewatching is useful for a number of problems we face in organizations and teams. For example, there are some individuals who, because of their type, are natural at engaging people, making them feel at ease and affirmed. There are others with a different type who are more reserved and who feel less comfortable relating directly with people. Some individuals are adept at dealing with changes in the organization and are willing and able to work against last-minute deadlines. Others cannot handle such situations. Some people like to generate ideas, explore the possibilities for the future, and look at the big picture, while others want to concentrate on the details in the here and now. All of these differences can be recognized by the skillful typewatcher.

The first step in typewatching is to discover our own preferences, to look at how they are formed, and what they mean in our lives. According to Carl Jung, the noted psychoanalyst, each of us is born with particular preferences that are reinforced and developed throughout our lives. According to type theory, there are four pairs of preference alternatives:

| | | |
|---|---|---|
| Extraversion | vs. | Introversion |
| Sensing | vs. | iNtuition |
| Thinking | vs. | Feeling |
| Judging | vs. | Perceiving |

Jung postulated that an individual's apparently random behavior was not random at all. Rather, when carefully observed, a pattern could be seen that reflected a person's preferences for getting energized, for taking in information, and for making decisions. The pairs cited above reflect such preferences. To make this idea more understandable, stop right now and write your name with your right hand, if you are right handed, and your left hand, if you are left handed. That was probably easy and comfortable for you to do. It didn't take much energy and you completed it quickly. Now sign your name with your other hand. While you could do this, it was probably more awkward and not as natural. It probably took you longer to complete and chances are the signature is not as legible as the first one. The point is that although we use both hands, we generally prefer one hand over the other. Because we rely more on the preferred hand, it is better developed than the other even though you can and do use your other hand for some things. That is the way it is with preferences. It doesn't mean that we cannot use our other preferences, but rather we tend to use those that are more comfortable for us.

# Determining Personality Type

According to Jung's theory and the theory underlying the MBTI, an individual's behavior is the result of preferences for taking in information (perception) and coming to conclusions (judgment). The best way to determine your type is to take the temperament indicator test. However, one can get a preliminary understanding of his or her type by matching one's preferences with the descriptions given for the different pairs. You may find that you relate to some or many words and behavioral descriptions of each pair. But more than likely, you will agree with more in one pair than the other. Identifying our type allows us to learn a great deal about ourselves in a nonjudgmental way. Unlike some psychological instruments, the MBTI does not deal with what is "wrong" with a person; there is no right or wrong way to be or to answer. All of the four pairs and the resultant 16 preferences have their own strengths, contributions, and pitfalls.

Type theory includes four pairs: Extraversion versus Introversion, Sensing versus iNtuition, Thinking versus Feeling, and Judging versus Perceiving. As you read the descriptions and the key words for each preference that follows, check the words and phrases that apply to you. We will deal first with the Extraversion/Introversion pair.

## Extravert—Introvert

This first pair addresses how you are energized. If you are an extravert, you draw your energy from people around you, from talking things out, and from taking action. You probably tend to talk first and think later and often don't know what you think or will say until you say it. A typical extravert knows a number of people and considers many of them close friends. If you are an extravert, you have no difficulty engaging in a number of activities simultaneously, such as reading a book, watching television, and listening to a conversation all at the same time. The extravert is easily distracted from the task at hand and may seek interruption as a diversion. Generally, extraverts are approachable and engaging, but may dominate conversations. Face-to-face communication is preferred to written. They like to generate ideas out loud in a group rather than by themselves. Extraverts respond quickly and like variety and action. They can be impatient with long jobs or assignments that do not seem to be going anywhere. The extraverted key player in a case management program will be visibly enthusiastic and prefer to work with others in planning and implementing the program.

On the other hand, if you are an introvert, you draw energy from within yourself and from quiet time for reflection on ideas. Unlike the extravert, you rehearse things before you say them and say things like "I'll have to think about that." You are often perceived as a good listener and have probably been called shy from time to time. You like to state your thoughts and feelings without interruptions and often wish you could present your ideas more forcefully. You prefer to work alone and to communicate in writing rather than face to face. You are able to work on one project for a long period of time with becoming impatient or bored. You may be enthusiastic and committed to the program, but your outward demeanor will probably not reflect it. Introverts have to work hard to show their feelings to others, but this reserve should not be interpreted as indifference.

Some key words that contrast these two preferences are:

| **Extravert** | **Introvert** |
|---|---|
| Active | Reflective |
| Sociable | Reserved |
| Outward | Inward |
| Breadth | Depth |
| Expressive | Quiet |
| People | Privacy |

Put an "X" by the description that fits you best.

| Extraversion | Introversion |
|---|---|
| E________ | I________ |

**Sources of Misunderstanding**

It is important to point out that extraverts may seem shallow to introverts and introverts may seem withdrawn to extraverts. Extraverts should not assume that because an introvert raised no objection during a discussion or in a meeting that he or she is in agreement with the points being made. Because it is generally easy for extraverts to raise issues or discuss ideas in a group, they assume that this is true for everyone. They also assume that because everyone had an equal opportunity to offer opinions and to offer objections, they assume agreement when none are presented. However, the extravert must realize that an introvert needs time to reflect on the discussion and should not be pressed to make premature comments.

Understanding the basic differences in style outlined above facilitates a smooth working relationship between all members of the case management team. Both preferences are important and contribute equally to the success of the project. One cannot say that an extravert will be more successful than an introvert in any of the key roles usually associated with a case management program. What can be said with certainty is that how they implement their roles will be completely different. Extraverts should be encouraged to plan when to switch from a speaker to a listener role and to build in time for interaction during meetings. Likewise, introverts should plan a time to switch from a listener to a speaker role. They can do this by saying "I have an opinion on that. Would you like to hear it?" and by allowing time in meetings for reflection.

## Sensing—Intuition

This pair of preferences focuses on what you pay attention to, your perception, and your way of thinking about things. In the June 1989 issue of *The Type Reporter*, Susan Scanlan wrote: "You could say that Sensing Types live in the valley. They farm the land and enjoy its bounty. They build a community; they trade with each other. Their interest is on the day-to-day survival of their family and their village." She goes on to say ". . . Intuitives live on the mountaintop. They look down and see miles and miles of land at once. They see how one community compares to another, the roads and waterways that connect them. Their interest is in studying the system and how it might be improved." Her conclusion is that if a road is not built between these two communities, neither can function optimally by itself. The sensing community can see only what is around them. They cannot prepare for what might or could happen. On the other hand, the intuitive community are stuck with their view of what is coming and cannot avail themselves of the bounty in the valley. In practice, this situation is reenacted numerous times when we say "Don't bother to tell Mary (sensing type) about any new ideas. She never listens to them." Or when referring to Karen (intuitive type), "She is always coming up with impractical ideas. She has her head in the clouds."

If you are a sensing type, you focus on facts and figures, what is practical, and what is going on in the situation right now. You look at specific parts and pieces and start at the beginning, taking one step at a time. You like procedures and established routines and prefer specific answers to specific questions. You give precise and clear instructions and get frustrated when others do not do the same or when they treat the instructions as vague guidelines. You have difficulty when someone says "Here is the overall plan, we'll fill in the details later." You focus on what works now rather than on how things can be improved. You seldom ask "What if?" You could develop a "If it ain't broken, don't fix it" attitude.

If you are an intuitive type, you focus on insights and possibilities and are always aware of new challenges. You frequently ask "What if?" You like opportunities for inventiveness and dislike doing the same thing repeatedly. Unlike the sensing type, you begin not at the beginning but at any point in the process. You will undoubtedly leap over steps, much to the chagrin of your sensing colleagues. You look at patterns and relationships and study the overall design to see how the parts may fit together. Because you dislike taking time to be precise, you may get your facts a bit wrong. You like change and variety and tend to think about several things at once. This characteristic may cause some to call you absent-minded. To the sensing type, the intuitive may seem fickle, impractical dreamers. To the intuitive type, the sensing person may appear to be materialistic and too literal-minded.

Put an "X" by the description that fits you best.

| Sensing | iNtuition |
|---|---|
| S________ | N________ |

**Sources of Misunderstanding**

More than any of the other preferences, differences between sensing and intuitive types are the source of most miscommunication, misunderstanding, defamation, and vilification in groups. The differences place the widest gulf between people. The sensing types notice what is actually happening and want to deal with that. They do not want to concern themselves with what might happen. In contrast, the intuitives seem to scan a room, a group, or a situation, trying to get a global picture of what is going on. They will frequently miss the details that are so essential to the sensing types. Even the language that inspires the intuitives has no meaning for the sensing types. In fact, the intuitives' penchant for metaphors, poetry, and other "esoteric" ways of communication causes the sensing types to solidify their impressions of intuitives as flighty, impractical, and unrealistic. Sensing types tolerate little "nonsense" at work, so the "idle" dreamings of the intuitives can cause them major discomfort. The differences between these two preferences can create hard feelings and great misunderstanding in a work group if everyone does not clearly understand and accept the differences in style. Good communication skills are important in all situations, but in dealing with the differences in this pair they are essential. The following guidelines are helpful when presenting material to, or trying to influence, or explaining to, or trying to understand:

| **Sensors** | **Intuitives** |
|---|---|
| Be factual, give details | Give the global scheme, the big picture |
| Think of a bottom-line reason for the change | Talk about the opportunities the project presents |
| Make up an action plan | Be confident & enthusiastic |
| Ask for the pitfalls | Talk about concepts |

Some key words that contrast the two types are:

| **Sensors** | **Intuitives** |
|---|---|
| Details | Patterns |
| Present | Future |
| Sequential | Random |
| Directions | Hunches |
| Perspiration | Inspiration |

## Thinking—Feeling

This dimension relates to what information you use to make your decisions and how you prefer to organize and structure that information. People who chose the impersonal way to make decisions are thinking types and those who chose the personal way are feeling types. Each person is capable of making decisions both ways, but they prefer one way over the other.

This pair of preferences is the only one of the four where a gender difference has been noted. It is hardly surprising to note that most women are feeling types and there is strong cultural sanction for this type of behavior for women. Most men, on the other hand, are thinking types. Again, there is strong cultural support for this kind of response for men.

If you are a thinking type, you use nonpersonal logic and objective information first to make your decisions and consider the impact on people later. You decide with your head and would rather settle a dispute based on what is fair and truthful rather than what will make people happy. You are concerned with truth and justice. You take the long view and see situations more as an objective onlooker. You enjoy proving a point for the sake of clarity, and it is not beyond you to argue both sides of an argument simply to expand your intellectual horizons. Because you are able to stay calm in most situations, people may see you as detached or cold and reserved. It is more important to you that you are right than it is to be liked.

If you are a feeling type, you consider people's feelings first before making a decision. You generally decide with the heart rather than the head and prefer harmony over clarity. You use personal values and convictions to arrive at your decisions and are concerned for maintaining harmonious relationships at all costs. You see things as a participant rather than as an onlooker and take an immediate and personal view of events and situations. You can be accused of taking things too personally.

When communicating with thinkers and feelers, use the following guidelines:

| **Thinkers** | **Feelers** |
|---|---|
| Be logical | Be personable and friendly |
| State principles involved | Mention relationships |
| Be well-organized | Indicate how it is helpful |
| List the costs and benefits | Show how it supports personal goals |

Some key words that contrast thinkers and feelers are:

| **Thinkers** | **Feelers** |
|---|---|
| Cool | Caring |
| Objective | Subjective |
| Impersonal | Personal |
| Analyze | Empathize |
| Criticize | Appreciate |
| Precise | Persuasive |

Put an "X" by the description that fits you best.

| Thinking | Feeling |
|---|---|
| T________ | F________ |

**Sources of Misunderstanding**

Sometimes the feeling types are seen as more emotionally sensitive than the thinking types. However, this is not necessarily true. Feelers may simply express their feelings more openly than thinkers, thus their emotional reactions are more apparent. Consequently, thinkers may be unjustly described as cold, reserved, or unemotional.

The thinking and feeling type differences may not cause serious problems in group work if there is a balance in the group. Once the thinking person realizes that the feeling type can make decisions based on logic rather than on feelings and vice versa, a good relationship can ensue. The thinkers have to learn not to trample all over people's feelings, while the feelers have to learn to deal with the tough issues.

## Judging—Perceiving

If you prefer a planned, organized life and prefer closure rather than leaving your options open, you are likely to be a judging type. It is important to understand that the meaning of the word, *judging*, as it is used in type psychology does not mean judgmental or critical. It means that you prefer an organized lifestyle, one that is "under control" and includes definite order and structure. You enjoy making decisions and like clear limits and guidelines. You like deadlines, make lists (and actually use them), and like to work things to completion to get them out of the way. In groups, you may push for closure before sufficient discussion has occurred because you like to wrap things up quickly. For the judging type, work comes before play.

If you are a perceiver, you prefer a flexible lifestyle, going with the flow, and leaving your options open. In contrast to the judging type person, you resist closure, wanting more data. While perceivers make lists, they use them as reminders of the things that they may have to do some day, maybe! Unlike the judging type, perceivers do not mind surprises and like to experience life as it happens. You can be easily distracted, frequently changing the subject in the middle of a conversation. You don't usually plan a task, but wait to see what it demands and then work frantically against the deadline. Perceivers will turn any work into play, and given the opportunity would rather play than work. Perceivers tend to usually make things less than definite from time to time, but not always.

Some key words that contrast judging and perceiving types are:

| **Judging** | **Perceiving** |
|---|---|
| Deciding | Inquiring |
| Planning | Absorbing |
| Organizing | Adapting |
| Scheduling | Changing |
| Structure | Flow |
| Deadlines | Discoveries |

Put an "X" by the description that fits you best.

| Judging | Perceiving |
|---|---|
| J________ | P________ |

### Sources of Misunderstanding

To the judging type, the perceiver may seem disorganized, messy, easily distracted, and irresponsible. To the perceiver, the judging type may seem demanding, rigid, and overly controlled. Js are more outcome oriented, whereas Ps are more process oriented. The difference in preference between this pair can cause a great deal of difficulty in group work. The Js are seen as "all work and no play" by the Ps while the Ps are seen as "not serious enough" by the Js. Both want to get the job done, but their approach is totally different. Most of the misunderstanding in the workplace seems to be between Js and Ps. The former deal almost exclusively with product, where the latter deal with process. There are some useful strategies to help avoid the inevitable problems between Js and Ps and to keep Js from jumping to "premature" conclusions. In working with Js, Ps should:

1. Give them new information in advance so they can have time to review it before any discussion.

2. Acknowledge their worthwhile contributions and ignore behavior that you may see as "aggravating."
3. Make it clear when you are just speculating and ask them to join in.
4. Ask them how they have reached their decision.
5. Ask them to organize the information gathering and review process.

Perceivers cause problems in work groups because they are all too eager to withhold a decision so that they can get another opinion, check another resource, do another draft, and discuss it some more. The guidelines for dealing with Ps are the same as those for dealing with Js, except in reverse.

1. Give Ps your *plans* in advance so they have time to think about them. Ask questions such as "What do you think the greatest problem would be doing it this way?" or "Do you think it would be impossible to do it this way?"
2. Acknowledge the worthwhile new information (as opposed to judgments) underneath the "aggravating" style you see.
3. Make it clear when you have to have a decision and *why*. Try to get Ps to set time lines and to tell you when they intend to begin.
4. Ask Ps questions that will lead them to think about the order and direction of their thoughts. When Ps tell you that they feel or think something is wrong but they don't know what it is. You could say: "There are many things that could be wrong. It could be the idea, the people, the market, or the wrong time. Do any of these stand out in your mind?"
5. Set up frequent feedback sessions so they can talk about what they are thinking.

## Summary and Conclusion

In working on problems or making decisions, the MBTI preferences can be used to help guide the process. The problem-solving process discussed here can be used to guide individual or team problem solving. Although the process seems simple, it can be difficult to implement because of people's tendency to skip over the steps that require them to use their least preferred preferences. The problem-solving model illustrated below is a circle to show that the process can start at any point and move in any direction until a decision has been reached. Adhering to this process will ensure that the views and opinions of individuals with all preferences will be included. Also below are some questions that can be asked at each step.

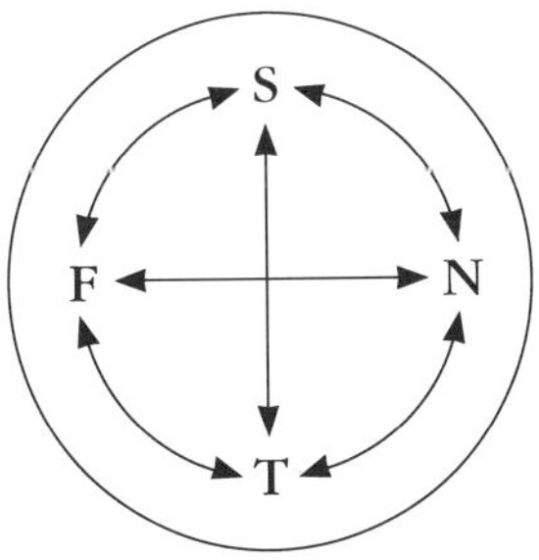


*Model adapted from Gordon Lawrence, *People Types and Tiger Stripes*. Center for the Applications of Psychological Type, 1982

**Sensing (S)**

What are the facts?
What is the situation?
What has been done to solve the problem?
What am I and other members of the team doing?
How would an outsider look at this situation?

**Intuition (N)**

What are the possibilities?
What other ways are there for solving this problem?
What do the data imply?
What are the implications beyond the facts?
What is this problem analogous to?

**Thinking (T)**

What are the pros and cons of each possibility?
What are the logical consequences of each possibility?
What is the cost of each?
What are the pleasant and unpleasant outcomes of each?
What is the consequence of not acting?

**Feeling (F)**

How much do I care about what I gain or lose in each alternative?
What are the values involved for each possibility?
How will the people concerned react to the outcome?
Who is committed to carry out the solution?
Will the outcome contribute to individual or group harmony?

(Hirsh & Kummerow, 1990, p. 32)

## References

Hirsh, S.K. & Kummerow, J.M. (1990). *Introduction to Type in Organizations*. Palo Alto, CA: Consulting Psychologists Press, Inc.

Keirsey, D. & Bates, M. (1984). *Please Understand Me.* Del Mar, CA: Prometheus Nemesis Book Co.

Kroeger, O. & Thuesen, J.M. (1988). *Type Talk*. New York, New York: Dell Publishing Co.

# 4

## Ethics

Vivian Tillman, RN, CIRS

"Having to do with right and wrong: of ethics or morality; in accordance with formal or professional rules of right and wrong"—(*World Book*). The definition of ethics also includes the study of standards of right and wrong—the part of science and philosophy dealing with the moral conduct, judgment and duties of ethics.

Ethics should be an easy topic to discuss, correct? *Wrong*! We all know what ethics are about, correct? *Not necessarily!* I will not be discussing ethics from an academic or legal viewpoint. I will be discussing ethics from my personal perspective, developed over the last 22 years as a medical case manager. I will express my point of view concerning the accountability and responsibility of your role as a medical case manager.

## Three Principles of Ethics

Three principles have influenced the shape of public policy on disability and overall case management: autonomy, beneficence and justice. Looking at each one individually, autonomy—"promoting independence"; beneficence—"promoting well-being"; and justice—"providing just allocation of resources to meet needs" is to see case management in a nutshell.

The specialty of case manager to date has not developed specific standards, canons, or rules for conduct of ethical behavior. In the individual specialties—nursing, social work, occupational therapy, physical therapy, or whatever the case manager's background is—you should know your own standards and code of ethics for your specialty. All registered nurses who have received their license either have a copy or can obtain a copy of these standards from their local Board of Nursing. The standards of conduct are reviewed while obtaining your education, whether it is in nursing or one of the other disciplines. We are each responsible for upholding our own personal and professional code of ethics. Case management is a very diverse and elusive term. Depending on your area of practice—hospital, insurance carrier, rehabilitation facility, or state agency—your role could be very different from that of individuals practicing in one of the other areas. Also, your background, whether social worker, registered nurse, vocational counselor, physician or other discipline, can be defined in very different terms. Looking at all these areas that can involve case management, it is very important that you know and are very comfortable with your own personal code of ethics.

# Developing a Code of Ethics

The need to develop a standard code of ethics appears to be overwhelming. Many professional magazines, newspapers, and professional journals are addressing the need for ethics, whether business, medicine, or government. You can find many articles about ethical principles and the need for those principles. This topic is also the subject of regional, national and international conferences. The topic is being addressed by attorneys, physicians, advertising agencies and many other groups who are attempting to identify ethical problems and how to solve them, how to promote ethics in the work place, how to formulate guidelines for dealing with ethical issues, and how to assess and develop ethical behavior.

There are times when promoting independence (autonomy) and promoting well-being (beneficence) seem to be at odds. You as the case manager utilize your experience and knowledge of the specific patient needs and have determined the course the individual should follow to promote his "well-being." But your client chooses to follow a different route or your account (employer) gives specific limitations. Is this an ethical dilemma? You must draw on your own ethical beliefs, what your role within the system is, what system-jurisdiction you are working in, and your accountability and responsibility in all of these areas. If you have not, you need to sit down and identify your own personal ethics. Would you work in a hospital that performs abortions? Would you accept a "bonus" for referring patients to a specific facility? Be aware of the specifics of your contractual agreement with your employer. Is the primary role to control cost? Is your role of limited involvement—transferring the patient from an acute facility to his home? Are you aware of the law and statutes governing the jurisdiction within which you are working? If you are providing assistance or have been hired by a government agency (Social Security, Welfare) or are working within an insurance arena (liability, workers compensation), you must be aware of the statutes, regulations and types of services your particular client is entitled to under the specific coverage. The patient is entitled to know what your role is, your obligations, and the direction in which you will be guiding your case management plan. Many times, as the patient moves from an acute hospital situation to a postacute rehabilitation setting or to re-entry into the work force and/or home situation, each stage can be very difficult and each "case manager" can present a different set of directions, all making this very confusing and bewildering to the patient.

Let's look at Case A: You are assigned to a patient who has just sustained his second back injury, resulting in surgery. He is fired by his employer. He is eligible for vocational rehabilitation after completing his medical recovery. Due to the patient's limited background in manual labor, it is obvious he should pursue a lighter type of employment and take advantage of his vocational rehabilitation opportunities. Within the jurisdiction of the patient's coverage, he is offered the opportunity to "settle" his case. In your opinion as case manager, due to the patient's medical history, do you feel he should pursue another vocational avenue and not "settle" at this time?

Now let's look at Case B, a young man who had a significant head injury, with resulting damage to his dominant arm. He went through the acute hospital rehabilitation program and was discharged to a postacute facility for cognitive training. He also received intensive physical therapy for his arm and recovered beyond the physicians' or any therapists' expectations. It was not an option to return to his usual and customary employment, so other vocational goals were developed. Specific job situations were developed, with starting salary at $14 an hour with the potential for $20 an hour. These were presented to the patient.

Regarding Case A: The case manager, being aware of the statute and regulations governing the jurisdiction under which the patient is covered, presents him with his options. As case manager, you are aware of the medical recommendations for future work and limitations regarding his back. From a philosophical perspective, and utilizing past experiences, you, as the case manager, feel the best approach would be vocational rehabilitation. Your role is to present the options, and then the patient makes his choice. The case manager needs to know when to "turn loose." Your obligation as case manager is to present the options and recommendations. If those options or recommendations are to be pursued, you can assist with that; otherwise, your job is done.

Regarding Case B: The patient's independence was being promoted. He was given all of the information regarding what he needed for his "well-being." He would be able to get back in the work force, utilizing his present skills with the potential for higher wages. In the case manager's judgment, the patient should have followed this course. The job of the case manager is to give all of the information and direction to the patient and then allow him to make his own choice. You need to look at the direction ethical behavior needs to proceed and to ensure that you are not compromising your ethical beliefs nor compromising the ethical beliefs of your employer or agency and not exceeding the jurisdictional framework.

You need to sit down and write your own personal code of ethics. When you accept a position or a contract with a firm to provide your services as a case manager, ask some questions. What is expected of you as an employee? Are there compromises expected? What are the directions, rules and regulations within the system-jurisdiction in which you are working? Is the bottom line to control costs? To what extent are you expected to control these costs? Is updated training-education provided and/or allowed within your specialty? Looking at case management, one role is to promote the independence and well-being of the individual and to provide a just allocation of resources to meet those needs. This is to be done in a cost-effective and efficient manner. Are you expected to compromise your own code of ethics to meet the expectations of your employer? Are you expected to deal with people whose values and behaviors are unethical? Are you expected to use the cheapest therapy source, when you know a more expensive program would provide better services with longer-lasting results? A case manager needs to make crystal clear to both her client and the recipient of her services what she perceives as the obligations and duties in her role as case manager.

As case managers, we are on the cutting edge. *Case Management* is the buzz word for the 1990s and can be very misleading. There are very few jobs where situational decisions can have such far-reaching effects. Because the term *case manager* can be applied to so many situations, each with its own definition, you need to know what your job description is and what jurisdiction you are working in. Are you reviewing medical bills? Are you looking at cost containment issues? Are you providing vocational assistance to help return an injured person to work? Are you doing discharge planning to get the person from an acute hospital into his home? In the case manager arena, there are many, many players—physicians, attorneys, various therapy modalities, state agencies—all involved at various stages or at one time. One of the case manager's duties is to bring all of these parties together at the same table, looking at and settling on an outcome objective, and getting the team to function as one for the best outcome for the individual. In the specific role and definition of your case management position, the objectives of the goals will include looking at autonomy, beneficence, and justice. How are these applied? And specifically, what is your role within these arenas?

# Legal and Ethical Issues

Legal and ethical issues can be confusing. Many times, issues may be decided by case law or statutory limitations. As an example, an individual may be injured in a serious one-car accident and need extensive rehabilitation. The limits of the contractual agreement for medical treatment is a certain dollar limit. Even though the cost may exceed the dollar limit, the individual has entered into a "contractual agreement" under which all parties must operate. You must adjust your role accordingly to the jurisdiction you are working within.

To summarize, the case manager needs to know the resources, must be able to adequately evaluate the resources, and must be able to make a quantifiable, objective recommendation to her employer, the recipient of her services, and other members of the team involved with this individual. This can be done by knowing her own personal ethics, the jurisdiction within which she is working, and helping all team members to objectively determine goals, action plans, and outcome.

# 5

# Putting Automation Systems to Work

Rufus S. Howe, RN, MN, FNP

It is clear that automation has made a significant impact on the health care industry. References to the cost-cutting, patient care enhancing and time-saving benefits of automating the *administration* of health care are not hard to find (Barry & Gibbons, 1990, Vanzandt & Johnson, 1986). In this chapter, an automated system is defined as using data retrieval and calculation systems to augment one's practice. This definition does not limit itself to the use of standard microcomputers and mainframes. Any tool, such as the new hand-held remote entry terminal that automates our service to the client, is worthy of examining within the same context.

The needs of primary health care providers are unlike those of hospital administrators. Most health care automation systems used today originated from patient billing systems. Administrative applications are much more concrete than health care applications. Considering this obvious disparity between approaches, health care workers ask tough—and sometimes unanswerable—questions when confronted with a change to automation; What is the "goodness of fit" of automation to health care? Which components of practice can be automated? What can we reasonably expect from such a system? What can health care workers contribute to this emerging technology? Will health care workers use such a system? The answers to these questions are not easily answered from a single perspective.

After a review of goals for automation, this chapter will separate, then bring together salient contextual variables influencing the transition to automated systems. Finally, strategies for change and implementation based on a review of current literature are suggested.

# Goals for Automation

Hospitals and health care workers have different agendas for an automated patient care package. Most current packages (not surprisingly) focus on administrative functions (Shannon, Dextrom & Fuhrhop, 1989). Health care workers realize that money, manpower, and supplies are important ingredients to support patient care. Health care workers also know that their primary mission is to care for patients. A change to automation must contribute to the improvement of care to their patients.

The automated system's goals are stated as those characteristics that enhance quality of care by:

- being patient centered
- designed for optimal efficiency and flexibility and intuitiveness
- providing for an accurate exchange of information
- providing a timely exchange of information
- automating routine functions such as drip rate calculation, charting input and output trends, or identification of high-risk populations
- empowerment of client and hospital personnel
- acting as a means of reflective and prospective research
- reducing redundant charting
- insuring legibility.

# Analysis of Contextual Variables

The context in which the change to automation takes place is crucially important. The sociocultural impact of automation cannot be underestimated.

## Sociocultural

In 1982, John Naisbitt announced in his book, *Megatrends*, the coming of the "information society." His primary fear was that the new technologies would depersonalize the service industries. Naisbitt called for a "high tech, high touch" approach. Health care is high touch, but what about high tech? Almost ten years later, many health care workers remain reluctant to get involved with the possibilities automation can offer.

Could it be that "technodread" accounts for much of the reluctance to incorporate automation into practice? Many health care workers practicing today were not raised with automation. Because of this fear of the unknown, some health care workers may feel intimidated and distrustful of this change (Barhyte, 1987). The same holds true for administrators who are leery of automation and may be the chief barrier to implementation (Barry & Gibbons, 1990).

Lastly, health care workers need to be convinced that automation will work to their advantage (Tortora, 1989). Data entry, for example, must be easier than manual charting (Johnson, 1987). The interface between the computer and user can be a potent distancing factor as well. Ideally, the software should remain "transparent" to the intervention. The provider should not feel as if the computer is the third party in the intervention. This is readily apparent when you consider the prevalence of the arcane and cryptic MS-DOS (IBM standard) command language used in most automated systems.

## Political

Political influences on automation are many and provide the stage upon which automation can become a possibility. Strong, consistent support from top-level management and physicians is paramount (Denger, Dee, & Walker 1988; Bauer, 1986; Yero, 1988).

Top administrators need to develop an automation policy that is accessible to the entire work force during its development (Graves & Corcoran, 1988). This cross-leveled approach to policy development ensures that the system is designed within the context of the organization's needs (Barry & Gibbons, 1990). The policy sets forth a unified show of support, purpose, and direction for the change to automation.

Nurses, the largest group of care givers in the hospital, must be allowed the opportunity for input into the design of the system (Johnson, 1987; Denger, Dee, & Walker 1988; Graves & Corcoran, 1988; Badger, 1988; Yero, 1988). Top management's empowerment of health care workers allows the design of their own system according to their needs (Johnson, 1987; Denger, Dee, & Walker, 1988). Health care workers, then, must feel that they are worthy partners in health care, and not the servants of past times (Badger, 1988).

It is apparent that in the final analysis, most systems fail because they do not consider the end-user (Ozbolt, 1986). Many systems are designed by those who are not familiar with the health care process (Johnson, 1987). Because most health care workers do not have programming skills and must rely on software programmers, they are not able to produce their own applications.

## Economic

The switch to automation has far reaching economic impact. In the Secretary's Commission on Nursing report on the nursing shortage, the members included computerization as a method to better utilize available resources (cited in Barry & Gibbons, 1990). Tortora (1989) points out that "the installation of computer technology in hospitals may represent the single most important cost-cutting tool available to the American health care system"

The banking industry, for instance, spends 7-10% on information technology, compared to 2.5% of hospital operating budgets. The economic impact of automation is further strengthened when one considers that 30% of nursing time is spent on information handling. Studies report nursing automation systems average a time savings of 1.5 hours per shift (Barry & Gibbons, 1990).

Nursing personnel are estimated to account for as much as 80% of a hospital's operating cost (Mowry & Korpman, 1987). Automation can increase productivity by scheduling nursing staff levels according to patient acuity, thus eliminating under- and overstaffing and depending less on high-cost registries. (Tortora, 1989; Vanzandt & Johnson, 1986)

## Ethical

The introduction of automation has brought on a deluge of largely unanswered ethical questions concerning privacy, confidentiality, and security. Romano (1987) states that "privacy concerns the disclosure of information, whereas confidentiality concerns redisclosure of that information." The provider-client relationship implies the provision of privacy to enable confidentiality. When the confidential data is entered into a computer (third party), the risk of disclosure to unauthorized persons increases. If the client knows that the data will be part of a hospital-wide computer record, this may alter the relationship in ways that have not been explored.

### Privacy

Because the computer will "remember" anything that it is told, it is tempting to capture a large amount of data whether or not it is pertinent to the situation. Certain data, such as political views, may not be appropriate to collect (Barhyte, 1987). For these reasons, a task force consisting of health care staff and ancillary personnel should determine which data elements should be stored (Johnson, 1987).

### Confidentiality

In most cases, anonymity is not possible due to the nature of the use of the data (Barhyte, 1987). Additionally, clients have the right to gain access to their files and be permitted to make corrections or additions to the record (Barhyte, 1987).

Automated reports, based on data entered by a variety of providers, bring an interesting ethical dilemma to light. Who *owns* the data if the report is generated from laboratory, nursing, and medical data? It is clear that the "ownership of [jointly authored] data needs to be resolved" (Barhyte, 1987).

### Security

A common source of resistance to automated patient information rests with the concept of "usage integrity" (Romano, 1987). In other words, who—besides the primary provider and the client—will have access to the information? Will the dietitian, for instance, be able to make corrections to nursing orders? For this and many other reasons, assigning access to computerized data should be done on a "need to know [and edit]" basis (Brooks, Semenuk, & Vaughan, 1988).

Other security considerations include the location of hardware, provision of limited personnel access to area, passwords, timed screens, and usage audit logs. (Barhyte, 1987; Romano, 1987).

### Service delivery

Health care providers will ask how their service to the client will be affected. As was alluded to earlier, automation should augment, not replace, judgment and intuition. In addition to the routine clinical data kept in the computerized health record, newer systems are employing knowledge-based capabilities. Knowledge–based systems are designed to serve as reservoirs of details pertinent to the case at hand (Badger, 1988). For example, imagine the utility of an online connection with lab values, client medical history, and current literature related to the client's situation.

Other service variables come in to play, such as the location of the data entry point. The further the system is away from patient care, the more likely an entry error will occur (Barhyte, 1987; Romano, 1987). Costly bedside terminals (some are hand-held remote units) that provide point-of-service entry are designed to reduce data entry errors. (Tribulski, 1989; Johnson,1987).

## Integration of Contextual Variables

As is usually the case, the contextual variables do not stand by themselves. The development and existence of an automation package often necessitates crossing departmental lines. Interesting political, economic, and cultural ramifications will emerge from this process. A common positive result of automation change is the discovery of unforeseen links between departments (Denger, Dee, & Walker 1988; Bauer, 1986). These newly recognized links can then be operationalized and used as sources to improve the system of health care delivery.

Political policies often impact on many aspects of organizational change. National, state, and local policy, for example, is not clear on the provision for the confidentiality of automated records (Romano, 1987). Because of this, it is left to local organizations to determine policy relating to access to computerized information.

# Strategies for Change

The greatest impact in both the perception and implementation of automation in practice will happen within schools of medicine and nursing. Faculty and students should be educated in automation concepts and design (Denger, Dee, & Walker, 1988). Incorporating automation in the curriculum will enable students to feel at ease with computers and allow a greater involvement in future system development and use (Barhyte, 1987).

The corporate climate must not be neglected. Providers must feel that there is political, economic, and sociological support to automate care (Yero, 1988). Yero also points out that this organization must have a positive experience with change in order to make a smooth transition to automation.

The use of teamwork and sound training has been emphasized throughout this chapter as a means of facilitating a smooth transition to automation (Denger, Dee, & Walker, 1988). Teamwork is essential because a comprehensive automation package will include other hospital services. And because automation affects everybody, the perceptions and needs of the team should be considered.

Avoid the temptation to do it all at once. To ensure the best chance of adoption, the integration of automation is best achieved when done in small, realistic pieces (Bauer, 1986; Yero, 1988). Remember, many health care workers are not familiar with computers and need to be sold first. A small, well-done application is better received than a large one with many bugs.

The introduction of automation will require training. In the absence of adequate computer literacy, individual training seems most effective—and the most costly. According to some, the training-the-trainer method is least effective (Johnson, 1987; Denger, Dee, & Walker, 1988).

With regard to design, most current nursing systems do not fit the intangible nature of health care intervention. Present systems are designed around routine assembly line tasks such as producing templates for a given disease. Ideally, systems should incorporate inductive decision-making tools such as online data bases and protocols, etc. (Ozbolt, 1986; Graves & Corcoran, 1988). The design should also allow for user modification that reflects the dynamic nature of practice (Graves & Corcoran, 1988).

To summarize this chapter, the concept of augmenting practice with automation is not new, but is still in its infancy in terms of its utility. Isolated systems are being developed that incorporate the routine functions of the traditional systems with more intuitive tools such as online data bases. Unfortunately, only a handful of case management automated packages exist. To this end, more work must be done to integrate computer literacy among health care workers, thus providing the tools to make an impact on a change that is inevitable—and will happen with or without our input.

## References


Badger, L. (1988). A nurse's view of technology. *Computers in Healthcare, 9* (2), 31-2.

Barhyte, D.Y. (1987). Ethical issues in automating nursing personnel data. *Computers in Nursing, 5* (5), 171-4.

Barry, C.T., & Gibbons, L.K. (1990). Information systems technology: Barriers and challenges to implementation. *Journal of Nursing Administration, 20* (2), 40-2.

Bauer, C. (1986). The moment of truth: a nursing station goes "live." *Computers in Healthcare,* 7 (12), 47,49.

Brooks, G. M., Semenuk, T., & Vaughan, V.S. (1988). Controlling information: Who, what, how?. . . computer access policy. *Computers in Healthcare, 9* (1), 16-8.

Denger, S., Cole, D., & Walker, H. (1988). Implementing an integrated clinical information system. *Journal of Nursing Administration, 18* (12), 28-36.

Graves, J., & Corcoran, S. (1988). Design of nursing information systems: Conceptual and practice elements. *Journal of Professional Nursing, 4* (3), 168-7.

Johnson, D. (1987). Decisions and dilemmas in the development of a nursing information system. *Computers in Nursing, 5* (3), 94-8.

Mowry, M. M., & Korpman, R. A. (1987). Evaluating automated information systems. *Nursing Economics, 5* (1), 7-12.

Naisbitt, J. (1982). *Megatrends.* New York: Warner Books

Ozbolt, J. G. (1986). Designing information systems for nursing practice: Data base and knowledge base requirements for different organizational technologies. *Computer Methods and Programs in Biomedicine, 22* (1), 61-5.

Shannon, M., Dextrom, N., & Fuhrhop, M. (1989). A proactive approach to computerizing nursing process: A management perspective. *Health Care Supervisor,* 7 (3), 71-81.

Tortora, M. L. (1989). Integrating computers into the nursing environment. *Nursing Forum, 24* (2), 8-12.

Tribulski, J. A. (1989). Why aren't more health care workers using this valuable tool? *RN, 52* (12), 54-9.

Vanzandt, B., & Johnson, J. (1986). Nursing systems and the art of nursing. *Computers in Healthcare,* 7 (5), 32-3.

Yero, M. (1988). Successfully implementing a point-of-care system. *Computers in Healthcare, 9* (2), 24-5.

# II

# SELF-CARE CASE MANAGEMENT

# 6

# Self-Care as a Part of Care Management

Kathleen C. Milne, RN, BSN
Ellen Radakovich, RN, MS, CNS

*The capacity for self-care may be the most fundamental and important determinant of health status. Maslow and others mentioned in this chapter have dedicated their entire careers to supporting and refining this notion. In reviewing the theoretical frameworks that influence health practices, it is clear that self-care plays a dominant role. One might, however, question the validity of incorporating an apparently uncontrollable variable, self-care, into the scheme of case management.*

*The authors of this chapter focus on the importance of recognizing the importance and facilitation of self-care among the elderly. The elderly population is held up as an exemplar because of its eventual loss of self-care capacity. One way these authors handle self-care facilitation is through their health care notebook. Although use of this notebook is not in itself the only answer, I believe it has added value to the clients' self-care capacity.*

*The authors have also threaded the concept of mutual respect, integrity, and advocacy throughout this chapter. I consider this consistent with our objective for self-care, which calls for optimizing "care within natural boundaries."*—R.S.H.

Advancements in disease prevention, medical treatment, and environmental living conditions have succeeded in increasing life expectancy for the elderly population. Concomitant with this expanded life expectancy are new physical, psychosocial, and environmental challenges facing the elderly. What has not changed is the desire of this population to maintain a life-style of optimal quality, characterized by personal independence and functional ability (Platakis, 1987). This *quality* of life surpasses the importance of *quantity* of life (Larson and Bruce, 1987). As a consequence, the health needs of the elderly are becoming more complex and require a multidisciplinary collaboration between the various health-related professions to meet these unique needs and to effectively educate this population in how to enhance self-care skills (Platakis, 1987).

Burnside (1988) believes that older adults have the capability and motivation to participate in self-care health-promoting activities if given supportive health education. In order for this education to be effective, the individual's internal motivation to acquire new knowledge, skill, and behaviors must be ignited or enhanced. This is achieved by 1) establishing a climate of collaboration, mutual trust, respect and support; and 2) involving the client in identifying his/her needs, developing strategies to meet these needs, and evaluating the effectiveness of the strategies (Redman, 1981).

In society's quest for efficiency, productivity, and avoidance of litigation, the elderly's basic right of participation is often removed. This holds true for competent elderly individuals as well (Eliopoulos, 1984). Health professionals, family members, and social service providers often develop and implement interventions based on what they perceive as "in the client's best interest." "What would *you* like?" is too often omitted from conservation.

The consumer of care management services becomes a client when he/she becomes dissatisfied or becomes incapable of meeting health and well-being needs due to social, medical, emotional, or environmental deficiencies (Eliopoulos, 1984; Carnevali & Patrick, 1979). The process of care management allows for the identification of specific health needs, location of appropriate services, and the creation and implementation of a plan to deal with the identified needs. The expected outcomes of care management are to:

- Maximize the health status of person served while enhancing quality of life
- Empower the person served by increasing the choices available to maintain his/her independence and control
- Prevent premature disability

Nurses are highly qualified care managers because their nursing and social education enables them to be the assessor, monitor, resource connector, and evaluator of the client's medical, nursing, psychosocial, or environmental status. Consequently, when a self-care limitation is identified in a client, the nurse/care manager is able to effectively determine the most appropriate intervention—"strengthening self-care capacity; removing or minimizing a self-care limitation; or acting for, doing for, or partially assisting" the client (Eliopoulos, 1984, p. 367).

The strengthening self-care capacity is the ultimate intervention toward promoting and achieving the maximum level of independence and quality of life. Many tools can be brought to bear in reaching this goal. The organization with which I am affiliated, Resource Connectors, Ltd. (RCL), a private health care management and consulting company, is guided by Orem's theory of self-care, Roy's theory of adaptation, and Carnevali and Patrick's nursing model/in maximizing the self-care capabilities of its clients.

Central to Orem's theory is the natural ability of a person to care for himself/herself and play a pivotal role in the development and achievement of a plan of care. Client care management based on Orem's self-care theory has exhibited increases in the client's choices and participation in a plan of care directed at reestablishing the client's self-sufficiency (Anna, Christensen, Hohon, Ord, and Wells, 1978).

Roy's model is based on Dr. Hans Selye's stress theory. According to Selye, the core of human life is the continual process of coping with ever-changing environmental stress, the process of adaptation. Man's ability to adapt to this dynamic environment is the driving force behind Roy's theory. Roy believes in the person's own creative powers, the belief that the person's own coping abilities will enhance wellness. The person is viewed as exhibiting purposeful behavior with the need, desire, and capability to learn how to effectively adapt to environmental stimuli (Janelli, 1980). Therefore, a person's drive to adapt to an ever-changing environment supports the desire to maintain an optimal level of self-care.

Carnevali and Patrick's (1979) nursing practice model states that "nursing's primary focus and area of accountability in providing health care is that of helping the individual and his family to manage the activities and demands of daily living as these affect and are affected by health and illness, at the same time taking into account the individual's lifestyle" (p. 7). This model is applicable from youth onward, but it clearly articulates the precarious situation faced by the aged in attempting to balance the stresses encountered in activities of daily living (ADL) with the tenuous coping resources and support systems (Carnevali and Patrick, 1984).

RCL completes a multidimensional assessment as base line data for its clients as part of the process of identifying current and projected needs. The functional assessment plays a primary role in this assessment. The functional approach is most helpful in assessing status and needs because 1) the elderly tend to define health in terms of functional ability; 2) the specific type of functional loss does not always determine functional impairment; and 3) no correlation exists between number of disease conditions and functional impairment (Matteson and McConnell, 1988; Kane, Ouslander and Abrass, 1989).

The domains of the functional assessment are physical, psychological, and social. More specifically, the physical domain reflects ability to cope with ADL and instrumental activities of daily living (IADL); the psychological domain reflects mentation, affect, and behavior; and interaction capabilities and quality of social support are addressed in the social domain.

# Health Care Notebook

RCL's "Health Care Notebook" (HCN) is a three-ring binder organized into sections with forms and educational tools that is used to detail the client's health care status, health and home maintenance needs and to provide a mechanism for continuity of care. This tool is applicable through the self-care continuum, dependent to independent.

The HCN is a tool for meeting identified client needs. It is a tailored health care management guide, with health being defined holistically. The client, care provider(s), and family and/or health professionals all use this resource. It provides a centralized location for accessing vital health information and for documenting, tracking, and communicating. It can be used in a variety of settings: self-care at home; by a client with several care providers (private, public or combination); by a client living with family and receiving regular private help; and by residents of foster homes and other facilities.

Components of the HCN include:

*Resource Module*. Contains demographics, family and social contacts, health care providers, medical and health benefits, and advanced directive information. It functions as an easily accessible "address book" containing important contacts for family and caregivers.

*Caregiver Module*. Lists caregiver tasks (daily, weekly, monthly) for ADLs, diet, activity, medication and other; measurable outcomes for client in the physical, psychological, and social domains. Includes a communication record (between caregivers); notable change record; medication record; and client expense record. It is used by caregivers to coordinate, document, and monitor care being provided.

*Health Care Module*. Contains client medical history, health care provider visit log, and health care provider visit form filled out for each appointment. It is used to track medical appointments and the client's health care needs.

## Case Example

The following case example illustrates the use of the HCN in a multigenerational home.

Mrs. F. is an 85-year-old widowed female who has been living with her eldest son, his wife, and three adolescent daughters for six years. A request for care management was received following a self-induced hot liquid burn on thighs and perineum. Normally, Mrs. F. has been independent with ADLs and IADLs, ambulatory, continent, and interacted with family. Mrs. F. limited her outside social contacts to weekly church services and hair salon appointments. At the time of the accident, the family noted increased confusion, inability to meet basic hygiene needs, increased isolation from family. Mrs. F. was evaluated by the geriatric assessment clinic and presented with few cognitive deficits, yet she was diagnosed as high risk for depression secondary to social isolation and a prolonged grieving process (her spouse died ten years prior). The adult son and his wife are frequently out of town on business and occasionally at the family vacation home. The grand-daughters are very active with extracurricular activities. Consequently, Mrs. F spent the majority of her time alone in her room on the top floor of the house.

RCL arranged for a private-care provider to come in daily to assist with personal care, meal preparation, home maintenance, and companionship; provide transportation to and from a senior day center; and to coordinate and track medical appointments. Due to the fluidity of this household, the HCN became an effective means for the care provider to maintain a daily log of tasks completed; to document the client's nutritional, cognitive, social, nursing, and medical status; and to communicate with the family. The notebook provided the client and family a means to share medical appointment information with the care provider; to communicate with the care provider; and to report Mrs. F.'s status and response to interventions provided. Health care providers used the information to provide historical data to facilitate assessment of current treatment plans and to communicate treatment plan recommendations. For the care manager, the data generated by the HCN helped piece together the "big picture." The HCN is an excellent means to track the client's verbalized needs, care provider role, medical needs, family ability to provide support, and to evaluate current interventions.

After one year, Mrs. F. returned to near base line in self-care and cognitive status. She continued to require daily assistance to meet IADLs and ADLs. Her family consistently uses the HCN for health monitoring, communication, and coordination and tracking of health care provider appointments. Care manager home visits have been reduced from weekly to monthly.

# Additional Self-Care Tools

Care managers have unique expertise in multifunctional assessments, problem identification and solving, negotiating the maze of health care and community resources, and networking and accessing a diverse group of professionals. This creates unlimited potential for community-based self-care education. Effective modes for educating the community are providing activities directed to the learning needs of clients and their support systems. Successful activities include conducting seminars, workshops, and classes at senior centers and community colleges and sponsoring health fairs and conferences. The goal of the sessions is to encourage persons to take control in decision-making rather than be a passive recipient of what others do to or for them. Topics of interest include how to hire a caregiver; managing chronic disease; housing options; advanced directives to physicians and health-care power of attorney; long-term legal and financial planning.

Conducting a family conference is another venue for transmitting self-care information. The problem-solving process provides a vehicle for education on disease processes, treatment and prognosis, societal myths, intervention options, self-awareness and coping skills, communication methods, and negotiating to reach family consensus. Checklists of critical facets of care needed can be used to guide clients and families during their investigation of housing and care options such as in-home care, foster homes, assisted living, intermediate care facilities, and skilled nursing facilities. This assembling of information increases the long-term success rate of the decisions made.

RCL is currently developing a "report card" for clients and/or their representative to evaluate the effectiveness of the established plan of care. Is the care manager creating an environment that enhances the *self-care* potential of the client? The purpose of the rating report by the client is to improve the care manager's skills in *listening* to the client's expressed desires and needs. How can one have the desire to do for oneself if one knows that someone else has already made the decisions?

# Vision for Self-Care

Health care in the 1990s will be characterized by limited resources, increasing incentives to manage health benefits, and consumers who want more control over their health care. In order to meet these and other challenges, providers will need to assist in the empowerment of their clients. Skills in win-win problem-solving and an increased orientation toward self-care will be crucial.

Providers will continue to face problems riddled with ethical issues, most of which they cannot address in isolation. An example is the need and use of advance directives. All people have the right and responsibility to be involved to the best of their ability in defining their advance directive wishes. However, they first need to understand the options in order to knowledgeably describe what they want. Education of clients about the health care system, health conditions, and options is critical in empowering consumers.

The conflicts experienced in health care are too often resolved with a win-lose approach. The "provider knows best" orientation has permeated professional training and practices, and at times inappropriately overrides an individual's health care preferences. Is it any wonder that client compliance is not higher? Self-care is supported when we 1) take advantage of teachable moments by educating our clients and families on options, consequences, and alternatives that are available; and 2) recognize and deal with conflict in a win-win fashion. By acknowledging that there is a partnership in health care, problems can be more readily identified and resolved. Additionally, the win-win process will lead to greater understanding of an individual's basic human needs, which influence behaviors and decision-making.

To be prepared for these changes and the requests from consumers, it may be necessary for health care providers to reevaluate their values and expectations. The following questions come to mind:

- Are we advocates for clients' rights? Do we clarify client and provider responsibilities? Are clients and significant others truly part of the decision making team?
- Have we incorporated self-care and educational opportunities into our practices?
- Do we understand which practices and tools work and when to use them?
- Are we evaluating health care based on providers' or client's goals?

The answers to these questions will require that we listen with a more involved and sensitive ear. Our role is not to take responsibility for our client's choices but to develop our expertise as facilitators in the decision-making process, thus empowering our clients to influence and direct their own care.

## References

Anna, D., Christensen, D., Hohon, S., Ord, L. and Wells, S. (1978). Implementing Orem's conceptual framework. *Journal of Nursing Administration*, November, 1978, 8-11.

Burnside, I. (1988). *Nursing and the aged: A self-care approach*. New York: McGraw-Hill.

Carnevali, D. and Patrick, M. (1979). "Health Care for the Elderly: Nursing's Area of Accountability", Ch. 1, 5-11. In: *Nursing management for the elderly*. Philadelphia: J.B. Lippincott Co.

Eliopoulos, D. (1984). A self care model for gerontological nursing. *Geriatric Nursing*, November/December, 366-369.

Fisher, R., Ury, W. (1981). *Getting To Yes: Negotiating Agreement Without Giving In*. New York: Penguin Group.

Janelli, L. (1980). Utilizing Roy's Adaptation Model from a gerontological perspective. *Journal of Gerontological Nursing*, 6(3), 140-150.

Kane, R., Ouslander, J. and Abrass, I. (1989). 2nd Ed. *Essentials of Clinical Geriatrics*. 61-69. New York: McGraw-Hill Book Company.

Larson, E. and Bruce, P. (1987). Health benefits of exercise in an aging society. *Archives of Internal Medicine. 147*, 353-356.

Matteson, M. and McConnell, E. (1988). Functional assessment. Authors, *Gerontological Nursing: Concepts and practice*. 57-91. Philadelphia: Saunders.

Platakis, J. (1987). Promoting health and wellness in the elderly. *Nursing Administration Quarterly. 14*(2), 40-43.

Redman, B. (1981). *Issues and concepts in patient education*. New York: Appleton-Century-Crofts.

# 7

# The West Point Experience

Karen Pugsley, RN, MSN
Rufus S. Howe, RN, MN, FNP

*In 1987, Karen Pugsley and I undertook a project that unpredictably became bigger than both of us. Our vision was to redesign a health care delivery system that started with the customer. Our idea was to allow our small community to tell us what they believed to be the most important health care services. Once these needs were identified, we made heavy use of computer data bases and health risk appraisal to track and identify those persons who may have needed more than the usual intensity of health care*—R.S.H.

The purpose of this chapter is to describe one U.S. Army hospital's effort to deliver health promotive health care in the face of shrinking resources and manpower—the Army Family Needs Assessment Program (AFNAP). AFNAP was (and is) an innovative health care delivery system that encorporates all four models of case management featured in this book. That AFNAP embraces the entire spectrum of case management is not unusual. What separates this system from the others is that the AFNAP—a largely hospital-based program—was designed from the self-care case management perspective. Frankly, the concept of case management was never mentioned during AFNAPs development. Sometimes the concepts come later.

The primary mission of the U.S. military medical system is to "conserve the fighting strength." For this reason, the military medical system must prioritize health care services to active duty service members. Family members of active duty service members are serviced next, followed by retired service members and, finally, their dependents. So there exists a "pecking order" of care that shapes the way military medicine is provided. This crucial point is often lost on many new service members and the newly retired, resulting in confusion and anger.

Availability of clinic appointments, surgery schedules, diagnostic procedures, and hospital beds are based on this priority list. Fortunately for those lower on this list, most medical care is still available in a timely fashion, but the system is fast becoming strained. Retirees and their dependents are more and more having to rely on CHAMPUS (a military supplemental health insurance for those under age 65) or civilian health insurance. Some military hospitals are no longer caring for certain retired populations.

The plan to downsize the military machine has caused considerable concern for health care providers, because the number of retirees and their family members will remain unchanged. Furthermore, some medical facilities have closed and more plan to close in the near future. These factors—prioritized medical care, non-availability of services to non-active duty personnel, and an overall reduction of medical services, have forced the military medical system to become acutely interested in health care delivery systems that support efficient patient management while improving access to care.

# Family Needs Assessment Program

The Army Family Needs Assessment Program was initiated in 1987 at the United States Military Academy, West Point, New York, in response to the above issues and a Department of Army Health Promotion Regulation, AR 600-63. AFNAP was implemented in a 65-bed community hospital situated in the rural area of West Point. The community hospital, called a MEDDAC in the military, offers a partial complement of services: orthopedics, pediatrics, obstetrics, opthalmology, urology, dermatology, and occupational health. The MEDDAC serves a population of about 25,000 persons, consisting of active duty and cadets (19%), family members (5%), and retirees and their families (76%). The MEDDAC is within 100 miles of major medical centers. The three goals of AFNAP were to provide:

1) early identification of selected risk factors using a health risk appraisal
2) timely and appropriate access to patient-selected options of health care
3) comprehensive patient-centered information systems to enhance quality improvement management platforms.

We were comfortable with the goals, but less comfortable with the path to reach them. Many (if not most) health care organizations respond to developing a health care delivery system by taking the "expert opinion" approach. The logic is that we in health care know best how to care for our population—even if the population isn't aware there is a problem. If the program fails, the blame falls on the non-compliant public. We identified three expert groups in this scenario—health care providers, community providers, and the target population. We refer to these groups as experts because from their perspective, they each know what is best for them or the patient.

Considering these three groups was our mandate while designing AFNAP. We either obtained or developed an instrument to obtain input from each of these groups—the health activities questionnaire, commander's questionnaire, and the Army's well check health risk appraisal tool.

The team approach was at the core of AFNAP and effectively brought together all disciplines within our health care system. The team approach provided a cross-sectional effort that improved the quality of AFNAP. Our AFNAP team consisted of physicians, nurses, administrators, and automated information specialists. In addition to individual team members, the AFNAP was also structured by organizational teams that helped clarify program focus and improve communication, thereby improving the system.

## Health Activities Questionnaires

The health activities questionnaire (Figure 1) was designed to determine the target population's perception of health-promoting and -demoting behaviors, and to seek input for access issues among the beneficiaries of the hospital. The questionnaire contained a series of open-ended questions that sought input about health-related topics from the target population's perspective.

The HAQ was developed by the MEDDAC and mailed to a random sample of 648 beneficiaries. Data from the HAQ were then carefully analyzed to established a marketing strategy and design appropriate programming.

Findings from the survey indicated program interest in exercise (62%), making better food choices (48%), weight reduction (39%), and stress management (23%). Respondents also indicated that they preferred self-help methods for altering behaviors (89%).

---

You have been selected to take part in a survey to find out what health interests you have. By helping us with this study, you will aid us in improving the medical care we give you. Please take a few minutes to answer the following questions and return them in the enclosed envelope.

1. What are you doing that keeps you healthy?
2. What are you doing that makes you sick or may make you die sooner?
3. How likely is it that any of the above habits will harm you? (circle the number that applies to you)

   not likely 1 2 3 4 5 extremely likely

4. What would you like to change to make yourself healthier?
5. What are the chances that you will be able to make these changes?

   none 1 2 3 4 5 extremely good

6. In the past, what health habits have you tried to change, how did you do it, and did it work?

   Tried to change How did you do it? Did it work?

   Example:
   Quit Smoking Cold Turkey No

7. How healthy do you think you are now? (circle one)

   poor 1 2 3 4 5 excellent

For the following question, think about your family, friends, coworkers, etc.

8. Who thinks you should make changes in your health habits and what changes do they want you to make?

   Who wants you to change? (Doesn't have to be a person, i.e., could be the Army)

   What behaviors do they want you to change?

   Example: Spouse and Army Lose weight

9. What is the easiest way for you to make changes? (Such as "on your own," "help from pamphlets," "in class")

*Continued on next page*

10. What would you like to see offered in a health promotion program?
11. If we offered health activities, what would be the best day and time for you?

## Demographic Data

12. Status (circle one):
    A. Civilian: GS-6 or below
    B. Civilian: GS-7 or above
    C. Family member of active duty: Enlisted
    D. Family member of active duty: Officer
    F. Active duty: Enlisted
    G. Active duty: Officer
13. Gender (circle one):
    A. Male
    B. Female
14. Age:

**Figure 1.** *Health Activities Questionnaire* (shown here in compressed format)

The commander's questionnaire design (Figure 2) was similar to the health activities questionnaire, but with a few administrative-type questions thrown in.

1. What do you think are the key components in a health promotion program?
2. What would you personally want to see included in West Point's health promotion program?
3. Where would you prioritize health promotion when considered in relationship to the installations mission?
4. In terms of combat readiness, what priority would you place on health promotion?
5. What role do you feel the command should play in health promotion?
6. What role do you feel USCC should play in health promotion?
7. What role do you feel Medical Services should play in health promotion?
8. What role do you feel community agencies (CRD, ACS, etc) should play in health promotion?

The population of West Point could be categorized into the following groups: cadets, active duty personnel and their families, civilian employees, and retired persons.

9. What health promotion activities, if any, should be provided by the installation to the cadets?
10. What health promotion activities, if any, should be provided by the installation to the active duty personnel and their families?
11. What health promotion activities, if any, should be provided by the installation to the civilian employees?
12. What health promotion activities, if any, should be provided by the installation to the retired?
13. AR-600-63, Army Health Promotion, dictates that the installation commander chair a health promotion council. It has been suggested that "key" installation leaders form a small executive team that directs the larger "working group." What are your thoughts on this matter?
14. How much are you willing to invest in installation time, money, and manpower to support health promotion?

**Figure 2.** *Commander's Interview*

## Health Risk Appraisal

The Army's health risk appraisal, an adaptation of the Rhode Island Wellness Inventory (Version 3.4), was used to begin a medical data base on the same target population. This HRA version was released in 1989 and included the Army's cardiovascular screening program.

Once the results were tabulated and analyzed, we set about reaching the three goals of identification, access, and a quality improvement-based management platform from which to operate.

## Identification

AFNAP enrollment involved inprocessing at one location only with three steps: completion of AFNAP forms and completion and review of the HRA profile. As personnel inprocessed through the military personnel office, an appointment was made for medical inprocessing. The military personnel office distributed a packet containing an information booklet describing health care options and containing AFNAP and HRA forms. The newly arriving family had an opportunity to review the health care options, choose the one that best met their needs, and complete the forms prior to the medical inprocessing appointment.

The HRA included a life-style questionniare and screening tests for elevated cholesterol, hypertension, and diabetes. An individualized health risk profile was printed and reviewed with clients by a health promotion counselor who also provided appropriate educational guidance.

A health promotion counseling tool was also used during the review session to assure that the counselors provided useful, accurate, and consistent information to all clients. The counseling tool was a flip chart that targeted the specific health risk areas identified in the HRA and was consistent with Army Regulation 600-63 (the health promotion regulation).

The well check clinic was the final step to AFNAP enrollment. At that time, the client's medical risk appraisal, consisting of health history and review of medical records, was seen and discussed by a nurse practitioner or an RN certified in physical assessment. A physical assessment was done as necessary. Appropriate referrals were then made. The client was assigned either to a designated primary health care provider or other support clinics and/or agencies. Referrals were expedited based on problem severity or the need for continued follow-up of a current medical regime. The screening process not only identified individual needs, but looked at the entire family structure.

## Access

An automated health care tracking system was the necessary link to effectively managing AFNAP. The software for user interface was developed to be as intuitive as possible by actively involving users of the system in the development of structure, wording of menus, data entry, screen design, and reports. The tracking process provided rapid access to patient information and was well received by the clinic staff.

Individual Zenith computers with 20 megabyte hard drives were used with the program. Though the computers were not networked at the start of this project, many of them were connected to a hospital-wide network. However, networking was still lacking and meant awkward information transfer problems when updating the various data bases.

The tracking system included three major modules:

1. The Health Promotion Center module stored incoming basic demographic data as well as health risks identified by the health risk assessment (HRA). The HPC used this module to make people aware of programs or services available.
2. The Clinical Support Division (the military counterpart to hospital administration) module matched patients and their families to appropriate health care providers. Treatment options were first registered in this module. The module provided a patient contact record which kept track of patient contacts—both good and bad. Contacts were considered as ongoing market research and used to better meet needs and interests.
3. The Clinic module contained the two modules named above but did not include the patient contact record. It was used to protect confidentiality. Core medical information found on the master problem list was also added by clinic staff.

We found that access is a two-way street. Typically, one may think of access from the direction of client to provider, but there are also problems in the reverse. The tracking software benefited both parties equally.

## Access from the Client Side

Beneficiaries were informed of the options for care: Family practice, general practice/pediatrics, internal medicine or CHAMPUS supplemental care. Information about various health care options was provided by video, pamphlets, and personal counseling. The pamphlet was given to beneficiaries at entry points such as the personnel office and army community services. The video was viewed at the time of enrollment. Finally, enrollment staff discussed the options, assisting beneficiaries with selection appropriate to the individual family needs.

AFNAP assigned the appropriate health care option to the client and family based on their choice and needs. A physician was designated by the clinical support division. Assignments were based on demand over the entire ambulatory system, thus balancing work load among providers and preventing overextension in any area.

# Quality Improvement Management

In order to administer the HRA, well check, and the health activities questionnaire, the hospital at West Point set up a health promotion center staffed by community health nurses and nurse practitioners. The health promotion center enrolled military beneficiaries, provided information about health care options and encouraged active participation in health care and health promotion. AFNAP included contracts between the consumer and the health care provider, timely and appropriate care, ongoing encouragement to alter modifiable health risks, and a central data base accessible to all health providers.

AFNAP enrollment and the HRA were offered to existing community members through a large community-based campaign. There was intense multi-media publicity about AFNAP, the HRA, and health promotion services, and a health promotion van visited all post housing areas during evening hours, screened residents for hypertension, elevated cholesterol and diabetes, conducted HRAs, and enrolled families in AFNAP. The health promotion van was well received, stimulating participation by 35% of the entire community.

As we stated earlier in this chapter, the AFNAP was built from the self-care perspective using the three major viewpoints—clients, providers, and community leaders. The primary care and episodic care models are fully supported by the enrollment process and tracking mechanisms. The episodic model is not as mature in its development—items such as critical paths and medical action plans are yet to be developed. The brokered care model is very much a driving force behind the day-to-day operation of AFNAP.

There is much left to be done at West Point to smooth out rough edges. Because the leaders embrace a quality improvement philosophy and their management platform supports close, accurate analysis, the prognosis for AFNAP is excellent.

## Community Leader's Survey

The Community Leader's Survey was designed to identify the perceptions and priorities of key leaders in the community. Formal and informal leaders were identified, and each was individually interviewed for 30 minutes. A standardized format was utilized and the community leaders' responses were taped and later transcribed. Specifically, areas of health promotion were addressed in the open-ended interviews. The community leader results were thoroughly analyzed and utilized along with the health activities questionnaire results to establish a marketing strategy and to design appropriate programming.

# 8

# Advice Nursing: First Step in Self-Management

Becky Mungai, RN, BA

*This chapter describes an excellent basis for organized self-care facilitation. As an advice nurse, Ms. Mungai clearly lays out her major functions, all of which aid the caller and benefit the hospital as well. The advice nurse complements our model in that she not only provides self-care information but also acts as a valuable link to case management dimensions.*—R.S.H.

## Overview

When a person has exhausted his/her own resources but is not quite ready to enter the world of health care, one way to maintain the self-care management role is to utilize an advice nurse.

An advice nurse has a multi-faceted role. In one short phone conversation she is capable of triaging a caller's symptoms and advising the caller when to seek medical attention and what to do at home in the meantime; referring the caller to a physician; scheduling the caller for a class the hospital is offering; giving health information; helping a first-time mother through the night with a sick child; offering reassurance to a caller waiting at home alone for 911 to arrive; or calling past callers back to see if they are satisfied with their physician and/or emergency room referral.

### Symptom-Based Advice—Using Protocols

The advice nurse uses a computer program comprised of protocols (guidelines) written by physicians and nurses who triage the caller's symptoms. Most programs set the protocols up into four categories: 1) emergent symptoms—seek emergency evaluation within 2 hours; 2) see physician within 24 hours; 3) make an appointment with your physician; or 4) home care—self-management.

## Follow-Up Calls

Most programs also provide an additional service of following up on emergent referrals within 24 hours. The RN calls the callers to ask if they sought emergent medical attention, if they were satisfied with their care, if they have any additional questions/concerns, if they need a physician referral for follow-up, and to remind them to call back if necessary.

## Health Information

By using medical staff-approved references and with some programs of computer-based information, the advice nurse answers callers' health information questions. These questions range from, "My child was exposed to chickenpox today. When should I expect her to break out and how long will she be contagious?" to "I read in the paper today that there was an outbreak of meningitis, what is that?" Some health information calls lead into symptom-based calls, such as when the caller asks "what is meningitis" and has a high fever, stiff neck, and rash. It is the experienced advice nurse who asks the caller "Are you having any symptoms that you're concerned about?" before going to the reference shelf.

## Class Registration

Many hospitals offer a variety of classes ranging from "How to tell a panic attack from a heart attack" to "How to speak so your child will listen, and listen so your child will speak". Most computer systems are programmed to allow the advice nurse to register callers for the hospital's classes. This is a very important opportunity for the advice nurse to assess whether it is wise for the caller to stay in the self-care mode or to seek primary care. A caller may call to register for a class such as "Carpal Tunnel Syndrome" when in fact they are experiencing numbness in the hand. The advice nurse would then look up "Neurological deficit" in the protocols and see that "numbness" requires an emergent referral, certainly not a *class*.

## Physician Referrals

It is when the callers have exhausted self-care options that they turn to the advice of a physician, linking self-care into primary care case management. The advice nurse has the ability to refer a caller to a physician by entering the caller's specific requirements, i.e., type of physician, gender, age, subspecialty, office hours, to name just a few. Some computer programs have the ability for the RN to place the caller's criteria in low, medium, and high categories—sorting the physicians accordingly.

If the caller calls during office hours the advice nurse attempts to make an appointment for the caller by placing a conference call to the physician's office.

If the caller calls after office hours or doesn't want an appointment, some programs call the callers back within a specific time frame of about three weeks to see if they made an appointment with the physician and if they were satisfied. If the caller is not satisfied with the physician, the advice nurse can refer them to another physician.

# Advice Nurse Performance

It is clear from the above examples that a good advice nurse must possess many qualities: triage nurse, counselor, teacher, community liaison, physician referrals, class registrant, and sometimes—a "detective". There are many instances that what a caller wants or is asking for and what he/she needs are two different things and only an experienced advice nurse can solve the puzzle. Take, for instance, the caller who wanted a class when she really needed an emergent referral, or a mother calling for the dosage of syrup of ipecac when she really needs the poison control center. It is the caller who is inappropriately trying to stay in a self-care mode that is the most difficult for the advice nurse to assess. It is up to the advice nurse to decipher what a caller is "really saying or asking".

One of the most important skills of an advice nurse is the ability to assess the caller's capability of understanding. The nurse doesn't want to talk at a level that is condescending, nor does the nurse want to "lose" the caller by "talking over their heads".

Another skill is keeping control of the conversation and conveying to the caller both the abilities of advice nursing and the limitations. For instance, an advice nurse cannot diagnose, prescribe medications or treatments, or give a prognosis. An advice nurse assesses the callers' symptoms as they describe them and, through the use of protocols, advises callers as to when and if they should seek medical attention. The caller always has the option of not taking the advice of the nurse.

Many hospitals are reorganizing the way they evaluate nurses. One hospital system is currently implementing a new strategy they are calling "Performance Management," in which nurses are evaluated on "job-specific accountabilities" that are weighted. This is a more objective evaluation. An advice nurse is evaluated by computer printouts, log notes, and/or taped telephone conversations.

# Benefits to Community, Physician, and Nurse

Advice nursing benefits the community far more than one would imagine. The advice nurse is often looked to as "the answer for it all"—health information, health advice, classes, physicians, counseling, child behavior consultant, and mental health consultant, to name but a few. The advice nurse fulfills most of these functions, and when it is something out of her realm, she almost always has a number to which to refer the caller.

Advice nursing is easily accessible—just a phone call away; it's free to the community; provides consistent information (all nurses at a given hospital use the same protocols); allows callers to stay in the self-care mode if they choose to or appropriately refers them into primary care case management.

The advice nurse is often the first step out of self-care. Many callers state that they feel better about "bothering" a nurse rather than a "physician". And when the caller appropriately calls an advice nurse, the physicians' valuable time can be spent attending to matters at their level. If the advice is to call their physician, the caller usually does so but if the advice is to use home care, the advice nurse has saved the physician's office a call. This is especially beneficial for the physician when the call is at 3 a.m.

When a caller is under current treatment for an illness or disease, the advice nurse refers the caller back to the physician. This is very important in maintaining continuity of care. Often when a prescribed treatment doesn't seem to be working, the public wants to try a new physician when many times the information that a treatment is ineffective is exactly what would lead the primary physician to a conclusive diagnosis.

Advice nursing is very fulfilling for the RN who enjoys seeing and experiencing the complete nursing process in a short time span. In one simple phone call the RN is able to assess, plan, implement, and with a follow-up call, evaluate and revise a nursing care plan. She is also able to use her knowledge and skills in counseling and teaching, thereby reaching a far more diverse and needy population than in any other area of nursing. Advice nursing is growing at a rapid rate. As more and more hospitals realize the benefits of a solid advice team, we will surely see advice nursing expanding.

# Benefits to the Hospital

The statistically proven benefits of advice nursing to the hospital are easier to measure than the empirical benefits. Most advice lines fall under marketing in the corporate structure. The hospital's main goal is to bring in revenue. It is fairly simple to measure the fact that physician referrals bring in revenue; that class registrations bring the public into the hospital system; and that symptom-based emergency room referrals bring in clear-cut revenue. But it is much less clear how health information and non-emergent symptom-based advice benefits the hospital. Many advice lines handle more symptom-based calls and health information than the proven revenue-producing calls. This poses a problem for the hospital as well as the advice nurses, often causing friction between the two. On the one hand, nurses want to give the public what they need (namely health advice), and part of the benefit to the nurse is providing that information free of charge. On the other hand, the hospital needs to see documented proof that the service is bringing in revenue.

This writer has been employed at three different advice lines in two different states. Two hospitals were private; one wrote its own protocols and had an independent system, while the other had a proven franchised system that is found at many other hospitals around the country. The third is a corporation of five hospitals which has recently implemented a new system that is also at many hospitals around the country. Its program is still in the infant stage.

It is very interesting to see the process of "proving" the worth of an advice line played over and over at each hospital. The hospital that devised its own system had the least internal opposition, was staffed according to call demand, and the nurses were paid and advanced as any other nurse in the organization. The second hospital has had its advice line for three and one-half years, and the nurses who staff it have spent most of that time "fighting" to be recognized as "full" nurses. They were left out of cost-of-living increases that were given to the other hospital nurses and each time had to write letters to the administration explaining their role. Just recently the hospital provided a budget to allow more staff to fill the call volume demands and compensate the advice nurses as "full" nurses. The third corporation of hospitals is just beginning its advice line and much work is still needed to get it going. The protocols, even though other hospitals around the country are using the same system, need revision and updating. The administration has yet to realize the importance of the service.

# Future of Advice Nursing

I believe the answer to providing a superior advice nursing line is to get the service out of marketing and into nursing, and to get the focus off revenue and into community service. But hospitals in today's economy cannot possibly do this. Many hospitals are already struggling financially. Possibly one answer is to find other funding for advice nursing. Each city could set up an independent network system that would give advice and refer callers to the closest, most appropriate service, hospital, or physician regardless of generating revenue. The service would operate on one set of protocols, thereby standardizing health care for an entire city. The funding could come from each hospital, the state lottery system, the state and or federal government by way of grants, and local businesses. The premise is: If we are not going to provide free or affordable health care to all people regardless of education, income, or insurance, the least we can do is provide a free health care advice line so they can better utilize the health care system. It's time we got away from how to make money and into how to save money. Providing the public with a system that appropriately assigns them to self-care or primary care should be the primary concern of the health care system and certainly the first step in case management.

# III

# PRIMARY CARE CASE MANAGEMENT

# 9

# Fundamentals of Primary Care Case Management

Rufus S. Howe, RN, MN, FNP

*Without doubt, ambulatory care now accounts for the lion's share of health care. It can be argued that this form of case management may potentially affect health care costs the most. This chapter supports the concept of the primary care case manager and proposes some innovative methods to "manage" primary care.*—R.S.H.

Primary care case management is not as well defined and studied as the rest of the case management models—as a brief scan of the table of contents will show. The reasons for this are many and will be addressed later in this chapter. The extremely scant literature on primary care case management is suggestive of the relative importance the health care industry (providers included) has placed on improving this aspect of health care delivery. Five well-known physician advocates of primary care case management and quality improvement were asked to submit a chapter to this book—four agreed to contribute, and one declined the offer. But six months and many communications later, not one physician was able to come up with a written word relating to primary care case management!

Aside from the frustration, there is another message that needs to be brought to the front. Even the "quality improvement physicians" are not able or willing to speculate on how primary care case management should play out and how it relates to other models of case management. What are we left with? We are left with me, a family practice nurse practitioner, explaining the salient features of this model. My hope is that you will use this chapter as a starting point.

# Background

According to our model, the objective of primary care case management is to provide assessment, diagnostic, and intervention services for those who have overwhelmed their self-care capacities. The supplier of this service must then be qualified to assess, diagnose, and treat. Based on our current health care structure, physicians, nurse practitioners, and physician's assistants fit this description. Alternative interpretations may include triage nurses who work from established algorithms or protocols and are given certain diagnostic and therapeutic privileges. Whatever the discipline, the primary health care provider in this model is in some way accountable for the complete routine care of the client.

For many years, a physician's practice was a sacred ground. There was no malpractice insurance to speak of. Patients were not the consumers they are today. One physician would never question (publicly) the practice of another because it wasn't "his business." Medicine was not yet to the high tech, high touch, competitive stage.

For some physicians, this "don't watch me" posture still exists, but their numbers are dwindling. Sharing practice patterns is now in vogue. Not only are physicians sharing their "pearls" with other physicians, they are beginning to incorporate ideas from other disciplines as well. So primary health care is moving in a new direction—from individual to professional community practice.

There is another change worth mentioning. Traditionally, primary care has occurred as a reaction to illness or injury. Sick people came to the doctor, who in turn reacted to their problem with a diagnosis and treatment. While sick people still present to the doctor's office, preventive care visits such as annual exams and Pap smears are fast becoming a significant part of the practice.

# Tools of Primary Care Case Management

For many, the tools of primary care consist of a collection of brief, terse notes, flow sheets and lab results loosely bound in the medical chart. Because of this tradition of brevity, many pertinent findings, therapies, and communications never find their way to the chart. Retrospective reviews (like those mandated in QA studies) become difficult if not impossible. Vital information is lost in the jumble.

Many of the tools of primary case management are already well developed, but perhaps not well coordinated. These tools should support proactive care, be based on state of the art standards of practice, and provide a system of documentation that lends itself to monitoring clinical practice.

The basic tools of primary care case management are described in the remainder of this chapter.

## Practice Guidelines and Protocols

Practice guidelines, protocols, or standard operating procedures can be thought of as the standard of practice for your community, state, or the nation. Several large medical organizations are aggressively trying to provide practice guidelines to standardize treatments and act as a basis upon which to build new knowledge.

## Flow Sheets, Problem Lists, and Medical Data Bases

Flow sheets, problem lists, and medical data bases all serve as summaries of the client's status. Risk factor reduction information such as Pap smear dates can be recorded in a clear, concise manner on a flow sheet, for example. Problem lists organize care for the clients and communicate the "big picture" for all health care team members. Whether manual or automated data bases assure that complete information exists for a client, one doesn't have to wade through the progress notes to search for family history or age of menopause, for instance. Unfortunately, as valuable as these simple tools are, they are the most neglected or underutilized.

## Critical Paths

Critical paths are not commonly found in the ambulatory setting. In the strictest sense, critical paths describe a process that starts, has midpoints, and ends. The episodic model of care fits well with this concept. Much ambulatory care ends only upon the client's demise. To see this point more clearly, let's take hypertension as an example. Once the diagnosis is made, the hypertension is a lifetime affair. Assessments and treatments are continually altered for the remainder of the patient's life. Because of this, ambulatory critical paths have a different time dimension. Instead of hourly or day parameters, time is measured as daily, weekly, monthly, yearly, or scheduled. The following format demonstrates what a portion of a hypertension critical path might look like.

| Daily | Monthly | Quarterly | Yearly |
|---|---|---|---|
| • Low-salt diet<br>• Take medications<br>• Exercise<br>• Avoid salt | • Blood pressure<br>• Weight | • At doctor visit review medications, signs and symptoms, habits<br>• Physical exam<br>• Lab work | • Risk factor reduction<br>• Pap smear<br>• Mammogram<br>• Rectal<br>• Cholesterol<br>• Blood glucose |

Notice that the critical path can be viewed as a summarized practice guideline. A critical path could be developed for each of the common diagnoses, then customized as necessary. To facilitate the client's self-care capacity, the critical path should be given to the client with any literature called for on the critical path. Doing this should help clients understand instructions, provide a ready source of expert advice, and clue them in on the regular cycle of their care.

An ambulatory critical path can also include episodic care if need be. Let's use an obstetrical case as an example. The time columns would be divided into the conventional prenatal visit schedule and end at the birth of the baby, discharge of the mother and baby to labor and maternity, then pick up again with post-partum and well child care. The perinatal chapter addresses this situation in detail and is an excellent example of how case management crosses heretofore uncrossable lines.

Developing these links in the critical path is essential to the continuity of care of the client as well as the consistency of care across providers. This linking is an obvious strength, but is actually quite hard to establish. Providers from different orientations are not used to working together—our present system doesn't support it.

## Referral Agreements

Referral agreements are a little-used tool in primary care case management. A referral agreement is a simple communication between a customer and a provider. The old adage "know your customer" plays out well here. Referral agreements set up a contract that lists the conditions of the referral. An example is in order: A nurse practitioner wants to refer a client to the urologist for evaluation of chronic urinary incontinence. The nurse practitioner calls the urologist to present the case and establish the referral. After ten minutes on the phone, the urologist accepts the referral and requests that a battery of lab tests be completed prior to the visit, and that the client present to his office with a full bladder.

This transaction could have been smoother with a referral agreement. The referral agreement includes the agreed-upon indications for referral, "set up" labs, and instructions, time frame for care, and the usual follow-up. Once this agreement is in place, the ten-minute telephone call is not necessary and the client's care is coordinated and efficient.

## Algorithms and Decision Trees

None of the above tools truly act in the process of decision-making. Algorithms and decision trees are decision-making tools. Most seasoned providers resist the idea of algorithms, stating that they are too "cookbook", and that "no single algorithm can accommodate the variation in presentations. There are, however, a growing number of such algorithms showing up in the literature.

Carmi Margolis, MD, from the Center for Health Sciences of Ben-Gurion University in Israel, is an outspoken proponent of clinical algorithms. Here's some of what Dr. Margolis has to say about algorithms:

- "It seems like a text describes one reality—in which the physician is a passive recipient of knowledge about diseases—while the clinician is required to function in a different reality—one that consists of making sequential decisions."
- "The main objection frequently raised to this seemingly drastic proposition (physicians as robotlike) is that algorithms will turn physicians into robots who do not think."

Debate over the clinical usefulness of algorithms continues. This debate is a healthy one, however. More work needs to be done to establish how algorithms fit in primary care. One tantalizing application is criteria mapping. Criteria mapping is a method of retrospective audit that examines each record in an algorithm fashion. This method tracks only salient features of care for a given case type and is tailored to the wide variance in patient responses to therapies.

To summarize the material covered in this chapter, full explanation of primary care case management is difficult given the newness of this approach. Primary care providers who use these tools should consider reporting on their effectiveness in clinical practice. Studies on health maintenance flow sheet performance have indicated a positive relationship to provider systems for health maintenance and client acceptance of screening. This is but one example of the growing body of knowledge in this area.

# 10

# Factors Affecting the Quality of Outpatient Cervical Cancer Screening

Rufus S. Howe, RN, MN, FNP
Robin Thomas, RN, MN, FNP

*On the surface, cervical cancer screening seems to be a "routine" office procedure. Yet, as this chapter illustrates, many problems still exist with the* process *used for such screening. Robin Thomas and I used statistical thinking (quality improvement methodology) not only to identify the salient fctors relating to cervical cancer screening but to propose a direction for improving the process.*—R.S.H.

Screening for cervical cancer is obviously a major component of a woman's preventive health care plan. Because cervical cancer is usually asymptomatic in its development, the woman will not be aware of the need to seek medical attention. By the time the woman gets a physical exam or symptoms appear, it may be too late for a positive prognosis. In fact, Mandelblatt (1989) points out that the most common characteristic of clients with invasive cervical cancer was that they had never been screened. The components of the screening process are well understood and studied. There is, however, the ongoing lack of coordination between provider, client, and health care delivery systems. The purpose of the study reported here was to evaluate the contribution of salient system variables that affect the quality of the cervical cancer screening process in a primary care setting.

## Significance of Problem

In the United States, nearly 13,000 new cases of cancer of the cervix are discovered each year (Silverberg & Lubera, 1988). In 1988, over 7,000 women died from cervical cancer (American

Cancer Society, 1988). For women who are diagnosed very early, the five-year survival rate approaches 100%, but only 40% of those with advanced cancer survive (Fink, 1988). The mortality rate is closely correlated with the timeliness of the Papanicolaou (Pap) test, a cytologic evaluation of cells found in the transition zone on the cervical os.

The Pap test is used for detection of cervical cancer, and is at the heart of the screening process. Evidence for the efficacy of the Pap test will probably never be studied in a randomized clinical trial due to ethical considerations. Indirect methods of evaluating the Pap test have shown it to significantly reduce the incidence of cervical cancer (Stenkvist, Bergstrom, & Eklung, 1984).

Risk factors and prevention strategies for cervical cancer are well documented. Mandelblatt (1989, p. 136), states, "Since the advent of the Pap smear in 1942, cervical cancer has become one of the most frequently screened-for diseases. Controversy still exists, however, as to the optimal frequency of administering this test." The doctor, nurse practitioner, and midwife are understandably confused. The data in Table 1 testify to the variations in screening guidelines encountered by providers.

**Table 1.** *Current Guidelines for Cervical Cancer Screening*

| Organization | Interval | Age at Onset | Age at Cessation |
|---|---|---|---|
| American Cancer Society and American College of Obstetricians and Gynecologists | Triennial; after three negative annual results | Onset of sexual activity | None; lifetime screening |
| U.S. Preventive Services Task Force | 2-3 years | 18 years | 65 years |

*Note*: From "Cervical Cancer Screening in Primary Care: Issues and Recommendations" by J. Mandelblatt, 1989, *Primary Care, 16*, (1), p. 140. Copyright 1989 by J. Mandelblatt.

## Literature Review

In a recent study by Woo & Woo (1985), comparisons were made between physician's recommendations, patient's desires, published guidelines, and actual practice. Their study found that there were discrepancies between these factors. Unfortunately, the sample was selected in a nonrandom fashion from an internal medicine clinic. This kind of sample is not representative of a normally distributed screening population (with varying amounts of active pathology). The authors acknowledged that the findings were generalizable to only their setting due to the nature of the patient population. In addition, no reliability or validity scores were mentioned for any of the instruments used in the study.

The patient sample was restricted to those followed on a regular basis in an internal medicine clinic. These patients were reported to have an increase in pathological problems and had adequate insurance coverage to pay for the screening evaluations. The authors mention that the study sample was probably different from groups who seek care on a sporadic basis. The conclusions drawn from this study were that the problem resides in the lack of an effective system for adequate screening to include reminders, cues, and cost/benefit ratios.

In another study looking at system characteristics of screening for cervical cancer, Wilson (1990) also used a survey design, but on a more "realistic" sample. Wilson's dependent variable was similar to the one proposed in this study—the number of women undergoing a Pap test in the previous five years versus the number who have never had a Pap smear. There was a practice improvement between the first and second surveys due to the adoption of a more consistent cervical cancer policy, and the addition of a call and recall system in many of the practices. Wilson was understandably impressed with his participants (physicians) for taking part in a potentially damaging inspection of their practice. Further, he stated that his purpose "was to stimulate interest and activity in cervical screening and to encourage practices to look at their own performance in more detail" (p. 377). The scientific rigor of this study was not high, but the goal of the study did not demand such depth. Certain aspects of the design were problematic, such as the sample selection, but overall, the study design and method seemed to fit the task and did a good job of describing the characteristics in question.

Measuring the quality of an ambulatory health care system is not as well understood in the health care arena as it is in manufacturing. One hospital's approach to this problem gives us insight into the complexities of the validity and reliability of measuring quality (Anderson, Benson, Schweer, Gartner, & Jay, 1989). Anderson et al set forth ten parameters of health care that are thought to encompass the determinants of quality. These parameters were placed in rank order in terms of impact on the client's health status and assigned weights upon which to compute a final program quality index (PQI).

The PQI was the measure of quality of a given system (one number, many parameters). The study included only hospital administrators, physicians, and specialists as expert judges to rank the parameters. There were no nurses, clinic support staff, ancillary services (pharmacy, lab, therapy services), or clients included in the ranking. This is unfortunate, in that the ranks are from a perspective that may or may not be representative of the entire system's impact.

# Conceptual Framework

Unfortunately, inconsistent recommendations are not the only problem with cervical cancer screening. There are many other variables that influence the quality of the process. For the purpose of this study, six major parameters are identified as being important to the success of the cervical cancer screening process. Within these major parameters, there are many influencing subsystems. Figure 1 illustrates these parameters in a modified cause-and-effect diagram and their subsystems and suggests relationships to the quality of the cervical cancer screening process. These factors were developed during a series of brainstorming sessions with a cross section of staff involved with the cervical cancer screening process.

## Setting

The setting for the study is a family practice clinic located in an urban area in the northwestern United States. The clinic staff consists of five family practitioners, one family practice nurse practitioner, one registered nurse, four medical assistants, one clinic administrator, and two receptionists. This clinic depends on a moderately large outside laboratory for Pap smear evaluation.

The clinic serves approximately 4,800 women who are considered "regular clients." All newly acquired clients are required to complete a personal health history form that includes biological, psychological, and, sociological data. Portions of this form are incorporated into a computerized client data base for tracking purposes. The personal health history form is located in the client's chart. The clinic staff follows the ACS recommendations (noted in Table 1) for cervical screening and have not added to it or amended it in any way. Due to the evaluative nature of this

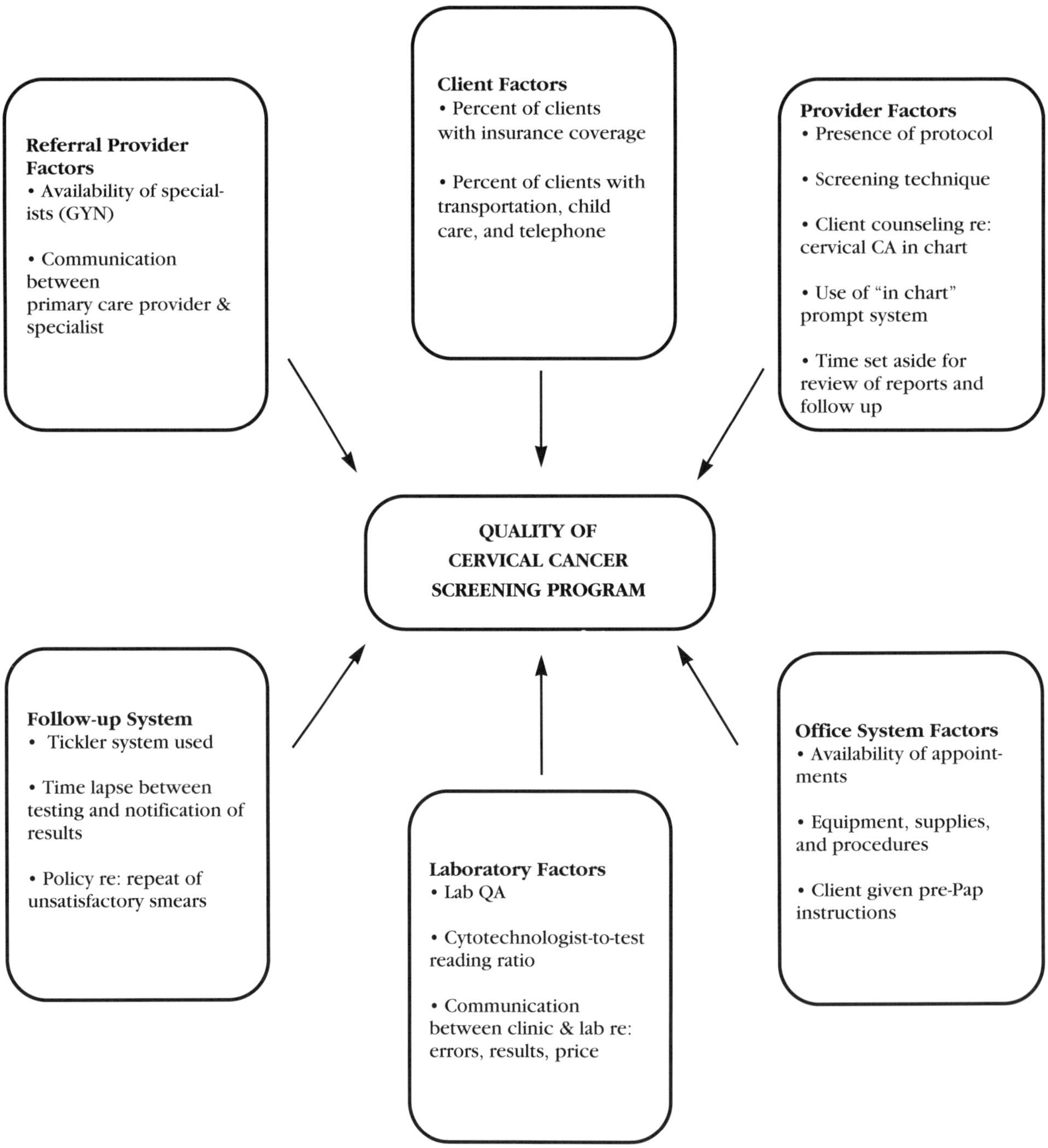


**Figure 1.** *System of factors hypothesized to affect the quality of a cervical cancer screening program in a primary care clinic*

study, the findings will be generalizable only to this primary care clinic. Factors thought to affect the quality of the cervical cancer screening program in this clinic are shown in Figure 1.

## Modified Mission Statement

What is the relative contribution of the provider, client, administrative, laboratory, referral provider, and follow-up parameters to the quality of the cervical cancer screening process?

For the purposes of this project, quality of screening for cervical cancer is defined as the ratio of women identified as needing Pap tests (per practice guideline) to women who have been identified but have not had a Pap test.

The clients for this study included women over the age of 17 who had completed the personal health history and had at least two visits to the health care provider. It was necessary that one of the visits included a basic physical exam and review of the client's medical history. This requirement ensures that the provider has had the chancc to review the client's record in some detail, and that the client has demonstrated the intention to establish a long-term relationship with that provider.

## Data Collection Methods

The investigators used multiple sources of data, including medical records, computer databases, self-reported health history forms, and observation. Table 2 describes the factors, parameters, criteria for evaluation, and instruments for input into the evaluation of the quality of cervical cancer screening.

To the degree possible, the sample of clients was randomly selected from a computerized list of women meeting the inclusion criteria noted in Table 2. To ensure an equal chance of selection, the last two numbers of the client case number were matched with a table of random numbers. If this was not feasible, the charts of the next 50 women who presented for Pap smears and met the criteria could be audited. The demographic profile of the "convenience" sample could be compared to the general clinic population to check its representativeness.

# Analysis Strategy

The following analysis is abbreviated for illustration purposes only and is fictitious. This explanation should help you to follow one thread of the overall project from describing and prioritizing the phenomena to seeking root causes and taking action.

Implicit in this study were the following objectives: 1) to enhance the health-promoting aspects of cervical cancer screening for the client; 2) to reduce the cost of cervical cancer screening; 3) to describe communication between consumers and suppliers; 4) to reduce the amount of waste, rework, and duplication in the system; 5) to develop instruments that adequately measure components of each parameter; and 6) to help establish a more participatory approach to system improvement.

The various aspects of each parameter will be computed on a standardized score and applied to an index based on 100. A score of 100 will be interpreted as meeting all the requirements

**Table 2.** *A Description of the Factors, Parameters, Methods, and Instruments*

| Factor | Parameter | Data Collection Method/Tool |
|---|---|---|
| Outcome variable<br><br>Quality of cervical cancer screening | Number of Pap smears performed to Pap smears required according to established guidelines | Probability sampling technique on 100 charts using the clinic's computerized data base. Search (inclusion) criteria will be: (Pap test done) Gender = female and age>17 and Pap = "yes" and Papdate = current date—5 years and Client visits>1. (Pap test not done) Gender = female and age>17 Pap = "no" and Client visits>1. |
| Client | Presence of insurance that covers routine screening and follow-up | Data base retrieval |
| | Percent of clients with transportation, child care, and telephone (Burack, 1989) | Chart audit using the client personal health history form (part of client record) for the status of these aspects of the parameter |
| Provider | Protocol | Documented evidence of a protocol based on ACS guidelines |
| | Screening technique (Helderman, Graham, Cannon, Waters, & Feller, 1990; Mandelblatt, 1989) | Inadequate smears/total of smears from cytology lab report |
| | Client counseling | Chart documentation of counseling regarding cervical cancer screening by stating "Pt. ed. re: Pap" in plan section of SOAP note. The treatment protocol will define what instructions to the client should include |
| | Time allowed for Pap test review and follow-up | Documented administrative time set aside in work schedule for this activity |
| | Client encounter prompt system which includes Pap test dates and results | Chart review for presence and completeness (current dates) of "in chart" prompt system (like a flow sheet) |

| | | |
|---|---|---|
| Referral provider | Availability of specialists to clinic | Documented list of at least three GYN cancer specialists available to clinic providers |
| | Communication between clinic providers and specialists | Evidence in chart of communication with referral provider to include consultation letters, results |
| Follow-up | Tickler system (Wilson, 1990) | Documented protocol of reminder system used by clinic |
| | Test-result-notification time frame | Chart review of test, result, and notification date |
| | Repeat smear policy | Presence of repeat smear policy in accordance with established guidelines |
| Administrative | Availability of Pap appointments | Review of provider schedule for first available appointments appropriate for Pap tests. Number should be proportionate to population at risk |
| | Equipment and supplies | Inventory list should include equipment and supplies necessary to perform Pap test according to guidelines |
| | Client pre-Pap instructions | Administrative staff able to produce a list of pre-Pap instructions given to each client upon making an appointment for a Pap smear |
| Laboratory | Quality control | Use of a certified lab (by the American Society of Cytologists or College of American Pathologists) that follows QC according to guidelines established by agency |
| | Cytotechnologist/ test ratio | Survey of number of Cytotechnologist-to-test ratio from lab compare with standards |
| | Lab-to-clinic communication | Communication log that includes date, time, result, and method of communication; also, presence of a written contract that documents agreements between the lab and clinic re: quality control, accuracy of evaluation, timeliness of reporting results, and levels of urgency versus reporting methods |

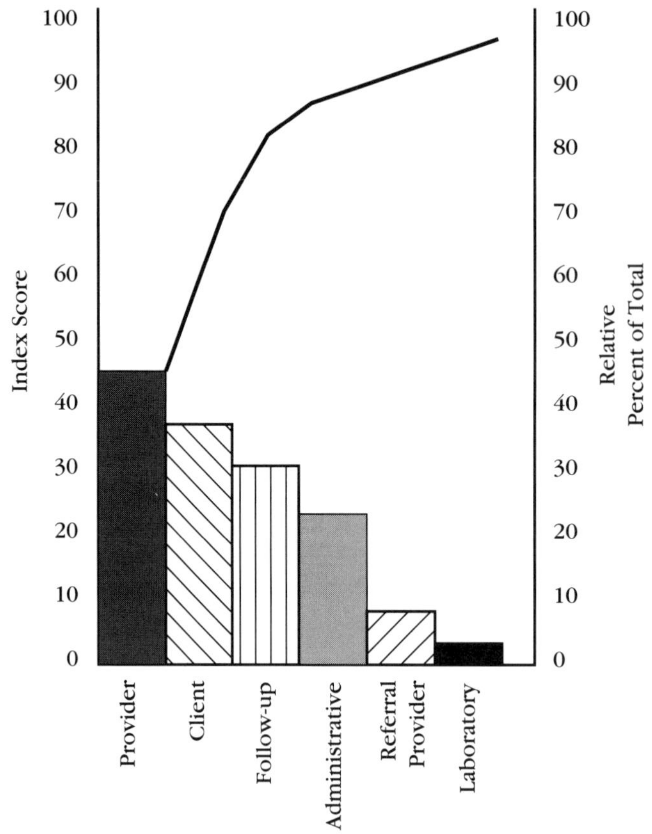


**Figure 2.** *Pareto by Phenomena. Relative contribution of factors relating to cervical screening process*

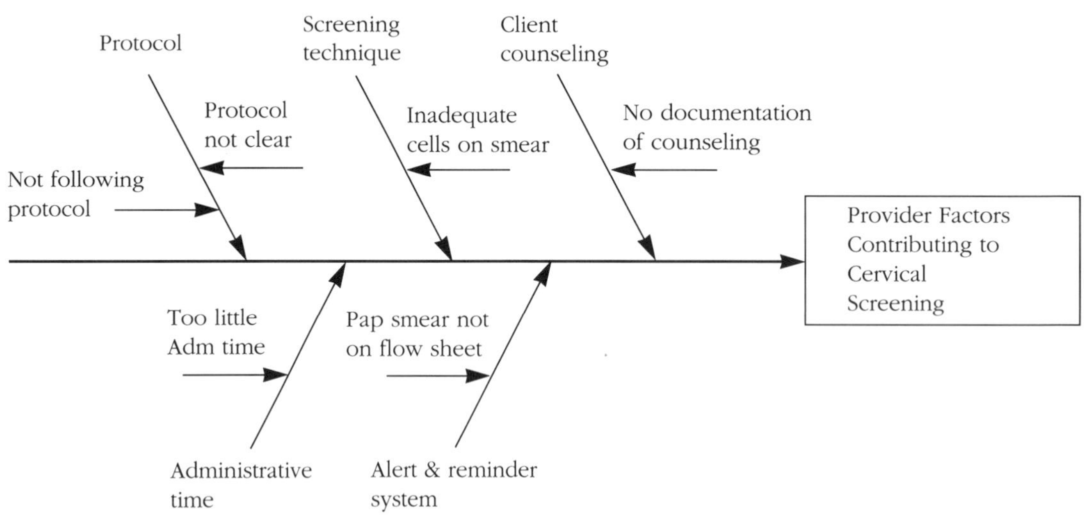


**Figure 3.** *Provider variables in cervical screening*

of that parameter. See Figure 2 for a detail of the findings. According to the Pareto Principle, factors that contribute to 80% of the total variation in the process should be attended to first. For the purposes of this project, the provider quality characteristic will be examined first. A criteria map of the cervical screening practice guideline provided the basis for chart auditing of the provider variables. The provider variables in question were detailed using a fishbone diagram (Figure 3). Once this fishbone was completed, a systematic audit captured data on each of the provider factors contributing to the quality of the cervical cancer screening process. A second Pareto chart was then constructed to prioritize the various causes of provider-related error (Figure 4).

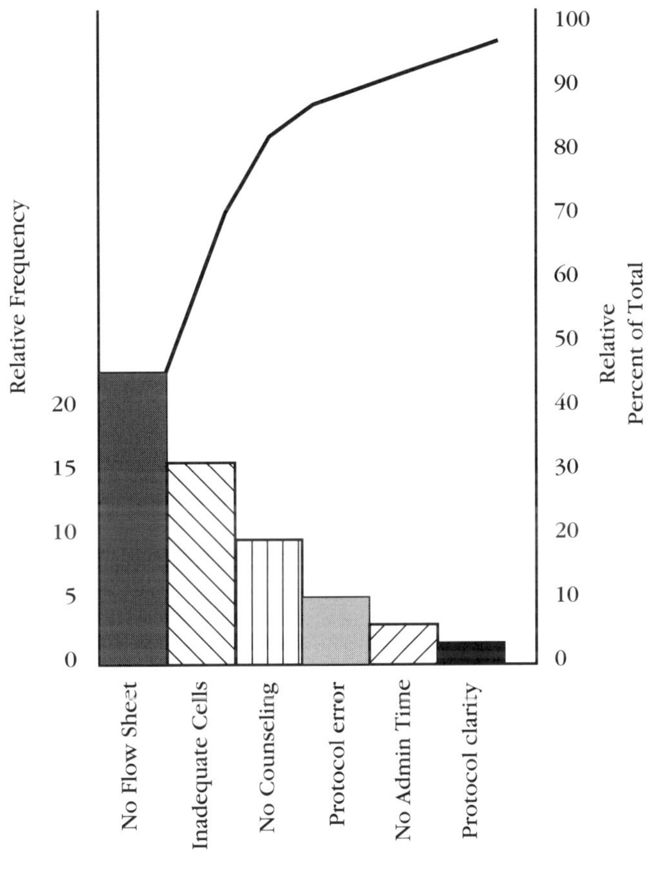


**Figure 4.** *Pareto by Causes. Relative contribution of cervical screening process failure*

## Potential Utilization of Findings/Summary

This study provides a relevant framework for system quality improvement. We recommend, based on the above findings, that:

- A flow sheet with "Pap smear" be placed in every female client chart on top of the progress notes.
- The clinic switch to a brush instead of a spatula to ensure adequate cells.

- A preprinted counseling sheet be inserted into the medical chart on every Pap smear appointment.
- The cervical cancer practice guideline be brought into a consensus within the group of providers to ensure a community standard of care.
- Administrative time be allocated to support and provider staff to update alert and reminder aspects of the medical chart.

In this study, the "health" of the cervical cancer screening system is expressed in the outcome variable and is "representative" of the six parameters. Once the relative contributions of each parameter are measured and then compared to the others, the clinic staff can prioritize and concentrate quality improvement efforts in a more cost-effective way. In this example, only the provider phenomena were detailed. Other phenomena, such as client or follow-up factors, would be handled in a similar fashion.

This study also seeks to explore the practicality of system improvement methodologies in terms of clinical decision making. Due to the complexities of ambulatory care systems and the myriad internal and external influences on those systems, it is usually impractical to apply the findings of one setting's audit to other settings. The practicality issue then becomes whether this exercise in quality improvement will positively affect the quality of the cervical screening process (Collier, 1990; Miller, 1989).

## References


American Cancer Society. (1988). *Statement by Dr. Harmon Eyre, national president, ACS*. New York.

Anderson, J., Benson, D., Schweer, H., Gartner, C., & Jay, S. (1989). AMBUQUAL: A computer supported system for the measurement and evaluation of quality in ambulatory care settings *Journal of Ambulatory Care Management, 12* (1), 27-37.

Benson, D. S., Gartner, C., Anderson, J., Schweer, H., & Kirchgessner, R. (1987). The ambulatory care parameter: A structured approach to quality assurance in the ambulatory care setting *Quality Review Bulletin, 13* (2), 51-5.

Burack, R. C. (1989). Barriers to clinical preventive medicine *Primary Care, 16* (1), 245-50.

Collier, J. (1990). Developmental and systems perspective on chronic illness. *Holistic Nursing Practice, 5* (11), 1-9.

Fink, D. J. (1988). Change in the American Cancer Society checkup guidelines for detection of cervical cancer *Cancer Association, 38* (127).

Helderman, G., Graham. L, Cannon, D., Waters, K., & Feller, D. (1990). Comparing two sampling techniques for endocervical cell recovery on Papanicolaou smears *Nurse Practitioner, 15* (11), 30-2.

Madlon-Kay, D. J. (1987). Improving the periodic health examination: Use of a screening flow chart for patients and physicians *Journal of Family Practice, 25* (5), 470-3.

Mandelblatt, J. (1989). Cervical cancer screening in primary care: Issues and recommendations *Primary Care, 16* (1),133-155.

Miller, J. (1989). Evaluating structure, process, and outcome indicators in ambulatory care: The AMBUQUAL approach *Journal Nursing Quality Assurance, 4* (1), 40-7.

Silverberg, E., & Lubera, J. A. (1988) *American Cancer Statistics, 1988, 38* (5). American Cancer Society.

Stenkvist, B., Bergstrom, R., & Eklung, G. (1984). Papanicolaou smear screening and cervical cancer: What can you expect? *Journal of the American Medical Association, 252,* 1423.

Wilson, A. (1990). Cervical cytology in the vale of trent faculty of the royal college of general practitioners, 1985-8 *British Medical Journal, 300,* 376-8.

Woo, B., Woo, B., Cook, E., Weisberg, M., & Goldman, L. (1985). Screening procedures in the asymptomatic adult: Comparison of physician's recommendations, patient's desires, published guidelines, and actual practice *Journal of the American Medical Association, 254,* 1480-4.

Woods, N. F. (1988). Using advanced statistical procedures. In N. F. Woods, & M. Catanzaro (Eds.), *Nursing Research: Theory and Practice* (pp. 420-2). St Louis: Mosby.

# IV

# EPISODIC CARE CASE MANAGEMENT

# 11

# Implementation of Episodic Case Management in a Managed Care Organization

Joyce Cardinal, RN, BS, CCRN
Vicky Knecht Kraushar, RN, MS
Teresa Wagie, RN, MS

*The three case managers at Emanuel Hospital, Portland, Oregon, have implemented a highly successful system for caring for inpatients. Emanuel shares the same problems that many other hospitals face—decreasing census and a large nonpaying clientele. The onus was on the leadership to transform health care delivery into a more cost-effective system while sustaining or improving the quality of care.*

*This chapter focuses only on implementing episodic care case management; no attempt is made to develop links to the other dimensions of our model. I have found that emerging case management systems first look inward, then as time and success permit, develop links to other care modalities. As this book goes to press, Emanuel is establishing links to pre- and postepisodic care. The authors of this chapter lead the reader through the steps necessary to implement episodic care case management. These case managers have, in my view, allowed us in the back door to see at first-hand what it takes to get this overwhelming task accomplished.*—R.S.H.

Health care in the 1990s is rapidly changing, forcing hospitals to evaluate patient care delivery systems. Changes in insurance reimbursement and the diagnosis-related groups (DRG) system have greatly influenced health care. It has become clear that health care professionals must work smarter in order for hospitals to remain in the health care business. Episodic case management and managed care produce quality patient care, and increase patient/family and practitioner satisfaction as well as reduce costs.

At Emanuel Hospital and Health Center, Portland, Oregon, case management has two focuses. First, a registered nurse in the role of case manager facilitates the development of critical paths and Multidisciplinary Action Plans (MAPs), follows complex patients to coordinate their care and assists with discharge planning. Case managers analyze variances from the critical path and work with other disciplines to make changes to reduce length of stay, as well as work toward efficiency and quality improvement. The second focus concentrates on staff nurse management of predictable case types utilizing critical paths and MAPs.

This chapter focuses on design and implementation of episodic case management/managed care in the acute care setting. Following are the steps required for implementation:

1. Financial analysis
2. Strategies for hospital staff and physician education
3. Development and refinement of episodic case management/managed care tools
4. Multidisciplinary reviews
5. Implementation of model
6. Catastrophic case management
7. Variances
8. Evaluation criteria for success of the model

# Financial Analysis

Emanuel Hospital and Health Center underwent a reorganization in the summer of 1990 and hired a consultant to assist in the implementation of case management. The consultant provided direction and information in the early stages of development of the case management model necessary to identify high-volume, high-cost, and low-reimbursement case types as well as quality of care issues for case type selection.

To determine which DRGs to begin with, the Medical Record Department provided us with a list of patients admitted to the hospital during the previous year. The list, grouped by DRG, also included primary diagnosis, length of stay, physician, payer source and patient charge. We averaged the length of stay and charge for each DRG. The next step was to rank the DRGs by volume and charge. Cross-referencing each DRG helped us to identify the top 20 DRGs by volume and charge. The top volume and charge case types were then ranked again by DRG reimbursement. We discovered, however, that we had to redo this ranking, utilizing actual reimbursement for accuracy.

In order to determine the actual cost of care provided we calculated the contribution margin ratio of all revenue-generating cost centers. The contribution margin ratio was computed by spreading the cost of running all nonrevenue-generating departments over the revenue-generating departments based on each department's percentage of overall hospital revenue.

We then took the cost of the nonrevenue-generating departments and allocated that cost to each of the revenue-generating departments based upon their contribution margin ratios. This gave us a cost-to-charge ratio that we were able to use to determine the daily cost for a patient on a specific unit and for diagnostic treatments. Our process for determining the cost-to-charge ratio was verified by our chief financial officer.

We compared our data to Medicare statistics for length of stay and reimbursement to determine how our hospital compared to the national length of stay and how our charges compared to reimbursement for Medicare. We found that our length of stay for most high-volume case types was actually under the Medicare length of stay; however, our cost was significantly higher than the Medicare reimbursement. This confirmed that our primary focus should be on resource utilization, with a secondary focus on length of stay.

Additionally, we analyzed current patient bills from the top 20 case types that were ranked by volume and loss to determine the percentage of each hospital department's charges and to look for any discrepancies in these charges by service. For example, supplies utilized by the operating room had a higher charge than the same supplies that were utilized on a medical/surgical unit. Historically, surgical charges were reimbursed at a higher percentage, thus explaining the reason for this practice; however, with DRG reimbursement and per diem rate reimbursement, separate departmental charges are irrelevant. This fact was communicated to the hospital's administrative staff in order to standardize charges between departments and to reduce total charges.

Based upon this financial analysis we determined which case types to begin development of critical paths for, with a strong emphasis on resource utilization. The challenge that faced us was to develop critical paths that would continue to provide quality patient care with a reduction in resource utilization.

# Strategies for Education

Prior to the development of critical paths and MAPs, we began educating the nursing leadership group on the concepts of episodic case management and managed care. At the first educational session, we shared our financial analysis and ranking of the prior fiscal year's DRGs in terms of volume and cost. This educational session assisted our group in determining which DRGs to use to begin the development process for critical paths and MAPs.

In addition to our own educational sessions with the nursing leadership group, we also invited an outside speaker to assist with the education process. Our speaker addressed the administrative staff, physicians, and all other hospital staff to reinforce how case management/managed care has been successful across the country, while stressing the benefits of this patient care delivery system.

During this same time period, we began making appointments with the medical chiefs of services and chairs of departments. We met with these physicians in their offices to begin familiarizing them with the concepts of case management and managed care. We attended their department meetings but found that as a group, they were unable to come to a consensus about this process and were skeptical. We found that by meeting with the physicians in their own offices they were more receptive to the concepts of our program and more supportive of the process.

Emphasizing that case management/managed care would be a process to facilitate care for patients throughout their hospitalization helped us obtain physician support. In addition, we stressed that orders would be carried out in a timely manner and the staff would be better able to anticipate the physician's needs. We emphasized variance analysis and resolution concerning system issues that physicians found problematic. We also asked the physicians for their input on system problems and took the critical paths back to the appropriate physicians for their input and approval. It was also suggested that preprinted orders could be drafted to match the critical paths.

We offered one-hour educational sessions to all employees within our institution to provide exposure to the concepts of case management and managed care. After the development of several critical paths, we presented an eight-hour workshop for the staff nurses designated as resource people on the units where case management would be implemented. The curriculum for this workshop included:

- Concepts of case management/managed care
- The tools of case management/managed care
- How to implement case management/managed care on the unit level.

In addition, the resource people were asked to develop critical paths using three methods of development.

We attended staff meetings on the units that were planning to implement case management and answered any questions that remained after the staff attended educational sessions. Another important issue included the education of the medical residents, because most of the patient orders were generated by them.

We found that with only three case managers following patients across multiple units, we needed to change our strategy in order to optimize the resources utilized in providing patient care by placing a single unit on managed care. We chose the orthopedic/neurosurgical unit for several reasons:

- The predictability of their patient population
- Support of the physician staff
- Limited residents on the service
- A strong integrative collaborative practice component
- The expertise of the nurses.

The educational needs shifted to a larger group of staff needing to be educated in the day-to-day utilization of managed care tools. Therefore, we provided three-hour workshops for all staff nurses on the orthopedic/neurosurgical unit. This provided baseline knowledge for all staff prior to the implementation of the model.

# Tools for Episodic Case Management/Managed Care

The tools of episodic case management/managed care include the critical path (Table 1), Multidisciplinary Action Plan (MAP) (Table 2), and the Variance Analysis form. Critical paths can be obtained by a variety of methods. One option is to purchase critical paths from various institutions. If critical paths are purchased outside of your institution, it is imperative to individualize them to meet your own health care team's practice patterns. Another method is to develop critical paths by doing a retrospective chart review of selected case types. A third way is to do a concurrent review of charts for patients who are presently hospitalized with a given diagnosis for which a critical path is being written. The last method is expert review. With this method the multidisciplinary health care team provides input for the critical path in an organized meeting.

We chose the method of retrospective chart review for our institution. Our development of the critical paths included utilizing our hospital's prior fiscal data for length of stay, since the Medicare length of stay was generally longer. The critical paths included the DRG number, diagnosis, a place for recording both co-morbidities (pre-existing medical conditions) and hospital-acquired complications in order to assist the Medical Record Department in abstract coding at discharge.

For the selected case types, we reviewed multiple charts under a specific diagnosis that met both the average length of stay and average charge for that case type. Areas of the chart abstracted for the critical path included:

- Physician orders
- Treatment records

**Table 1.** *Critical Path*

| | | | |
|---|---|---|---|
| **CRITICAL PATH**<br>**EHHC** | **CASE TYPE: DRG # 209 TOTAL KNEE ARTHROPLASTY/REVISION (R) (L)**<br>**Comorbidities:**<br>**Complications:**<br>**Code Status:**<br>**Allergies:**<br>**ANTICIPATED LOS: 6.0 DAYS**<br>**#PER MD ORDER** | | |
| **HOSPITAL DAY**<br>**UNIT** | **Preadmission**<br>**Preadmission Program** | **Admission/Preop**<br>**Orthopedic/Neurosurgical** | **Admission/Postop**<br>**Orthopedic/Neurosurgical** |
| **DATE** | | | |
| **CONSULTS** | Social Services # | Chaplain, VNA# | PT ordered#, O.T. ordered# |
| **DIAGNOSTICS** | CBC with Auto Diff#<br>Protime#, PTT#, ESR#<br>Chem Profile - Acute#<br>Urinalysis#, ECG#, CXR# | Type & Cross for __units#: | A&P/Lateral XR of knee (PAR)# (17 inch film)<br>Daily Protimes# |
| **PROCEDURES**<br>**TREATMENTS** | Alert blood bank of autologous blood collection#<br>Preop instruction sheet given<br>Instruct:<br>Antiseptic cleansing prior to surgery<br>Presence of tubes<br>CDB<br>Ankle pumps<br>Measure for:<br>Knee immobilizer# | Vital Signs Q 8H<br>I & O<br>IV site care<br>Measure for:<br>Antiembolic stockings; place on patient and send with pump to OR# | Vital signs per P.O. protocol<br>I & O<br>Foley or straight cath PRN#Hemovac/Drain#<br>IV site care<br>CDB/Incentive spirometer#<br>Epidural protocol#<br>Pulse oximeter#<br>$O_2$#<br>Antiembolic stockings#<br>Knee immobilizer#<br>Elevate affected extremity<br>Ankle pumps<br>Transfuse# |
| **HYGIENE** | | | |
| **MEDICATIONS** | Instruct:<br>PCA pump#<br>PCA pump brochure# | Antibiotic IV on call (or send) to OR#<br>Other medications# | Antibiotic IV x 24H#<br>Analgesic IV/IM PRN#<br>Coumadin per pharmacy#<br>PCA Pump#<br>Other medications# |
| **IV** | Instruct:<br>Presence of IVs | IV fluids# | IV Fluids# |
| **ACTIVITY** | Instruct:<br>Postop positioning/CPM#<br>Durable medical equipment | Activity as tolerated# | Bedrest/Turn Q 2H#<br>Start CPM 0-30°# |
| **DIET** | Instruct:<br>NPO past midnight | NPO# | Clear liquid diet#<br>Advance diet as tolerated# |
| **DISCHARGE PLAN** | Home assessment | | |
| **PATIENT/ FAMILY TEACHING** | Surgical waiting area<br>Visiting hours<br>Smoking policy | CDB/Incentive spirometer#<br>PCA pump#<br>Ankle pumps | CDB/Incentive spirometer#<br>PCA pump#<br>Knee immobilizer#/CPM# |
| **ASSESSMENTS** | D/C Planning Sheet<br>Surgical records completed<br>Abnormal diagnostics called to MD | Admission Form completed<br>Notify resident if: | Medical/Surgical Flowsheet<br>Notify resident if: |

**Table 2.** *Multidisciplinary Action Plan (MAP)*

| | | | | | | |
|---|---|---|---|---|---|---|
| MAP<br>EHHC | CASE TYPE: DRG # 209 TOTAL KNEE ARTHROPLASTY/REVISION (R) (L)<br>Comorbidities:<br>Complications:<br>Code Status:<br>Allergies:<br>ANTICIPATED LOS: 6.0 DAYS | | | | | |
| **PATIENT CARE** | **SHORT TERM GOALS**<br>**Key: M = Met R = Resolved * = see Progress Notes/Flowsheets** | | | | | |
| **DAY/DATE** | **Preadmission:** | | **Admission/Preop** | | **Admission/Postop** | |
| **PHYSIOLOGICAL:**<br>Neurovascular Impairment | | | Performs ankle pumps correctly | | Performs ankle pumps correctly<br><br>CMS good to lower extremities | |
| Musculoskeletal Impairment | | | | | Tolerates 0-30° flexion on the CPM machine | |
| Skin impairment | | | | | Dressing is clean, dry and intact | |
| GI impairment | | | | | Nausea controlled | |
| Pain | Pain level & coping style identified | | | | Pain controlled | |
| **PSYCHOSOCIAL:**<br>Support systems | Identifies social/family support | | | | Expresses anxiety appropriately | |
| Coping mechanisms | States concerns about hospitalization | | | | Coping mechanisms remain effective | |
| **ENVIRONMENTAL:**<br>Safety issues | Verbalizes home safety issues | | Functions safely in hospital | | Uses knee immobilizer safely | |
| Equipment needs | Identifies current use of any equipment | | | | States rationale for CPM | |
| **SELF-CARE:**<br>Interference with ADLs | Identifies current activity level<br><br>States understanding of postop positioning | | Verbalizes correct activity precautions | | Verbalizes correct activity precautions | |
| **EDUCATIONAL:**<br>Special learning needs | States knowledge:<br>Antiseptic cleansing<br>NPO status<br>Smoking policy<br>CDB technique<br>PCA pump | | Performs CDB/IS<br><br>States knowledge:<br>NPO status<br>Correct use of the PCA pump | | Performs CDB/IS<br><br>Verbalizes and performs correct use of the PCA pump | |
| **DISCHARGE PLANNING:**<br>Follow-up care | Verbalizes possible need for NH placement or VNA at D/C | | | | | |
| Goals/Outcomes | Yes☐ No☐ | | Yes☐ No☐ | | Yes☐ No☐ | |

| Initials | Signature | Initials | Signature | Initials | Signature | Initials | Signature |
|---|---|---|---|---|---|---|---|
| | | | | | | | |

- Educational documentation
- Therapist's notes
- Progress records.

We reviewed an average of 10% of charts for patients admitted with the selected diagnosis on the critical path for the previous year.

After abstracting the charts, we placed items that occurred 100% of the time on the finalized critical path. Our goal was to have a common critical path per case type and not physician-specific critical paths. Items that occurred more than 50% of the time, but less than 100%, were also placed on the critical path, but with a symbol to indicate that these items were by specific physician order. The critical path did not replace written physician orders, but assisted in standardizing the use of resources for a patient under a specific diagnosis, as well as making the patient's care needs more predictable for the health care team members. The critical path also helps expedite the patient's progression throughout his/her hospitalization by providing discharge planning. For example, on admission, a patient with a hip fracture who undergoes an open reduction internal fixation surgical procedure has an initial discharge plan completed. On postoperative day number four, an evaluation for a skilled nursing facility is completed to finalize the discharge plans.

### MAPs

Once the critical paths are reviewed by the multidisciplinary team, MAPs are developed utilizing a problem list, with expected patient outcomes identified by the multidisciplinary health care team for the specific case types. Like the critical paths, the outcomes identified on the MAP show logical progression toward discharge. The problem list of the MAP was categorized under major subheadings according to the standards for patient care established by the Joint Commission on Accreditation of Healthcare Institutions (JCAHO). Discharge outcomes also established included the Oregon Medical Professional Review Organization's (OMPRO) discharge criteria. These OMPRO criteria were included to ensure that patients were medically ready for discharge. Additionally, this ensured that the resident staff was writing discharge summaries justifying patient discharges when OMPRO criteria were not met. The other major benefit of including OMPRO discharge criteria was maximizing the hospital's reimbursement for Medicare and Oregon Welfare Department patients.

The MAPs are reviewed each shift during nursing report; however, each discipline has the responsibility of addressing achievements of outcomes for the specific patient for each area of expertise. Codes have been established to indicate if an outcome has been met, if the problem has been resolved, or if the plan for achieving the outcome needs to be revised. In addition, the nursing staff on the evening shift has the responsibility of evaluating whether or not the outcomes established have been achieved for the last 24-hour period.

## Multidisciplinary Reviews

Once the critical paths and MAPs were drafted into a final format, multidisciplinary reviews were held. These multidisciplinary reviews had experts from all the disciplines involved with the patient's care review the critical paths and MAPs. The goals of the multidisciplinary review included:

- Reviewing the present practice patterns.
- Suggesting methods to improve quality of care.
- Suggesting ways to streamline resource utilization resulting in cost-effectiveness.

Once the revisions were made on the critical paths and MAPs, physician input and approval were obtained. We provided the physicians with clinical data and literature to ease them into agreeing to the recommended changes in their practices made by the multidisciplinary health care team. For example, the use of metered dose inhalers (MDIs) was instituted on day one of the hospitalization, if indicated, in addition to the aerosol nebulizer for the patients admitted with simple pneumonia. The aerosol nebulizer was discontinued for all patients on day three, with MDIs continued until discharge as needed. This change in physician practice addressed both quality improvement for the patient as well as cost containment in regard to resource utilization.

The last tool is the Variance Analysis form, which tracks deviations from the critical path that cause delays or deviations in patient treatment and/or discharge. This form allows all members of the health care team to identify the type (system, patient/family or practitioner) and cause of the variance, as well as to suggest methods of getting the patient back on track with the critical path. The case manager analyzes the variances in order to correct system problems/weaknesses and to identify practitioner educational needs.

Many revisions occur during the development and implementation of the critical paths and MAPs. A trial period for actual use of these tools should be allowed before secondary revisions are made. With the use of these tools, resource utilization can be streamlined, yet quality of patient care can be improved.

| DATE/TIME INITIALS | VARIATION | CAUSE | ACTION TAKEN |
|---|---|---|---|
| | | | |

| Initials | Signature | Initials | Signature | Initials | Signature |
|---|---|---|---|---|---|
| | | | | | |
| | | | | | |



**Figure 1.** *Variance Analysis Form*

Episodic case management/managed care has positively affected health care delivery at Emanuel Hospital and Health Center. We believe that the multidisciplinary review is the key factor behind the success of our program.

After the first draft of the critical paths and MAPs, a multidisciplinary team was organized to review each discipline's current practice patterns and resource utilization for each specific case type. Members of the team include any discipline directly or indirectly involved with the patient's care: nurses, pharmacists, occupational therapists, physical therapists, clergy, dietitians, speech pathologists, respiratory therapists, admitting clerks, preadmission nurses, interns/residents, and social workers. The goals of these reviews were to examine current practice and determine ways to improve on the quality of that practice in a more cost-effective manner. Changes on the critical paths were supported by consensus among team members, other clinical experts, and research data.

The benefits of conducting multidisciplinary reviews were to provide an atmosphere to promote teamwork, collaborate on ideas to improve quality of care, and reduce both resource utilization and duplication of services. The benefit to each team member who participated in the reviews was that he or she was able to see how his or her interventions influenced the rest of the health care team members' relationships to the patient. Patient problems/needs and outcomes were also identified on the MAP by each discipline for each specific case type that was presented.

After the critical paths and MAPs were revised with the multidisciplinary team's recommended changes, they were taken back to the physicians for their input and approval. When recommendations were made to alter current physician practice patterns, literature to support the changes was provided for the physicians. For example, we recommended that the orthopedic surgeons at our institution decrease the use of prophylactic intravenous antibiotic therapy in elective surgical procedures. The antibiotic therapy was changed from 48 hours to 24 hours postoperatively, which benefited the patient by reducing the risk of chemical phlebitis and pseudomembranous colitis. This change also benefited the hospital by reducing pharmacy costs and nursing time for medication administration.

Another positive change that occurred during the multidisciplinary review was the recommendation that all patients with chronic illnesses be evaluated for pneumonia and flu vaccine during their hospitalization. This had positive benefits for the patient since perhaps a second illness could be prevented. The benefit for the hospital was that a second admission could be prevented for a patient with an underlying chronic illness.

Finally, the multidisciplinary review provided an atmosphere to discuss appropriate teaching for patients based upon the diagnosis of the patient on admission. All disciplines discussed what they would teach the patient and on what timeline.

# Implementation of Model

Once the critical paths and MAPs were developed for the chosen case types and staff education was completed, episodic case management/managed care was ready for implementation on the pilot unit. Prior to the actual start date, certain logistical questions needed to be answered, such as where would the critical paths and MAPs be stored on the nursing unit, who would stock them, and where would they be kept once they were initiated for a patient.

We chose to stock the critical paths and MAPs in a designated file cabinet on the nursing unit. Initially, the case managers were responsible for restocking, but as more case types were developed, it became clear that it would make more sense to have them reproduced and distributed from our central printing department.

In order to promote collaborative use of the critical paths and MAPs, we chose to keep them on a clipboard at the patient's bedside. This promoted easy access to the current care plan for all health care team members, and also provided an overall view of how the patient was meeting the individualized daily goals set by the multidisciplinary team members.

The initiation of the critical path and MAP ideally began at the point of entry into the hospital system. The point of entry could be the preadmission program, where the patient was seen on an outpatient basis prior to hospitalization for an elective surgical procedure. Initiation of the critical path/MAP could also occur on the day of admission in the Emergency Department or on the admitting unit. The critical path/MAP selection was made by the admitting nurse or floor nurse.

Once the critical path and MAP were selected based upon the admitting diagnosis and the initial assessment of the patient was completed, the bedside nurse reviewed the critical path and made modifications to the plan of care as appropriate. The bedside nurse also reviewed the critical path with the attending physician and/or resident within the first 24 hours of admission. The critical path did not replace written physician orders, but served as a guide for writing them. After the initial 24-hour period, any changes to the critical path were noted as variances. The critical path was then utilized for nurse/physician rounds and nursing intershift report on a daily basis to keep the patient on track as well as to identify and resolve variances. The case managers monitored the system from a distance and were there on the floor during the initial stages.

In addition to daily use of the critical path and MAP, multidisciplinary discharge rounds were performed on a weekly basis on identified patients who were not following the critical path or were having difficulty meeting their goals. This multidisciplinary meeting provided an opportunity to discuss discharge teaching needs and to assist in determining realistic discharge dates for complex patients. With a collaborative approach and timely goal setting, we believed that quality patient care could be provided with appropriate resource utilization, even for the most complex case types.

Another part of our case management/managed care model was to provide multidisciplinary case conferences to discuss an individual patient with complex discharge needs with the health care team as well as the patient's family, when appropriate. These meetings provided the members of the health care team, as well as the family, a forum to address treatment options and answer specific questions regarding the discharge plan. The meetings were facilitated by a case manager, who assisted in keeping the meeting within a predetermined time frame, yet assured that questions were answered and a new plan realistic for the patient was developed to address variances that occurred.

Finally, to make the episodic case management/managed care model work, the case managers were available for case consultations with any member of the health care team when a patient had a variance that prolonged treatment and/or delayed discharge. Case consultations were short and had the goal of developing a plan to correct the variance(s) or intervening to correct a system variance viewed as interfering with the health care team's ability to deliver quality patient care.

# Catastrophic Case Management

After developing critical paths for some of the simple case types, we identified certain case types that did not fit the conventional critical paths. However, these patients, who use a great many resources, were in need of case management. An example were patients admitted under DRG # 2, Craniotomy for Head Trauma, Age >17. We had a high volume of these patients, with long lengths of stay at high cost to the institution. Reimbursement for this case type was only 34% of our charges.

We developed a critical path for the patient with craniotomy for head trauma, but found so many patient variances that the nursing staff found this critical path too confusing. We began to look at other methods of managing these patients. A form was developed to help track these patients and closely monitor resource utilization. Initial family contact was made by the case manager soon after admission of the patient with head trauma. The case manager assessed the family's educational needs and provided initial education. The case manager also initiated appropriate therapies and a rehabilitation consultation when needed.

We found that discharges were often delayed because we did not have a good method to determine the patient's medical readiness for discharge. To correct this, we called skilled nursing facilities and rehabilitation centers in the area to determine their admission criteria. We then developed discharge criteria for traumatic brain injury patients being sent to these facilities and for patients being sent home (Tables 3, 4, and 5).

We set up weekly multidisciplinary rounds, where weekly goals were set for each patient. The case manager began talking to families about discharge as soon as the patients were transferred out of the intensive care unit. As soon as a discharge destination was determined, the multidisciplinary team had a conference with the family to discuss discharge planning. During this conference the disciplines working with the patient communicated their role in the patient's care, the goals set for the patient to achieve, and the patient's progress thus far. We tried, as a team, to help the family understand and accept the discharge plan for the patient. If a patient was to be discharged to home, the case manager arranged teaching sessions for the family before discharge. Our case management model for these patients required a team approach, including not only the multidisciplinary team, but also the patient's family.

This case management model for the patient suffering head injury was adapted for the patient with catastrophic illness or injury.

**Table 3.** *Discharge Criteria (Skilled Nursing Facility)*

1. Afebrile, off or on antibiotics.
2. Stable vital signs.
3. Suctioning no more than every 2 hours.
4. Tolerating oral feedings or tube feeding via PEG, gastrostomy, JJ or nasogastric tube. If nasogastric tube is being used patient is not at risk for pulling tube.
5. Restraints used for patient safety. A plan of care regarding restraints must be a part of the discharge summary. (i.e., restraints may be off when family is in the room.)
6. No purulent/bloody drainage from incisions or wounds.
7. No CSF leak.
8. Staples or sutures out.
9. Electrolytes within normal limits.
10. Reculture of sputum, blood, and urine within one week of transfer. SNFs will not accept patients with cultures positive for MRSA. If patients have positive cultures with any organism other than MRSA, contact nurse epidemiologist.

**Table 4.** *Discharge Criteria (Rehabilitation)*

1. Must be able to actively participate in 3 hours of therapy a day.
2. Afebrile, off or on antibiotics.
3. Stable vital signs.
4. Tolerating oral feeding or tolerating tube feeding via PEG, gastrostomy, JJ or nasogastric tube. Patient with nasogastric feeding tube should not be at risk for pulling tube.
5. Weight bearing for head injury patients unless Rehab stay is for family training.
6. No purulent/bloody drainage from incision or wounds unless able to be contained.
7. Must have a discharge destination other than a nursing home.
8. Seizures must be controlled by medication.
9. Must have PT and PT evaluations before Rehab consultation obtained. Speech consultation must be obtained for head injury patients.
10. Special considerations for ventilator-dependent patients per psychiatrists.

**Table 5.** *Discharge Criteria (Home)*

1. Afebrile.
2. Stable vital signs.
3. No purulent/bloody drainage.
4. Stable on oral diet (tube feeding only with family training).
5. Trach out.
6. No IVs or IV medication within 24 hours of discharge.
7. Rancho Level 6 or 7 only discharged after family conference. All Rancho Level 6 patients being discharged must have Rehab consultation before being discharged to determine if appropriate for inpatient or outpatient Rehab or to recommend appropriate follow-up.

## Variances

There are three types of process variances: system, patient/family, and practitioner. On the back of the critical path sheet is a Variance Analysis form (Figure 1). A list of variance codes developed in conjunction with the Medical Record Department's coder abstractors are utilized for trending purposes. For example, under a system variance, equipment failure or inability to get operating room time is included. A patient/family variance may involve the patient and/or family not being able to decide to have a certain procedure performed. An example of a practitioner variance is different physician specialists writing conflicting orders for a patient.

Once the variances have been compiled into the appropriate classification of their type, the case managers examine trends or significant system variances that contribute to delay in treatment and/or discharge. If a system variance occurs that could have an effect on a large number of patients, an action plan is established and the variance is dealt with in a timely manner. For example, it was noted that a patient on the medical unit had an order for a physical therapy evaluation, pending discharge, on a Friday afternoon. The physical therapy department saw orthopedic and

**Table 6.** *Types of Variances*

| System Variances | Patient/Family Variances | Practitioner Variances |
|---|---|---|
| Internal:<br>Equipment failure<br>OR time unavailable<br>Trauma pre-empt<br>Department closed<br>External:<br>Rehab transfer delayed<br>SNF placement unavailable<br>Equipment needs not met (i.e., brace) | Patient:<br>Fever<br>Infection<br>Ileus<br>Fall<br>DVT<br>Unplanned return to OR<br>Family:<br>Not available to take patient home<br>Unable to make decision on procedure | Physician:<br>Consultant MDs write orders that conflict<br>Covering MD not willing to discharge<br>RN:<br>Failure to properly prep patient<br>Omission<br>Commission<br>Ancillary Staff:<br>Procedural error |

burn patients only on the weekend, and new evaluations only on Monday. The patient on the medical unit was seen on Tuesday morning and discharged that afternoon—a four-day delay in discharge because of an existing policy.

The case managers noted this significant delay and met with the manager of physical therapy to solve this problem. It was agreed that in the future, all evaluations that need to be done to assess patient safety prior to discharge would be given priority on the weekend, as long as the person entering the order into the computer system noted that the evaluation was pending discharge.

If it is noted over time on pre-established critical paths that consistent variances occur that indicate a change in physician protocol, then the critical path is revised accordingly after discussion with physicians. A wait of several months is suggested before such revisions are made.

In the event that a patient develops several variances from the critical path, any member of the health care team may consult a case manager for assistance in formulating a plan to correct the variances or for coordinating a multidisciplinary patient care conference. Patient/family variances, although significant, may not always be avoidable, and the critical path may need to be modified to adapt to the change in patient condition.

# Criteria for Success

When implementing episodic case management/managed care, it is important to develop measurable and realistic criteria to evaluate the success of the model. We developed evaluation criteria that encompassed outcomes in terms of patient care quality, financial results, and levels of satisfaction.

The patient care quality improvements included:

1. Improved documentation of patient pain control
2. Improved documentation of patient education
3. Decreased infection rates for IV-related phlebitis
4. Consistent documentation of patient discharge planning
5. Decreased number of readmissions to the hospital (with the same DRG) within 30 days after discharge.

The financial outcomes included:

1. Decreased nursing overtime (measured in one-hour blocks)
2. Decreased (or same) average length of stay for all selected case types compared to previous year's fiscal data
3. Decreased (or same) average charges on all selected case types (including ancillary department charges such as pharmacy, laboratory, and physical therapy) compared to previous fiscal year's data
4. Increased (or same) percentage of reimbursement from charges for selected case types compared to previous year's fiscal data.

The satisfaction outcomes included:

1. Increased nursing satisfaction
2. Increased physician satisfaction
3. Increased patient/family satisfaction
4. Decreased time for conducting patient discharge rounds on the nursing units.

Baseline data in the above-mentioned areas were collected prior to implementation of the episodic case management/managed care model. The financial outcomes were evaluated at both 6- and 12-week periods after implementation, whereas the patient care and satisfaction criteria were evaluated after the 12-week period only. These findings then were compared to the baseline data previously collected.

An example of a patient care outcome that indicated improved discharge planning involved the Social Service Department's new practice of seeing or telephoning elective orthopedic surgery patients prior to their admission. On one occasion, a patient who was scheduled for a total knee replacement and would not be able to return home after the surgery discussed discharge destination with the social worker. The patient was provided with a list of skilled nursing facilities and given the opportunity to tour and choose the facility she wanted prior to admission to the hospital.

Physician satisfaction was monitored by giving all the involved orthopedic surgeons satisfaction surveys prior to and three months after implementation of episodic case management/managed care. We surveyed the physicians in the following areas: physical therapy, occupational therapy, nursing, dietary, and pharmacy; and the Social Service Department's involvement in discharge planning. Physician satisfaction increased in all areas after implementation of case management/managed care, with the most significant increase in the area of discharge planning. We believe by involving Social Service with patients prior to admission, physician and patient satisfaction increases and clinical outcomes are improved as well (Figure 2).

Nursing satisfaction was measured by providing the staff with a questionnaire prior to and three months after the implementation of the case management/managed care program. This questionnaire had 32 questions in the areas of collaboration, documentation, nursing process, patient/family education, and professional development. Again, all areas improved from the baseline data collected, with a return rate from nursing staff of 74% (Figure 3).

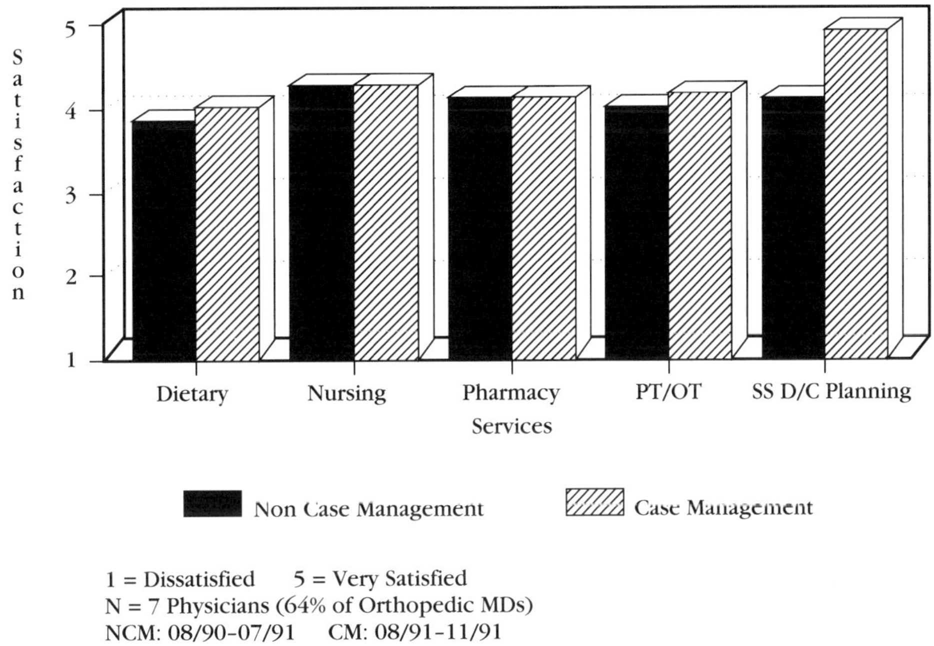


**Figure 2.** *Physician satisfaction (by services)*

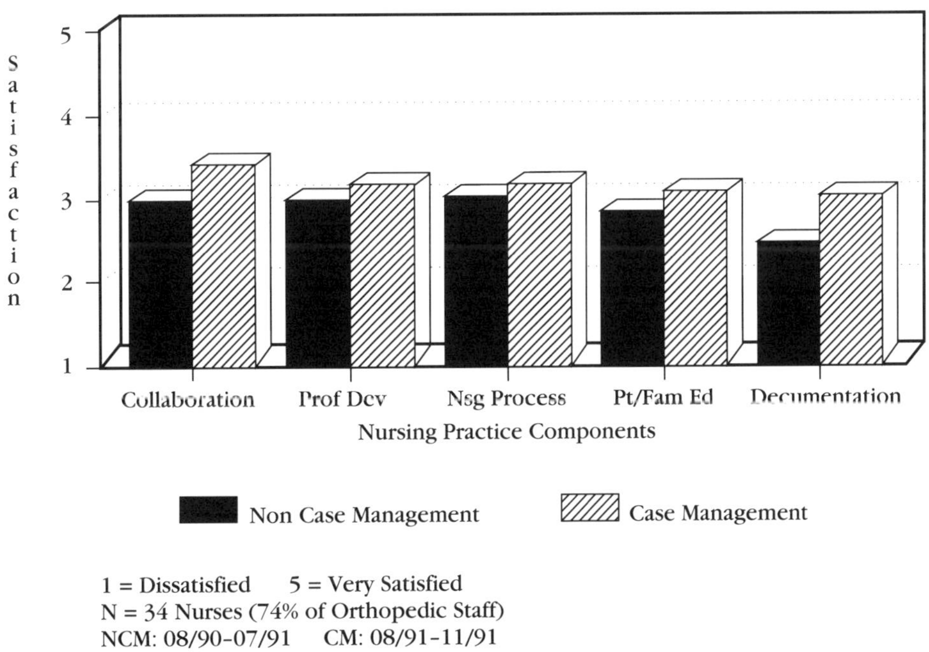


**Figure 3.** *Nursing satisfaction (by nursing service components)*

In all 12 case types involving our pilot unit, length of stay decreased. The most significant decrease was in the number of hip fracture patients who underwent an open reduction internal fixation procedure. Length of stay decreased from eight days to six days due to earlier discharge

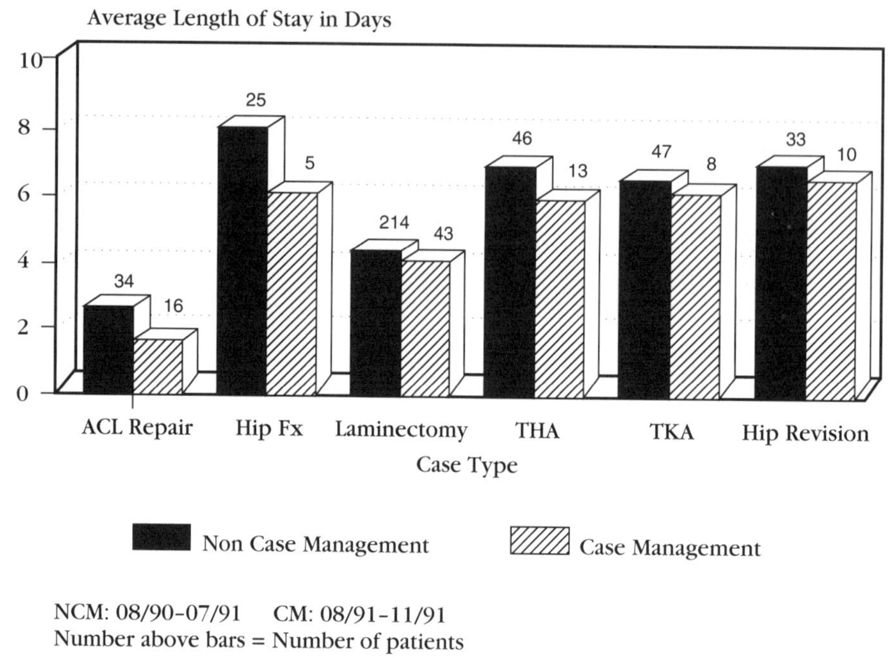


**Figure 4.** *Average length of stay per patient (by case type)*

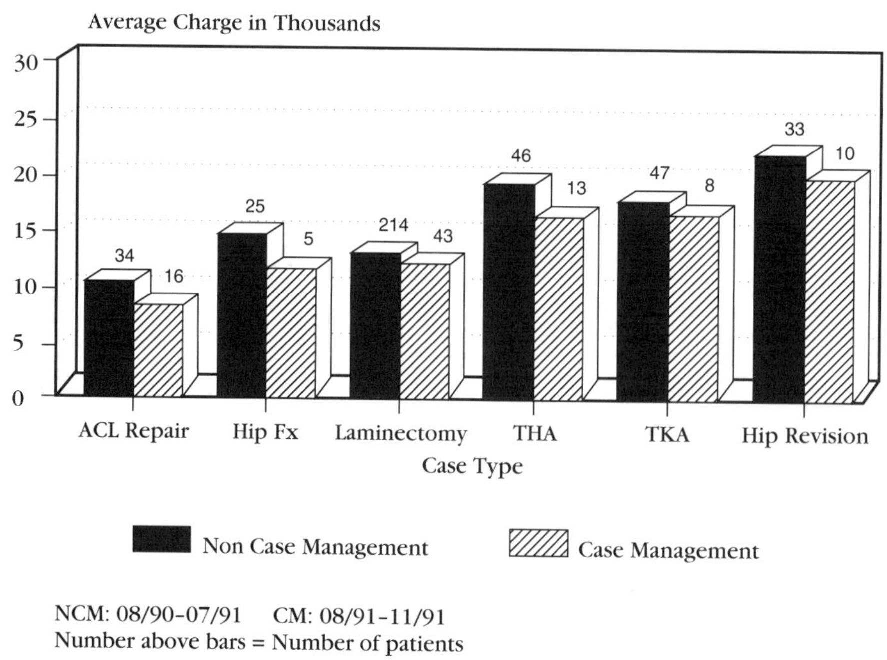


**Figure 5.** *Average charge per patient (by case type)*

planning and earlier involvement with physical therapy. Not only does this have a positive financial impact for the institution, but it also improves clinical patient outcomes (Figures 4 and 5).

Due to the success with the pilot unit in terms of quality improvement in patient care, practitioner satisfaction and financial outcomes, we believe that episodic case management/managed care can be adapted to other services within our institution. We have already begun implementation of this model on our surgical/gynecology unit and are working with our Family Birth Center staff to expand this program into that unit.

In addition to implementation of this program in our own institution, we have begun to consult with other hospitals within our own Legacy Corporation as well as other hospitals in the Pacific Northwest. We strongly believe that the Emanuel model for case management can be adapted to any health care setting and used with any nursing patient care delivery model. Continuous quality improvement in patient care is the priority while implementing such a program; a secondary benefit is institutional financial success in the 1990s.

# 12

## Acute Care Case Management

Virginia Del Togno-Armanasco, RN, MN

*In this chapter, Ms. Del Togno-Armanasco presents an example of episodic care case management that is worthy of examining because it works. As with the Emanuel group (chapter 11), the focus is on delivering high-quality, cost-effective care that is collaborative. The two programs have some superficial differences, however. Tucson Medical Center's critical paths are largely developed through the nurses' expert review, whereas Emanuel's are developed through retrospective chart audit. Both methods appear to work equally well. Tucson Medical Center's critical path and MAP format are quite different (columns instead of rows for tasks), but again, both methods seem equally effective. Tucson Medical Center's use of patient/family information books and discharge sheets adds a dimension of self-care to the episodic environment.*—R.S.H.

Motivated by a reimbursement system that paid a predetermined amount based on the diagnosis-related group (DRG) into which an illness fell and by contracts with HMOs and PPOs, Tucson Medical Center (TMC) was challenged to seek new ways to provide quality patient care in a fiscally responsible manner. (Del Togno-Armanasco, Olivas, & Harter, 1989). After researching the most promising systems for providing high-quality care in the mid-1980s. TMC decided that the key figure in any system aimed at achieving its objectives in an effective and efficient manner would be the registered nurse. The RN seemed to be paramount in the process because of his/her professional practice focuses on collaborating with all disciplines and coordinating the care required and specified by each physician. Developing a patient care delivery system to facilitate RN professional practice while using the knowledge and skills acquired in nursing education would be beneficial to the patient, nurse, physician, and the hospital. Such a process would support the staff nurse at the patient's bedside in collaborating with all clinical disciplines and coordinating the care needed for each patient for the entire episode of illness. At the same time, appropriate service delivery would be coordinated by the staff nurse through multidisciplinary care planning by the clinical care team. The end result would be coordinated care delivery process using standardized resources (services and treatments) within an appropriate length of stay. (LOS). Thus, the reputation TMC enjoyed for care excellence would be maintained or even enhanced. We named this process *collaborative* (to denote its multidisciplinary focus) *nursing* (to denote the RN as the coordinator of the acute care process) *case management*.

# Methodology

Developing a new patient care delivery system involved administrative support and commitment of top management. The task was accomplished by a planning committee comprising all clinical and support disciplines. Examples of departments represented on this committee were Nursing, Medicine, Social Service, Respiratory Therapy, Education, and Information Resource Management (computer department). From Nursing, representatives from all levels and all shifts were sought. Although the committee was large, it permitted a forum for all disciplines to have input into the development of the new patient care delivery system and to have access into guiding its evolution. It also assured the buy-in by all involved participants as the final product was developed with their guidance and support. These two factors—support by top management and buy-in by the other departments providing patient care service and support—were essential in the development of TMC's collaborative nursing case management.

Once the overall program for restructuring the delivery of patient care was determined, the planning committee identified the structure, process, and outcomes for the program. Table 1 specifies those developed and implemented at TMC.

After the conceptual activity was completed, two demonstration projects were implemented. These programs allowed us to test our assumptions and fine-tune our process and forms. We discovered that although the core concepts we had identified were universal, their application varied. This variance reflected the physician partners, the patient population being case-managed, and the nursing culture on the unit. Our five core concepts of collaborative nursing case management were stated as follows:

1. An identified nurse(s) is responsible for the coordination and collaboration of the care process and the multidisciplinary team.
2. A written process of care is based on the various components of care and the time or date each is to be provided. This provides a multidisciplinary, preplanned process that promotes a continuous quality improvement process. It is more useful and interactive than the traditional patient care plan.
3. The care process is based on (a) a diagnosis or DRG and/or (b) a physician(s) practice pattern.
4. The care process includes the entire episode of care from the point where the decision to admit is made until the patient is able to resume care responsibilities upon discharge.
5. A multidisciplinary care process includes all members of the clinical team who normally provide care for patients admitted with a particular diagnosis for an identified physician.

These core concepts may be summarized in a statement that collaborative nursing case management is a written core protocol based on the expert clinical nurse's knowledge of the care expected and planned for a particular group of patients for a specific physician, and that when this protocol is committed to paper, all nurses providing care for the patient can fully participate and contribute to facilitating the patient's care process.

As our experience with case management expanded, staff nurses who were working on developing and implementing the programs at the unit level offered suggestions on how the forms designed for the program could be made more "nurse-friendly" and save time in planning, delivering, individualizing, monitoring, and documenting care. Thus, as new aspects of the case management program are implemented, we refine the forms to meet the needs of each patient

**Table 1.** *Nurse Case Management Program Development Guidelines*

| Structure | Process | Outcomes |
|---|---|---|
| Program goals and objectives | • Develop | • Overall direction for the nursing case management program is specified |
| Standardized forms | • Formulate<br>• Approve | • Needed information is recorded consistently |
| Diagnosis-related groups (DRG) for hospital | • Identify high-volume DRGs for hospital<br><br>• Select DRGs that may have the most impact on patient care quality and resource utilization | • Most frequently admitted types of patients are identified<br><br>• Quality of patient care is improved or maintained while accomplishing appropriate resource utilization |
| Unit/DRG implementation | • Explain NCM program/model to physician(s) who admit patients with identified DRG(s)<br><br>• Develop collaborative case management plan (CCMP) for identified DRG<br><br>• Develop CarePlan MAP© for the identified DRG<br><br>• Develop patient teaching/orientation material/discharge instructions for the identified DRG | • Commitment, cooperation, and collaboration is achieved in planning and implementing program<br><br>• The expected patient's response to illness through the identification of nursing diagnoses, long- and short-term goals, the self-care actions of the patient, and the actions of the nurse, physician, and other disciplines are specified on the CCMP<br><br>• Identify nursing diagnosis and patient-expected outcomes/goals. Specific interventions for the delivery of care for the patients admitted with a specific DRG are identified in a day-by-day format according to category of care<br><br>• Patient orientation and educational information are available for patient use |

population as defined by the nurses providing care in that area. Our latest major revision involves merging the requirements of a plan of care, as defined by Joint Commission on Accreditation of Healthcare Organizations, with the multidisciplinary interventions of our first form. We see our overall program as a process that is continually being fine-tuned to reflect the needs of the patient as all clinical disciplines strive to provide quality care in a fiscally responsible manner.

**Table 1 (cont.).** *Nurse Case Management Program Development Guidelines*

| | | |
|---|---|---|
| Communication plan | • Develop methodology for assignment of nurse care manager (NCM) and associate care providers<br>• Identify meeting frequency for NCM for group practice or unit task force<br>• Develop methodology for regular collaboration between NCM, physicians, and other disciplines<br>• Develop reporting format/methodology | • NCM and associate care providers are identified and roles clarified<br>• Meeting times are specified and utilized, relevant patient/clinical team information is communicated<br>• Collaboration times are specified and utilized, relevant patient/clinical team information is communicated<br>• Report format/methodology is utilized for communication of relevant patient and team information |
| Evaluation | • Identify criteria for evaluation based on the program's goals and objectives<br>• Develop or adapt evaluation tools to measure identified measurement criteria<br>• Develop measurement sampling schedule to achieve desired information<br>• Conduct and evaluate program information<br>• Reevaluate program based on outcome criteria | • Pertinent measurement outcomes will be identified to determine the program's effectiveness<br>• Appropriate measurement outcomes will be measured effectively<br>• Relevant information will be obtained on a standardized timetable<br>• Program's effectiveness will be determined<br>• Program will be adapted to meet the needs of all participants |

# Tools and Forms

Our case management program started out with two basic tools/forms identified as essential to the delivery of collaborative care. These are the Collaborative Case Management Plan (CCMP) and our Multidisciplinary Action Plan (MAP). The CCMP displays our standard of care specifying the interventions by all participants based on the nursing diagnosis/patient problem. It acknowledges the contributions made by the patient as well as the clinical disciplines to resolve each nursing diagnosis/patient problem. Table 2 is an example of a CCMP for one nursing diagnosis/patient problem (neonatal hyperbilirubinemia). Its strength lies in the fact that it represents how each team member's actions contribute to the resolution of nursing diagnosis/patient problems. Like all standards of care, it is a reference document.

The second basic tool/form developed for this program, the MAP, was designed to guide the caregivers in the process prescribed by the multidisciplinary team for a patient admitted with a particular DRG/diagnosis. The MAP specified what should happen on each day of hospitalization. Most times this is a daily time frame. For certain DRG/diagnoses that require a longer hospitalization, the time frames are converted to steps or milestones to be accomplished. Regardless of which time frame format is used, the care categories are listed as interdependent and independent actions to reinforce the professional aspects of the staff nurse role.

In 1991 TMC decided to merge the traditional care plan concepts with the MAP because the nursing actions listed on the MAP were a restatement of the nursing actions from the traditional care plan. (Gwozdz & Del Togno-Armanasco, 1991). The new tool/form that resulted was designated as a CarePlan MAP©. In addition to becoming the plan of care, the CarePlan MAP serves as our basic documentation form. Table 3 is an example of the front page of a CarePlan MAP specifying the nursing diagnosis, outcome expectations/goals, and the documentation of the achievement/nonachievement of these goals at discharge. As such, the CarePlan MAP promotes and complements the concepts of total quality management by quickly enabling identification of the results of the care process through the measurement of the patient expectations or outcomes of care.

Tables 4 and 5 are examples of interventions identified by the multidisciplinary team as appropriate to facilitate the patient's progress toward the achievement of the goals specified on the front page of the CarePlan MAP. Table 4 shows the interdependent actions, while Table 5 displays the independent actions. Each action is referenced to the appropriate nursing diagnosis/patient problem by a superscript notation at the end of the action statement. Some statements have more than one reference number, indicating that the action facilitates the resolution of more than one nursing diagnosis/patient problem. Signature lines are provided so that the nurse can quickly document the care delivered on a particular shift or care interval. Interventions not provided as planned are noted with an asterisk at the end of the statement and an explanation on the last sheet of the CarePlan MAP. This indicates what was individualized, why these actions were necessary, and what, if anything, will be done to maintain the patient on the desired care process. Table 6 is an example of this form.

Other printed materials we find invaluable are preprinted doctor's orders, patient education booklets, and discharge instruction sheets. Once the multidisciplinary team decides on the actions and their sequencing for patients admitted with a particular DRG/diagnosis, preprinted doctor's orders can be developed. Among the advantages of preprinted orders are that they eliminate the need for a physician to rewrite the same order for each patient in that DRG, orders are legible, and inadvertent omission of orders is prevented.

Patient education booklets and preprinted discharge instruction sheets facilitate the exchange of information between the nurse and the patient/family. Patient education booklets in-

**Table 2.** *Nenonatal Hyperbilirubinemia Collaborative Case Management Plan*

| Nursing Diagnosis | Patient Short-Term Goals | Parent Care Actions | Nursing Actions | Physician's Actions | Actions of Other Departments |
|---|---|---|---|---|---|
| Alteration in metabolic function related to:<br>• overproduction of bilirubin<br>• impaired excretion of bilirubin<br>• deficient conjugation of bilirubin<br>*As evidenced by:*<br>• dark urine<br>• feeding difficulties<br>• jaundice<br>• high-pitched cry<br>• lethargy<br>• seizures<br>• other________<br>________<br>________<br>________ | Infant will have inadequate metabolic function and be free of signs and symptoms of hyperbilirubinemia as evidenced by:<br>1. Total serum bilirubin level of less than ________<br>2. Ability to tolerate feedings<br>3. Pale yellow urine<br>4. Lack of:<br>• jaundice<br>• lethargy<br>• seizures<br>5. Normal tone of cry<br>6. Other________<br>________<br>________ | | 1. Assess and record:<br>• Infant's skin color every shift<br>• Any neuro changes & vital signs every 2 hours<br>• Signs and symptoms of alteration in metabolic function<br>• Bilirubin levels when ordered *(Notify physician if increased)*<br>2. Keep infant unclothed under phototherapy lights with eyes covered. remove mask for short periods so nurse or parents can hold & comfort<br>3. Keep accurate intake & output record characteristics or urine & stools<br>4. Prepare infant & family for exchange transfusion if necessary<br>5. Other________ | 1. Orders lab work, photheraphy lights<br>2. Performs exchange transfusion (if necessary) | *Lab*<br>Draws heel stick blood work<br><br>*Blood bank*<br>Prepares blood for exchange transfusion |

**Table 3.** *Care Plan MAP© (Lumbar Laminectomy with Fusion)*

| Nursing Diagnosis<br>Patient Problems | Outcome Expectations | Expectations Met at Discharge<br>Yes No Nurse's Signature |
|---|---|---|
| Potential anxiety related to hospitalization and/or surgical procedure | Patient and/or family will verbalize or exhibit decreased anxiety | ___ ___ ________<br>Date:________ |
| Potential alteration in sensory perception related to disease process and/or surgical intervention | Sensory impairments recognized and managed. Circulation, sensation & movement of affected extremities within normal limits | ___ ___ ________<br>Date:________ |
| Potential alternation in comfort: pain related to surgery | Patient verbalizes absence or decrease in pain level & actively participates in care | ___ ___ ________<br>Date:________ |
| Potential ineffective breathing pattern related to anesthesia & pain | Patient will maintain normal respiration pattern for patient | ___ ___ ________<br>Date:________ |
| Potential for fluid volume deficit related to NPO status, blood loss, and/or nausea & vomiting | Adequate hydration & vital signs within normal limits | ___ ___ ________<br>Date:________ |
| Potential for infection related to surgical intervention, decreased mobility, and/or urethal catheterization | Patient will remain afebril & free from infectious process | ___ ___ ________<br>Date:________ |
| Potential altered elimination: constipation related to anesthesia, decreased mobility, and/or pain medication | Patient will have bowel movement prior to discharge | ___ ___ ________<br>Date:________ |
| Potential for urinary retention related to anesthesia, decreased mobility, and/or disease process | Patient will return to normal voiding pattern prior to discharge | ___ ___ ________<br>Date:________ |
| Potential knowledge deficit related to home care & discharge | Patient will verbalize and/or demonstrate understanding of all written & verbal discharge instructions | ___ ___ ________<br>Date:________ |
| **Additional Problems** | | |
| ■ ________<br>________<br>________ | ________<br>________<br>________ | ___ ___ ________<br>**Date:**________ |
| ■ ________<br>________<br>________ | ________<br>________<br>________ | ___ ___ ________<br>**Date:**________ |

**Table 4.** *Interdependent Actions Based upon the Human Response to Actual or Potential Problems (Lumbar Laminectomy with Fusion)*

| Hospital Day | Consults | Tests | Activity/ Rest | Medical Interventions | Medications | Nutrition | Nurses' Signatures |
|---|---|---|---|---|---|---|---|
| Pre-operative testing: outpatient<br>Date:____ | Chair back brace with Tucson Limb & Brace | • CBC<br>• Lytes<br>• EKG > 40 years<br>• Autologous blood<br>• Type & screen | | | | | ________<br>________<br>________ |
| Day of surgery pre-op:<br>Date:____ | | | Up ad lib | | As at home | NPO | ________<br>________<br>________ |
| Day of surgery: post-op<br>Date:____ | | | • Log roll every 2 hours<br>• Bed rest<br>• Cough & deep breathing every 2 hours<br>• Bed position of comfort<br>• Stand to void | • Foley catheter<br>• TED hose if ordered<br>• Reinforce dressing: Do not reinforce<br>• Notify MD for:<br>—saturation of dressing times 2<br>—temp > 102° F<br>•SCD times 3 days<br>• Throat lozenges PRN<br>• Laxative of choice | • IV<br>• Analgesics IM<br>• Antibiotics: Kefzol 1.0 GM IV every 8 hours times 6 doses (if patient not allergic)<br>• Antiemetic PRN<br>• Reorder & start meds as at home<br>• Antipyretics T [illegible]01° F | • Clear liquids after 6 hours<br>• Advance as tolerated | ________<br>________<br>________ |

Identify items not provided as planned with (*)
Enter explanation in the individualization/variance section on last page

form the patient/family about the usual course of hospitalization for a person admitted for a particular type of care. The booklets also inform the patient/family about the anticipated length of stay and give special information they will need to participate in care during hospitalization and at home. The discharge instructions assist the nurse in documenting information provided to the patient/family. The nurse simply notes on the discharge plan that the discharge instruction form was used; this helps to eliminate the need to list individual instructions each time a patient with a certain DRG is discharged.

**Table 5.** *Independent Actions Based upon the Human Response to Actual or Potential Problems (Lumbar Laminectomy with Fusion)*

| Hospital Day | Assessment | Discharge Planning | Teaching | Psychosocial | Self-Care | Nutrition |
|---|---|---|---|---|---|---|
| Pre-op testing: outpatient Date:_____ | | | | | | ________<br>________<br>________ |
| Day of surgery pre-op: Date:_____ | Baseline<br>•vital signs<br>•neuro signs<br>•voiding status<br>•bowel sounds<br>•breath sounds | Needs identified by admission information | •Logrolling<br>•Good body mechanics[2,3]<br>•Cough & deep breathing[4,6] | •Assess anxiety level<br>•Assess family dynamics<br>•Interventions as needed[1,9] | Self-care | ________<br>________<br>________ |
| Day of surgery: post-op Date:_____ | •Vital signs<br>•Neuro signs<br>•Dressing for drainage<br>•Voiding status<br>•Breath sounds<br>•Bowel sounds | | Implement post-op teaching[9] | •Assess anxiety level<br>•Assess family dynamics<br>•Interventions as needed | Assisted coughing & deep breathing | ________<br>________<br>________ |

Identify items not provided as planned with (*)
Enter explanation in the individualization/variance section on last page

# Outcomes

The nursing care management program at TMC grew out of a research base. Research/outcome questions developed as the program evolved were as follows:

1. Are patients who have an identified nurse care manager coordinating their care more satisfied with their hospitalization experience than patients not receiving this service? (Patient satisfaction is measured by a subjective patient satisfaction questionnaire.)
2. Are physicians who have an identified nurse care manager coordinating the care of specific patients more satisfied with the care provided by the hospital? (Physician satisfaction is measured by a subjective physician satisfaction questionnaire.)
3. Are nurses who are identifiable to the patient and the physician as "the" nurse coordinating their care process more satisfied with their ability to provide patient care than

**Table 6.** *Interventions Not Provided as Planned*

MAP reviewed by:

Nurse case manager:

____________________

Date: ____________

Associate case manager:

____________________

Date:______________

Associate case manager:

____________________

Date:______________

| Date | Individualization/ Variation | Cause | Action Taken | Signature |
|---|---|---|---|---|
| | | | | |

those nurses not functioning in that role? (Nurse satisfaction is measured by a subjective nurse satisfaction questionnaire.)

4. Do nurses functioning as nurse care managers perceive that they function in a more autonomous professional model of providing patient care than nurses not functioning in this role? (Nurses' perceptions of a more autonomous professional model of providing patient care is measured by a subjective nurse satisfaction questionnaire. It is also measured objectively by examining nurse retention and performance appraisal data.)
5. Is the LOS for patients receiving nurse care management provided within the time span identified and planned by the care management team more often than the patient not

receiving this care planning process? (LOS is measured objectively by examining hospital financial records.)

6. Are resources (supplies, tests, procedures) used more efficiently by patients receiving nursing care management than by patients not enrolled for this care planning process? (Resource utilization is measured objectively by examining hospital financial data.)
7. Are individual quality management outcomes for patients on nursing care management more consistently achieved based on the nursing diagnosis identified in the patient's plan of care than other patients?
8. Are quality management outcomes evaluated and documented as to their achievement on the patient's plan of care more consistently on nursing case management patients than on other patients? (Quality management outcomes are measured objectively by measuring the achievement of outcome expectations at discharge.)
9. Is discharge planning accomplished and in place prior to the patients' discharge more consistently among patients on nursing case management than among other patients? (Discharge planning is measured objectively by auditing the patient care record.)

Our research included a review of satisfaction data from patients, physicians, and nurses as well as financial data related to length of stay and costs of providing care, and quality outcome data. (Del Togno-Armanasco, Harter, & Goddard, 1991). To date we have documented that patients who receive care in our case management program at TMC are more satisfied with their nursing care than patients receiving traditional care. We have also documented that the LOS for each patient group being case-managed has decreased. The decrease in LOS varies according to patient population and anticipated total LOS. For patients with an anticipated LOS of ten days, the actual LOS has dropped approximately two days. Patients with a three-day LOS now stay about two and one-half days. Specific examples include:

| | | Length of Stay (in days) | | |
|---|---|---|---|---|
| **DRG #** | **Diagnosis** | **Anticipated** | **Current** | **Decrease** |
| 209 | Total knee replacement | 10 | 7.61 | 2.39 |
| 209 | Total hip replacement | 10 | 7.46 | 2.54 |
| 105 | Valve replacement | 10 | 8.5 | 1.5 |
| 107 | Coronary bypass | 10 | 8.5 | 1.5 |
| 335 | TURP with complications | 3 | 2.21 | 0.79 |
| 335 | TURP without complications | 3 | 1.86 | 1.14 |

Our experience shows that once the multidisciplinary team decides on the care the typical patient admitted with a certain diagnosis is to receive, designates when such care should be provided, and furnishes copies of the plan to all individuals participating in care delivery, care is actually delivered in a more coordinated fashion and the LOS decreases. Generally, the cost for providing such care also decreases. The only instances of slightly higher costs involved increased use of expensive technology. In those cases, we believe costs would have risen more if collaborative case management had not been implemented.

In summary, collaborative case management in the acute care hospital makes sense if it is developed with the support of administration and with the input of the multidisciplinary team involved in the care of a specific group of patients. The process should be coordinated by a professional nurse and should be thoroughly documented so that all persons participating in care delivery have access to the expected outcomes and interventions as arrayed by category of care and time.

## References

Del Togno-Armanasco V., Olivas G., Harter S., "Case Management: A Bottom-line Management Care Delivery Model, Part I: The Concept," *Journal of Nursing Administration*: 1989, 19:11:16-20.

Del Togno-Armanasco V., Olivas G., Harter S., "Case Management, A Bottom-line Management Care Delivery Model, Part II: Adaptation of the Model," *Journal of Nursing Administration*: 1989, 19:12:12-17.

Del Togno-Armanasco V., Olivas G., Harter S., "Developing an Integrated Nursing Case Management Model," *Nursing Management*: 1989, 20:5:26-29.

Gwozdz, D. T., Del Togno-Armanasco, V., "Streamlining Patient Care Documentation," Journal of Nursing Administration 1992 22 (5), 35-39.

Del Togno-Armanasco, V., Harter, S., & Goddard, N.L. Cost and Quality: Are they Compatible?. In P. Schroeder (Ed.). *The Encyclopedia of Nursing Care Quality: Vol. 1 Issues and Strategies for Nursing Care Quality* (pp. 25-42). Gaithersburg, M.D.: Aspen Publishers, 1991

# 13

## Building Momentum for Case Management

Colleen M. Lucas, RN, MN, CNS
Dana Underdahl, RN, BSN
Judy McGee, RN, BS

*The key word for this chapter is* perception. *The authors, who are all intimately involved in episodic care case management in a very large hospital, discuss the "political" aspects of implementation. Although this chapter does not discuss the "how to's" of critical paths, MAPS, or variance charting, it may be the most important chapter to read for those considering implementing case management in a hospital.*
—R.S.H.

In the spring of 1990, the Department of Nursing at Good Samaritan Hospital and Medical Center in Portland, Oregon, made the commitment to implement case management. We see case management as a clear, logical, thoughtful approach to addressing many of today's care delivery issues. The underlying principles and patient-centered focus for managing cost and quality outcomes are consistent with the demands of the health care market. The model recognizes and promotes nursing as the key position for coordinating care within and across delivery settings. Case management provides structure and order within a disorganized, resource-constrained care delivery system.

While many leaders agree with our view of case management, others are doubtful. Why aren't all hospitals jumping on the bandwagon to implement case management? Why does implementation of the model take so long, and why are there so many struggles along the way? How can the introduction of case management be facilitated? A thorough understanding of the struggles and strategies in implementing case management is essential in order for potential difficulties to be anticipated, addressed, and resolved.

The authors of this chapter appreciate the encouragement and direction of our consultant, Dr. Kathleen Bower, who guided us through many junctures in our journey.

From our experience, we have identified three major variables which influence the ease and success of implementation: 1) how well the language and models used to describe case management are understood by all; 2) the readiness to make an institutional commitment to case management; and 3) the ability to see opportunity in change.

# Understanding Case Management

## What It Is

### The Meaning of Words

In the introduction of any change, words are used to describe the new idea and tell how it is different from the systems currently in place. Remember that words are symbols, and the terms used to define and describe case management will have a strong influence on how quickly agreements are reached. Cavalier selection and definition of terms increases the cost of the change process. Terms that are used interchangeably, or are loosely defined, result in vague understanding and misconceptions. Preconceived notions will predominate and associated emotional responses will surface.

Examples of commonly misunderstood nomenclature are: managed care, case management, variance, and variance reporting. These terms may carry negative connotations associated with utilization review, budgets, and brokered care case management. The traditional interpretation is gatekeeping, or policing of practice through external cost control and internal reporting mechanisms. The emotions associated with gatekeeping are anger and frustration. Providers feel loss of control over selection of treatment alternatives while still being held accountable for treatment outcomes. Common responses are, "I feel my hands are tied," and "This is cookbook medicine."

A third emotion is fear of economic considerations overriding quality of care. Reports on length of stay, variance days, and cost control reinforce a focus on achieving financial goals.

### The Power of the Observed

The transition from existing practice models to case management is shaped by definitions of the what (characteristics of case management), the why (mind sets, beliefs, philosophy), and the how (concrete examples). If the model is not clearly defined, the working definition will remain elusive in spite of the project coordinator's and staff educator's efforts to enlighten. Staff may try on and model new behaviors, but these behaviors may not concur with the department vision or goals. The behaviors will reflect individual beliefs about what case management is and what is observed in others.

Both positive and negative reactions to new practices reinforce the perception of what case management is. For example, the nurse who perceives the major role of the case manager as financial may focus more on communicating the payer's authorized length of stay and meeting utilization criteria. As the nurse begins wearing the utilization review hat, case management will be perceived as a new name for an old game, i.e., utilization review. In this case, perception is reality. The nurse *is* performing utilization review. Case management will become utilization review as nurses observe and mirror the role.

A contrasting example is the nurse who perceives the major focus of case management as facilitating transitions from caregiver to caregiver and setting to setting. In the belief that continuity of care is dependent on collaboration and clear communication across settings and between caregivers, this nurse positions him- or herself to provide a consistent source of information about the patient and treatment goals. The nurse makes preadmission contact with the patient to better anticipate care needs; collaborates with other team members in establishing a plan of care and evaluating patient responses; and follows up with patient contact after discharge. The team evaluates plan effectiveness in meeting discharge and post-discharge outcomes. Evaluation results are used for initiating care revisions to improve outcomes for similar patients. In this example, case management again becomes what it is perceived to be by the features and outcomes that are observed in practice. This time, however, the observed behaviors reflect the envisioned model—continuous quality improvement through team collaboration, patient-centered care and practice based on outcome evaluation.

## What It Is Not

The transition from existing models to case management must address not only the what (characteristics) but also the why (mind sets, beliefs, philosophy). Practitioners are at risk of developing erroneous perceptions of case management when exposed to isolated elements of the model prior to formal education. Hearsay and indirect experience may feed personal bias. The result is an attitude that the observed features represent the entire model.

Physicians may perceive that case management is:

- Standing orders
- Control of practice
- Nursing's attempt to run the show
- Nursing's attempt to gain power
- Yet another bureaucratic infringement on their practices

Nursing staff may perceive that case management is:

- "Old forms in new clothes"
- A new way of giving shift report
- Elitist roles for favored nurses
- Management's latest "hot" idea that will die from apathy and neglect
- Another project to keep management doing "make-work" activities
- A grand idea that won't work in the "real" world
- A fancy new name for the same old thing
- A return to a prior nursing model, team nursing
- A potential rescue from bedside nursing; a "time-out" job

Interdisciplinary support staff may perceive that case management is:

- Nursing's attempt to take over and direct everyone else's practice
- A new label for "good ole" discharge planning
- A nursing model that really won't affect them except in peripheral ways
- Nursing's way of trying to get recognition for the hard work nurses do

- Nursing's way to gain "favored child" status with administration
- Nursing's attempt to *finally* get their act together

Convincing practitioners that case management isn't the embodiment of their fears and negative or erroneous expectations requires specific strategies for introducing and supporting change.

## Common Misconceptions About How Case Management Works

Clear definitions and concrete examples of how case management will be played out will facilitate a consistent and common understanding among all team members. In spite of educational strategies, misconceptions will evolve as the introduction of similar or simultaneous agendas compete for staff attention. The paradigm shift in thinking will remain incomplete, contributing to four common misconceptions about how case management practices work.

**Misconceptions**

Case management philosophy supports a *service-focused* environment. Each service defines how, when, and in what manner care aspects (services) will be provided or available and at what price. The financial health of the department is dependent on how many service units are provided and the charge for each unit. If the service volume decreases, the revenue contribution likewise decreases. Therefore, the well-being of the department hinges on maximizing the number of services provided and the charge for these services.

**Reality**

Case management is most successful in a *patient-focused* environment. Patient needs determine how, when, and in what manner care aspects (services) will be provided. The financial health of the institution depends on the achievement of outcomes mutually defined by customers and providers, via the efficient delivery of care at competitive prices per service unit. Therefore, financial well-being hinges on doing the job better, not in charging more.

**Misconceptions**

Case management is compatible with *parallel practices*. Each service/discipline addresses isolated aspects of care and independently identifies patient goals. Care is documented on discipline-specific records to track service charges, to monitor unique quality indicators, and to protect the discipline's domain of practice. Departments may be proficient in their own practice, yet unaware of how their role influences the big picture. Patients may be discharged unprepared for the transition to independent care because departments did not know when the patient was going home or the identified discharge needs did not fall into their domain of practice. Other patients may have the same assessments completed by several disci-

**Reality**

Case management depends on *collaborative practice*. Assessments are coordinated across disciplines and reflect a holistic evaluation of the patient. Team members identify, mutually influence, and set priorities for goals. Each caregiver contributes to and follows the team's plan of care rather than inventing strategies with each patient interaction. The plan, anticipated patient response (outcomes), and patient progress are clearly communicated verbally and on an interdisciplinary care record. The record reflects each team member's contribution to the patient's progress, the real value of this contribution (patient response), and the care needed and provided in getting the patient ready for the transition to home or other

**Misconceptions (cont.)**

plines, and have two or more disciplines providing the same aspects of care. Overall, patient charges may far exceed reimbursement received as each department attempts to substantiate its revenue contribution via the charge mechanism.

**Reality (cont.)**

care setting. Patients' expectations are met or exceeded, since the care is efficiently executed, timely, and meets their needs.

Case management requires changes in *staffing patterns and practices*. Nurses are asked to do more than previously and therefore more and different staff will be needed. Comments frequently heard are: "We don't have enough CNAs for it to work"; "I have too many part-time nurses for it to work"; "My staff will all want to be case managers so they can have weekends off"; "My budget won't support it."

Case management requires redefinition of *roles, relationships, and responsibilities*. The emphasis is on *common* interests and methods to achieve these. The nursing team and the interdisciplinary team have common goals and share the work and recognition in achieving these. Mutual value and respect promote a spirit of collaboration. Specialized roles may be defined to further streamline care, promote patient progress, and prevent overlap and gaps in care.

Case management is a method of care coordination designed to reduce the cost of care that will ultimately *reduce the quality of care* as well. Low cost = low quality.

Poor quality is not affordable. Doing it right the first time *increases quality and reduces costs*. Case management promotes consistency and continuity of care, reducing care gaps and redundant activities. Complications or problems that do occur are identified early and promptly treated.

# Strategies for Creating Understanding

1. Identify terms currently used in your institution for utilization review and in reviewing and reporting clinical, financial, and satisfaction outcomes. Determine the explicit and implicit meaning of each of these terms for the involved disciplines. Example: Some of our physicians were sensitive to the word "complications." In DRG (diagnosis-related groups) language, a complication is defined as an occurrence that is likely to extend the length of stay by at least one day in 75% of the patients experiencing the same event. To physicians the term was more than a description of the impact of an event, as it conveyed inappropriate care followed by increased reporting and scrutiny of practice.
2. Select and define terms for your case management model and use them consistently. Example: The term "variance" was already in use at our facility to describe noncompliance with budget and payer-authorized hospital days. The strong negative connotations did not dissipate when a new definition of the term was provided. We replaced "variance" with "exception," a more neutral term.

3. Validate congruence between the implicit and explicit meaning of each term with all involved disciplines. From our experience, all disciplines struggle with giving up their own definitions and terms to come to agreement on a common language. To provide a forum for interdepartmental communication and planning, we established a coordinating council of department heads.
4. To keep the project focused, create and share a vision of what the end product will look like. Likewise, set a clear goal that anchors project development and implementation into an existing system. During the planning process it is easy to get distracted by other changes and pressures. Without a clear goal and vision to check the focus of the project, it is possible to end up with a different product than what was intended. Our goal was to change nursing practice so that continuous quality improvement and cost-effective actions became part of what every nurse did with every patient every day. A distraction for us was the perception that everyone implementing case management had the same goals, thus the same results ought to be expected.
5. Provide structure and direction by translating abstract verbiage into concrete behaviors that the staff can try on and model. The structure includes policies, procedures, and tools (forms) that "flesh out" the framework. The amount of structure must be delicately balanced with the ability to maintain flexibility. The process and structure must make sense and be applicable at the bedside. If not, it will lack sufficient credibility to inspire innovative ways to change the system and will be seen as unrealistic management directives for change. When our new forms were introduced, nurses used the forms according to the established rules, but over time gradually created their own rules. The nurses discovered that what had meaning and value on first look was really quite limited in its bedside application. With their insight and energy, the documentation system was revised to reinforce and support the expected changes in practice. The product is a multidisciplinary care record that facilitates concise documentation of the *entire* nursing process. This time, rather than adding more forms for more responsibilities, we condensed the paperwork process, deleting three forms.
6. Provide role-playing opportunities and case reviews to practice and strengthen desired behaviors and problem-solving skills.
7. Define roles and titles for your case management model. Clarify differences and expectations of each role. Be sensitive to the possible meanings associated with role titles. Some titles may be viewed as subordinate to or of lesser value than others. These titles may interfere with achieving and maintaining mutual value and respect among all staff. Example: For some, the title of *case manager* may imply more than care management and may include nursing management responsibilities for supervising other nurses.
8. Determine the criteria for selection of case managers based on the skills and experiences required to fulfill the role (i.e., communication, collaboration, team roles, planning, assessment of patient care needs).
9. Remain open to role evolution as experience accumulates and effectiveness can be evaluated. We found that our expectations of case managers changed over time.
10. Support and develop required skills for each role. We developed a clinical management skills curriculum for all nurses to further build skills in negotiation, supervision, delegation, conflict resolution, teamwork, communication, discharge planning, family intervention, and ethical reasoning. Additional classes for case managers include evaluation of practice, role development, negotiation, effective presentations, and team building.

11. Market the desired perception. Use testimonials from patients, nurses, physicians, and other team members that describe individual experiences with case management and how these experiences were meaningful in meeting specific needs. Our staff writes articles for our biweekly nursing newsletter, makes teaching videotapes, and is developing informational packets on case management and nursing for physician's offices. Additionally, we have written articles for the medical staff newsletter, the corporate newsletter, and presented grand rounds for medical and house staff. Remember to communicate, communicate, communicate.

# Readiness and Commitment

The evolution of a new idea into a winning project occurs as a result of the planning, communication, and decisions along the way. Staff involvement and productivity will be greatest when a common vision for the project is created, communicated, and reinforced regularly. In developing the vision, two questions need to be answered. What are the values driving the design concepts? What are the primary motivators, and who is providing the driving force for the change? These are essential questions to be answered not only in the early stages of the project but also when the project bogs down and bench mark decisions are required.

# Influence of Values and Culture

The institution's values and culture will directly influence the success of the change initiative. The design of a new care delivery model must integrate the stated philosophy and values and must recognize the cultural attributes that will affect the project. Answers to the following questions will guide assessment and assist in the strategic planning and timing for the project.

- Is the institution in a financial survival mode or are activities well underway to improve market share? The emphasis here is on whether a new project will receive needed attention and financial support in uncertain economic times. If the institution is struggling to survive, resource constraints may be too tight to feed the project.
- Does the institutional environment nurture colleagueship or territoriality among services and departments? Do department lines create barriers to change? Does senior management work as a team? The working relationship of the team at the top influences the amount of collaboration and teamwork that occurs throughout the institution. The successful implementation of case management depends on interdepartmental teamwork. Powerful turf warriors will sabotage the best-intentioned plans unless they perceive that there is more to gain from involvement than undermining the project.
- Are risk-taking behavior and innovation rewarded or punished? An environment that supports initiative and creativity reduces the fear of failure and helps to maintain the

necessary energy level to keep the project going. If there is greater risk with failure than with maintaining the status quo, the impetus for change will be thwarted.

- What is the general understanding of and commitment to continuous quality improvement? Without a good understanding of continuous quality improvement, departments will continue to inspect for quality and react to problems. Case management requires a broader scope, focusing on meeting the expectations of the customer through continuously improving processes and performance. These improvements are achieved through a view of the entire picture, as seen by the customer, and interdepartmental collaborative actions that change the picture.
- How fast or slow is the response when necessary change is identified? Any change needs to occur quickly enough to maintain the interest but slowly enough to manage change responses. How many steps are involved in the idea approval process? Will all of the enthusiasm for the project be expended in merely gaining permission to try something new? Once the project is under way, additional changes need to be expected and quickly instituted. Project momentum will be lost if delays occur from unanticipated problems and unclear decision approval processes.

# Need for Institutional Commitment

A key element in the success of major organizational change is senior hospital management commitment and prioritization of project success across departmental and service lines. The commitment is communicated via change-oriented directives from authority figures empowered to influence others. The department and organizational commitment is validated through the provision of time, money, and expert resources for project development and implementation. Paying lip-service to the change without allocating resources devalues the importance of the project.

Accountability must be clearly defined at all levels and across departments. The importance of stating clear expectations cannot be understated or undervalued. Most employees will judge the priority of the project by the number of resources assigned and the clarity of the message regarding their involvement. Sidestepping clear articulation of accountabilities will result in confusion, delays, and the need for renegotiation. Participation will be perceived as optional. Enthusiasm will be lukewarm and progress half-paced at best.

Suppose that a single department wants to implement case management. Such a decision is commonly in the purview of department heads. If the project is designed and owned by a single department, it is viewed by others as a parallel and peripheral function that does not require their participation or involvement. Comments such as "It may be on your agenda but it's not on mine," are communicated verbally, while the nonverbal message is "And it won't get on my agenda until it's on my boss's agenda." Such comments predominate in environments where parallel practices are the rule. Is top level commitment required for case management to work in this situation? Definitely! Case management is patient focused and not a single discipline practice. It is effective in improving outcomes and reducing costs only when the professional team works collaboratively. When administrators endorse the department's autonomy to make the change but fail to make it a priority for other departments, the potential impact of the change is weakened and the required effort increases. When the institutional commitment is made, agendas are developed to reach common goals. Collaboration thrives, and the effect of the change is powerful.

# Strategies for Establishing Readiness

1. Know your mission. Be sure the goals are clearly understood and the scope of the project is defined from the outset. Scope creep, the most common reason for delayed projects, occurs when the project focus broadens to include unanticipated or indirectly related issues. Our greatest project delay occurred from an unanticipated change in project direction. As we began to change the thinking about how nursing was practiced, we uncovered strong dissatisfaction with our documentation system. Nine months into the project we found ourselves needing to revise all of our documentation tools.
2. Know where the boundaries of one's authority and responsibility end and another's begins. Determine how extension of the project beyond one's boundaries will be negotiated or how department interfaces will occur. Turf battles occur when the project focus begins to encroach on another department's or service line's area of responsibility without a predetermined management plan. We established an interdepartmental coordinating council to anticipate areas of department overlap and develop collaborative action plans.
3. Build the foundation for case management on the strengths of the culture and values of the institution. A project that builds on strengths identified by staff will be able to capitalize on staff investment in the project. Use brainstorming techniques to stimulate creativity and idea development. Focus groups or roundtable discussions are a good place to start. Select criteria that reflect these values to later determine project success.

   In addition to brainstorming, we developed a questionnaire and conducted guided interviews with 50 staff members, representing all shifts and all specialties. From the interviews, we determined that whatever model we came up with should:

   - Promote quality from the perspective of the patient, family, nurse, and physician
   - Improve interdisciplinary collaboration
   - Attract and retain satisfied professionals
   - Be flexible and forward-looking
   - Maximize efficient use of labor and supply resources to reduce expenses
   - Involve patients and families in their care
   - Improve continuity and consistency of care

4. Develop the structural support for the change process. Identify the key people to be assigned to the project and the roles of each. Establish a steering committee to guide the development of the project and serve as a clearinghouse for decisions and direction. Make sure those invested with the power to steer decisions provide a balanced representation of those to be affected by the change. Our steering committee com-

prises 85% staff and 15% clinical nurse specialists and nurse managers. A project coordinator provides administrative support to the committee and nursing units. The committee guides procedure and tool (form) development and provides project consistency and continuity across units.

5. Develop a strategic plan to guide the project within and across departments. Having a department plan for what needs to be done, who is responsible, when the activities need to be completed, and the milestones along the way will provide direction for each of the units in developing its plans. We started out with an 18-month plan for project development which was developed by the steering committee. A few months into the plan, the long-term plan was converted to a fast-track plan. This allowed us to test ideas and critical paths while other aspects of the project were still being developed. Later, we found ourselves adrift because we had not gone back to revise the original plan as the project unfolded. Continual attention to the strategic plan and milestones is required in evaluating staff's threshold for tolerance and in determining when to relax timelines. It is estimated that 20% of a project coordinator's time is spent developing and revising the plan.
6. Hire a consultant to guide and review strategic plans, and provide observations of progress along the way. An outside consultant provides a fresh perspective and incredible insight into the issues that are slowing or interfering with progress. Recommendations are more readily heard from an unbiased outside voice. Additionally, the consultant more readily listens to issues raised by staff because there is no investment in the specific project. In consideration of our values and culture, the consultant we hired worked with the project team in addition to holding project review sessions with unit nursing staff and managers. A big barrier for us was staff accountability for completing critical paths according to our stated guidelines. What we learned was that even though the responsibilities were clear, no one was being held accountable for closing the accountability loop. Clear expectations of staff and managers, continuous feedback and reinforcement, and incorporating expectations into the performance review process were used to close the loop. Other assistance received from the consultant included: how to sell the vision to other team members; ways to incorporate variance analysis into continuous quality improvement; role differentiation of the case manager and staff RN; development of educational materials; and strategic planning.
7. Use real data to document the reason for and results of change. In addition to charges/costs and length of stay, develop data bases to track rates of infection, falls, readmissions; time lapse from writing of discharge order and actual discharge of patient; understanding of and follow-through with discharge instructions; change in self-care abilities from admission to discharge; and satisfaction of patients with management of chief concerns such as pain, fear, and communication with significant others.
8. Establish a kick-off day to present the vision and goals to all departments. Having all departments hear the same message at the same time avoids departments not knowing how they will be affected or involved in the project.
9. In developing collaborative agendas, begin with identifying and reaching agreement on common interests and goals. Avoid focusing discussions on the activities of one department. Such discussions reinforce parallel agendas and "for your information only" sharing that does not require group action. Once common goals have been identified, action plans can be negotiated.
10. Create case management reporting mechanisms that require accountability for outcomes at all levels (staff, managers, department heads, vice presidents). Reporting sys-

tems that focus primarily on budget compliance will devalue case management by reinforcing the notion that case management is a budget-dependent and expendable (finance-driven) model.

# Seeing Opportunity in Change

The introduction of case management threatens the status quo for physicians, nurses, and interdisciplinary support staff alike. Historically, the department structure has provided the organizational framework for hospitals. This structure has created department boundary lines driven by budget expectations and volume targets. On the outside, all disciplines appear to agree on the goal of meeting patient needs, but the process looks more like a competition for the patient's time and attention. The patient is in the position of becoming a victim of fiscal and volume goals rather than an individual with specific needs. Conflict arises as hospitals switch from the traditional department organization structure to more innovative patient-centered structures. As the pressure and challenge to break down department barriers increases, the reflex to push back and resist intensifies. Fear in leaving behind what is perceived to be working well creates a monumental barrier to successful change.

The marketing of case management must address the fears of each group and define for each the features of change that will most benefit their practice.

# Strategies for Supporting the Change

1. Assist physicians, nurses, and interdisciplinary support staff in identifying their greatest hopes and worst fears for case management. Conduct interdisciplinary meetings or focus groups.

   Give each participant two cards, one containing the statement "My greatest hope for case management is . . ." and the other the statement "My worst fear about case management is . . . ." Have the group complete the statements on the cards. Collect the cards and collate them with the group.

   a. Tally the greatest hopes first. Discuss how these hopes will be achieved with case management implementation (i.e., how the dreams will become reality). We found common hopes to be "meeting the needs of the patient instead of the system," "a professional practice environment," "satisfied professionals and consumers," "less paperwork," "more time to do patient care," and "greater autonomy with more individual accountability." Include these greatest hopes in the indicators of success to be used for evaluation. Also, use the hopes to describe the vision of what the change will look like. As people visualize themselves in the new picture, they will begin acting as though the change has already occurred and the hopes have been realized. Example: Our vision was satisfied professionals with increased control over patient care time, improved interdisciplinary collaboration, streamlined communication processes, and better patient responses. As nurses visualized this picture of themselves and others, there was a graphic shift in mind sets from "It won't work" to "It has possibilities" to "I like it and it will work if we design it together."

b. After identifying the greatest hopes, tally the greatest fears. Ask the group if there are any more fears that are not on the list. Emphasis on getting a complete survey takes the focus off the reporting individual and reduces the risk in disclosure. These steps legitimize fear and recognize it as real. When fear is faced, the emotional response to the fear is released and dissipates. Discuss with the group the importance of identifying the fears so that measures can be taken to prevent them from becoming a reality. Outline specific steps that have already been implemented to assure the success of the project.

   We found the fears to be the antitheses of the hopes. Common fears for us were that "the staff won't be satisfied, understand it or accept it," "we won't coordinate well enough with other team members," "it will be threatening and people won't want to try it," "increase paperwork," "another addition to nursing's already heavy load."

2. Schedule a special meeting or hold a retreat, coupled with the expectation of clearing calendars and attending. Setting aside a special time to introduce the change and initiate planning will focus attention. Present a clear message when introducing the change and achieve consensus on the need for change before the end of the meeting. The meeting agenda should include:

   - Where we've been (history)
   - Why we can't afford to stay there (motivation for change)
   - Why now is the best time and why proactive change provides choices in selecting the path to be followed
   - What the survival requirements are and the ultimate vision

3. Determine the readiness of the group to proceed with integration. When we tried this, management group members were asked to anonymously rate their readiness to proceed, using a scale of one to ten, with one indicating "not ready at all" and ten indicating "I'm ready to do my part and be a cheerleader for others". Eighty-two percent of our management team rated their readiness at eight or higher; 50% rated themselves as nine or ten. No one rated him- or herself below six. Comments were, "I feel I am very ready to be a cheerleader for case management; "enthusiastic with increased knowledge but still skeptical"; "it will work." The process recognizes individual readiness as an essential criterion for successful implementation and provides valuable information regarding the readiness of the management team to move forward as a whole.
4. Empower staff to participate and own the development and implementation process. Staff is the best resource in designing a product at the bedside. Empowering staff creates knowledgeable informal leaders who will sell new concepts and procedures to peers.
5. Identify the customer. The patient is the primary customer in case management. Plan to involve the patient in the care process. Focus project design and decisions based on the patient involvement and expected outcomes.
6. Clearly spell out "what's in it for you" and design marketing strategies to advance case management goals. Some examples of benefits for target groups are:

**For the patient:**
involvement in the plan
continuity of care
less anxiety
quicker recovery

**For the hospital:**
increased patient satisfaction
attraction of new patients and doctors
decreased staff turnover
decreased costs

**For the nurse:**
professional acknowledgment
continuity of care
improved collaboration
job satisfaction

**For the physician:**
more efficient use of time
improved collaboration
fewer system problems
fewer phone calls from:
—health team members
—patients after discharge
—utilization review staff

The amount of change in health care today challenges and actually threatens long-term project development. At the same time, we know that without major system change, the cost and quality marriage will never occur. A vision to design a futuristic acute care delivery model using the concepts of case management provides the impetus necessary to orchestrate system change. Such a change will streamline the care process and link hospital acute care with existing expanding pre- and postcare arenas.

In initiating the change process, planning and consistent communication are critical. Management will be expected to lead, facilitate involvement, and maintain a project focus. Strategies for successful implementation are: use case management language and models that are understood by all; communicate an institutional commitment to case management that builds on institutional values; create an environment that embraces change as opportunity and hope.

Lasting positive organizational change is a long-term commitment, a journey from a previous era to a new beginning. The energy and stamina to develop, implement, nurture, and continuously cheerlead the process may falter at many junctures along the way. Expect to dedicate time to keeping the project fresh and exciting. Each time the concepts expand into a new area, the labor process starts all over again. The good news is that with each expansion, new cheerleaders emerge and the previous hard work is recognized, validated, and celebrated.

# 14

# Inpatient Flow Management: A Collaborative Approach

John C. McDonald, RN, MS, CPQA

*In this chapter, Mr. McDonald introduces the concept of patient flow-through service lines. In his model, the patient's care is viewed as linear progression from preadmission planning all the way to discharge back to the primary care physician. This "clinical production line" is consistent with our model for case management in that there is a logical progression of care, at least from self-care to primary care to episodic management. As usual, brokered care is left to its own devices. Because Mr. McDonald is affiliated with a very large hospital, his function must be extremely well organized in order to maintain control over case management activities. His model for reviewing care and utilization of resources is exceptionally well thought-out and applicable to organizations of all sizes.*—R.S.H.

Patient flow management is a collaborative approach for performing case management. Founded on the principles of *total quality* or *continuous quality improvement*, it is the ultimate way to measure/review the effectiveness of a health care facility's patient care delivery system.

It is important to have a way to view the complete health care delivery system so that the process—how a patient is moved through the health care facility—can be measured, studied, and improved upon. The patient flow management system outlined in this chapter has been developed by focusing upon the need to provide the most efficient, effective, and safe patient care possible (see Figure 1). This can be done when service areas work together. Each service area has the same ultimate case management goal, which is to meet the *clinical* and *customer-oriented* needs of patients. To accomplish this health care quality goal, hospital departmental walls must be brought down and people must be willing to work together in teams. When physicians, nurses, physical therapists, respiratory therapists, diagnostic specialists, quality and utilization review specialists, and other support personnel work together, care is improved.

When monitoring a patient's movement through the hospital, two perspectives of case management should be considered: the *hospital-wide systems/processes* and the *direct patient*

The author would like to thank Ms. Judith Wooten, vice president, Baptist Memorial Hospital, for her recommendations and editing skills which greatly assisted me in writing this chapter. I am grateful to Ms. Karen Farley Corken and Ms. Linda Freshour for their assistance in proofing the chapter. Last but very importantly, I would like to thank all those at Baptist Memorial Hospital who are dedicated to the process of case management and committed to meeting, beyond their expectations, the needs of our patients.

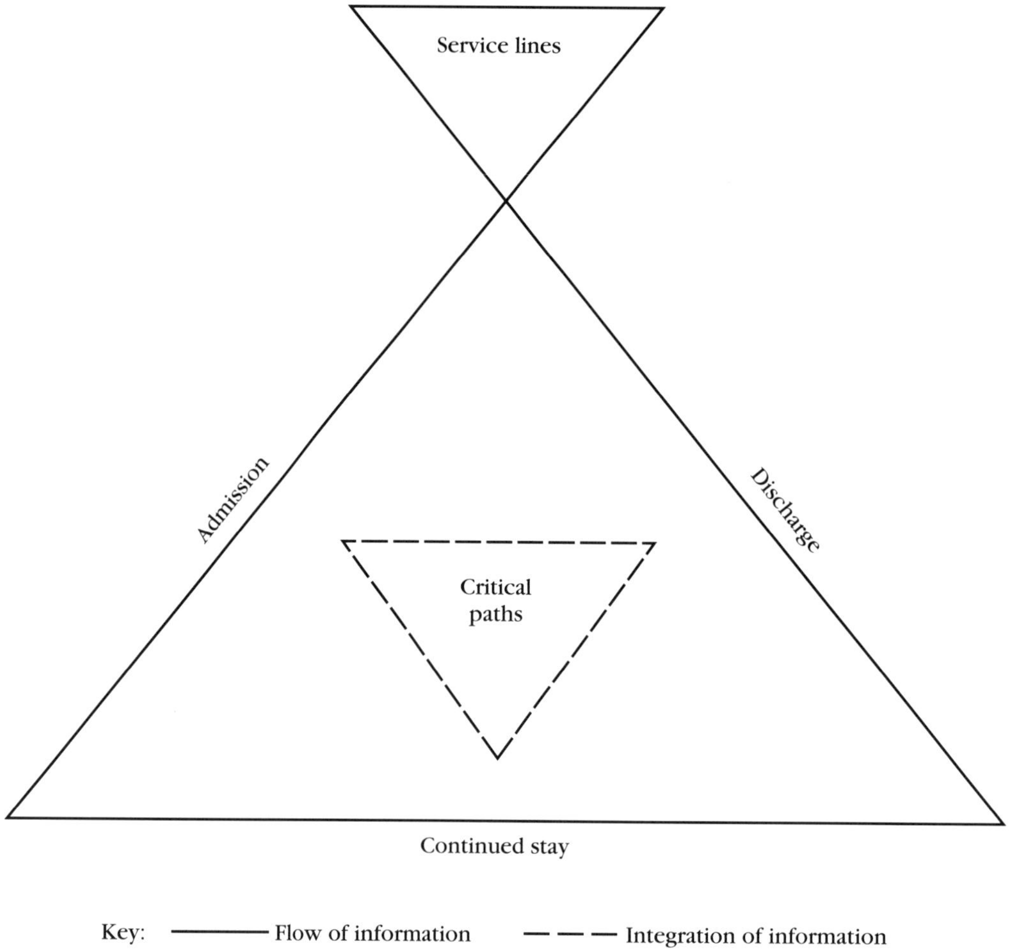


**Figure 1.** *Patient flow management diagram*

*care delivery system* or *critical path*. The broader concept is the hospital-wide admissions, continued stay, and discharge preparation process. The direct care viewpoint is the snapshot day-to-day organization of patient care based upon the physical, emotional, and spiritual (actual and perceived) needs of the patient. Many hospitals have long thought in terms of the big picture as utilization management but have just recently begun to think in terms of organizing direct patient care into clinical/critical paths. If one is industrious enough to think about making improvements in patient care from both processes—utilization management and critical paths—then *service line management* can be appropriately developed. Service line management in hospitals, what is often called product line management in other industries, is the process of viewing and organizing patient care across departmental lines and usually is implemented with marketing principles in mind. Whatever you choose to term your plan for case management, all efforts must be under the umbrella of patient flow management—a collaborative team approach—to be successful (see Figure 2).

Only recently have hospitals begun to address the efficiency of delivering patient care in

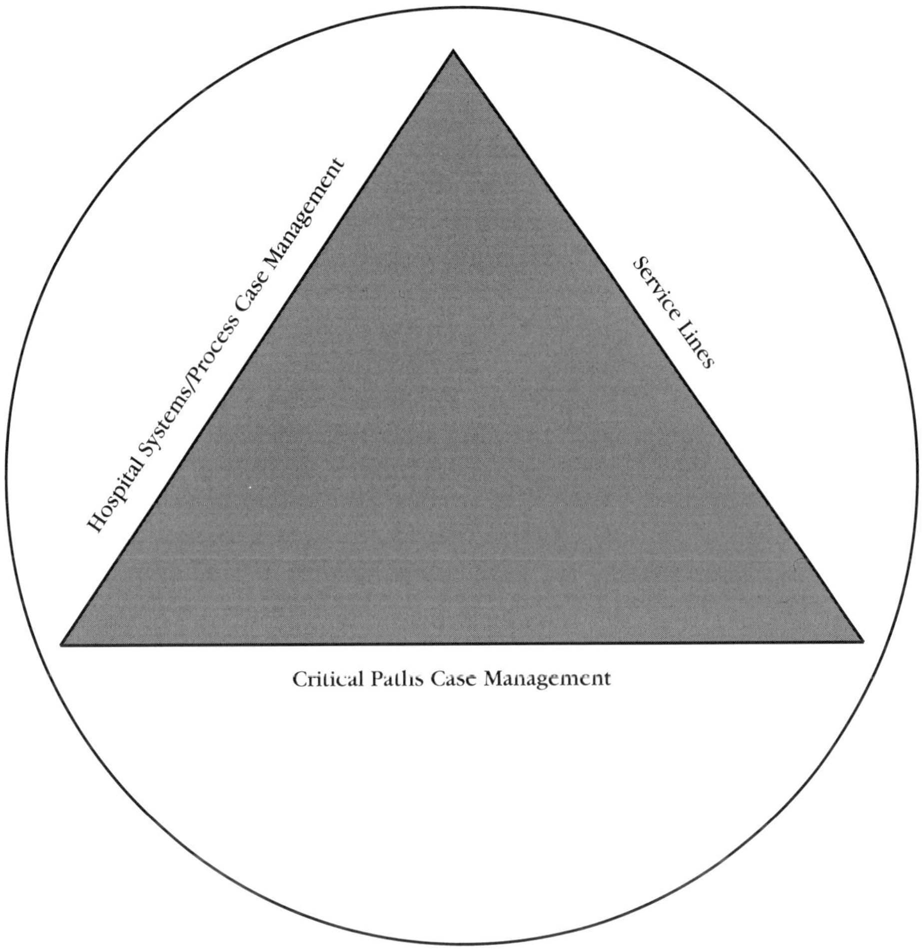


**Figure 2.** *Baptist Memorial Hospital patient flow management collaborative care process*

any complete and real terms. In most cases, this delay has been due to a lack of motivation. However, with increased financial burdens being placed upon hospitals and physicians, greater awareness of the public and payers regarding the connection of cost and quality, and the U.S. industry paradigm shift to total quality management or continuous quality improvement, hospitals and their respective medical staffs are beginning to wake up and take notice. Health care administrators and providers alike are starting to think in new terms of customer satisfaction and process or systems evaluation. The importance of team effort and the need to do things in the *best* way possible the *first* time are also beginning to be recognized. The purpose of the patient flow management process is to address these new ideas through an organized approach of reviewing hospital-wide and direct patient care efforts and seeking ways to improve upon them.

As we review case management, we will explore the need for hospital-wide systems/process management plus individualized or focused patient case management, and then examine the relationship of these elements to service lines. We will also investigate how to bring the two efforts together into one organized patient flow management process/plan.

# Hospital-Wide Case Management

Hospital-wide case management consists of three distinct yet integrated functions, all of which must be in place for the hospital to guarantee that the needs of the patient, physician, nurse case manager, and payer are met. These are preadmission planning, concurrent or continued stay review, and discharge preparation.

## Preadmission Planning

This function began in order to meet increasing third-party payer admission requirements to assure reimbursement. Preadmission planning is usually done by nurses who are knowledgeable about third-party admission criteria. These nurses work with the admissions staff to assist physicians with the preadmission certification process. This is usually done by receiving clinical information from the physician or office staff regarding the potential admission. An additional motivation for preadmission is to optimize payment from Medicare and other fixed third-party payment systems. This can be done by recommending to the physician that the patient be admitted to the most clinically appropriate and cost-efficient level of care. If data are kept regarding admitting levels of care needed, hospital-wide case management can be improved. This can be done by assisting the hospital with identifying the need for new or expanded levels of care and speciality beds based on the analysis of data regarding the clinical picture of patients presenting themselves to the facility.

## Concurrent or Continued Stay Review

Once the patient is admitted to the hospital, the concurrent review process assists the physician and hospital in proactively identifying quality and utilization concerns.

In this system, review nurses screen current charts to pinpoint problems that may affect the efficiency of care or outcome for a particular patient, such as orders that have not been properly carried out, system delays in providing diagnostic or therapeutic services, clinical risk issues, discharge planning needs, and inappropriate utilization of ICU or other specialty beds. Depending upon the nature of the issue, the nurse may either bring it to the attention of the appropriate caregiver so that action can be taken immediately to address the problem, or simply abstract the information for use in medical staff and hospital quality improvement activities.

## Discharge Preparation

As the third component of the hospital-wide case management system, discharge planning looks beyond the confines of the hospital to project what an individual patient will need to maintain the level of wellness achieved and continue a smooth recovery after discharge.

The key to effective discharge preparation is coordination, and the goal is for everything to be in place by the time the patient is ready to leave the hospital.

# Patient Flow Monitors

Many issues should be considered when looking at how a patient moves through a hospital system of care and what problems could occur. There are *four* patient flow or hospital-wide case management monitors to consider and attempt to improve upon: 1) appropriate levels of care are available based upon the resource needs of the patient's illness; 2) quality patient care is being delivered in a timely, effective, and safe manner; 3) care and services are driven by and delivered based upon the clinical picture and needs of the patient; and 4) preparation for discharge to home or to the appropriate level of care is coordinated prospectively. All of these areas should be monitored to assure that the patient needs to be in the hospital and that there are no delays either in providing appropriate health care or in timely discharge.

Team effort is an absolute must when trying to figure out how to monitor the above and take appropriate action when indicated. A team of physicians, clinicians, hospital management, fiscal services personnel, and other support staff will be needed to brainstorm on what indicators are most appropriate to monitor these four areas. It will be advantageous for a hospital to automate these monitors by developing a coding system and using the review specialists in the preadmission and concurrent review processes to abstract the information for later analysis (see Figure 3). It is also preferable to do most of the monitoring on a concurrent basis because quality and case management intervention can be done proactively while the patient is still in the hospital.

In regard to the first monitor, levels of care, it is important for the team to identify what levels presently are available in the hospital and what levels are needed to take care of patients presenting themselves to the facility (see 100 and 200 series codes, Figure 3). With monitor number two, which identifies issues related to timely, efficient, safe, and quality patient care, it is important for the team to brainstorm on how the hospital's patient care delivery system might not always be performing at its greatest potential and develop indicators around its findings (see 500 series codes, Figure 3). For monitor three, delivery of care based upon the clinical needs of the patient, most hospitals and their medical staffs have adopted nationally recognized criteria such as those being used by most state PROs and private insurance companies. However, when compared to any criteria that have been developed, clinical judgment will always play the primary role in evaluating the health care needs of any patient.

Appropriateness of a given service must also be considered when evaluating the clinical needs of the patient. There are many ways to determine the clinical appropriateness of a surgery and/or a procedure, as well as many ways to evaluate the appropriateness of other diagnostic and therapeutic regimens such as blood usage, drug usage, and diagnostic testing. Whatever method is used, the key is to have the hospital's physicians agree on the criteria being used to monitor the appropriateness of patient care. When necessary, peer judgment is used for problem-solving.

Monitor number four, discharge preparation, will take a group effort to identify areas of concern with the discharge preparation process. Not only should the team understand and monitor the effectiveness of the hospital's discharge preparation process, but some standard should be used to measure the timeliness of discharge as well. It will be important for any discharge preparation process to incorporate criteria that have been developed internally by patient care units for transfers and guidelines that have been developed for discharge to other appropriate levels of care.

Levels external to the hospital, such as nursing homes, are often difficult to access and can cause many placement concerns for hospital patients needing a non-acute level of care. This may lead to problem-solving activities beyond the walls of the hospital. Once the above has been done and hopefully automated, the real problem-solving activities begin with regard to patient flow management.

**100 Series**
**Actual Level at Admission**

| | **Acute Setting** |
|---|---|
| 100 | ER Outliners |
| 101 | Regular Room |
| 102 | Telemetry |
| 103 | Subacute |
| 104 | CCU |
| 105 | CCU Transitional |
| 106 | CVICU |
| 107 | CVICU Transitional |
| 108 | RICU |
| 109 | MICU |
| 110 | SICU |
| 111 | Neuro ICU |
| 112 | Neonatal ICU/SNICU |
| 113 | Nursery |
| 114 | Observation with subsequent inpatient stay (NON-PSYCHIATRIC) |
| 115 | Chronic |
| *116* | *Psychiatric / Geropsychiatric (obsolete)* |
| 117 | Recovery Room |
| 118 | Inpatient Hospice |
| 119 | Diabetic Unit |
| 120 | Addictive Disease Unit |
| 121 | Open Unit/Psychiatric |
| 122 | Closed Unit/Psychiatric |
| 123 | Geropsychiatric |
| 124 | Interim Care |
| 125 | Observation with subsequent inpatient stay (PSYCHIATRIC) |
| 126-138 | TBA |
| **139** | **Acute care for Pre-admission** |

PA PHYSICIAN ADVISOR
TBA TO BE ANNOUNCED

**200 Series**
**Needed Level at Admission**

| | **Acute Setting** |
|---|---|
| 201 | Regular Room |
| 202 | Telemetry |
| 203 | Subacute |
| 204 | CCU |
| 205 | CCU Transitional |
| 206 | CVICU |
| 207 | CVICU Transitional |
| 208 | RICU |
| 209 | MICU |
| 210 | SICU |
| 211 | Neuro ICU |
| 212 | Neonatal ICU/SNICU |
| 213 | Nursery |
| 214PA | Observation with subsequent inpatient stay (NON-PSYCHIATRIC) |
| 215PA | Chronic |
| *216PA* | *Psychiatric / Geopsychiatric (obsolete)* |
| 217 | Recovery Room |
| 218 | Inpatient Hospice |
| 219 | Diabetic Unit |
| 220PA | Addictive Disease Unit |
| 221PA | Open Unit/Psychiatric |
| 222PA | Close Unit/Psychiatric |
| 223PA | Geropsychiatric |
| 224PA | Interim Care |
| 225PA | Observation with subsequent inpatient stay (PSYCHIATRIC) |
| 226-239 | TBA |
| | **Non-Acute Setting** |
| 240PA | SNF |
| 241PA | ICF |
| 242PA | Rehabilitation |
| 243PA | Home Health |
| 244PA | Home - OUTPATIENT Diagnostic |
| 245PA | Hotel - OUTPATIENT Diagnostic |
| 246PA | Hospital - OUTPATIENT Diagnostic (Self-Care) |
| 247PA | OUTPATIENT - Other |
| 248PA | Observationon ACUTE unit with no subsequent inpatient stay |
| 249PA | Ambulatory Surgery |
| 250PA | Mental Health Facility |
| 251PA | Vocational Rehabilitation |
| 252PA | Boarding/Care Home |
| 253PA | OUTPATIENT/Home Health Hospice |
| 254PA | Home |
| 255PA | Observation on PSYCHIATRIC unit with no subsequent inpatient stay |
| 256PA | Psychiatric Day/OUTPATIENT TREATMENT |

NOTE: ANY NEEDED LEVELS CODED 240-256 WILL ALSO BE INTERPRETED AS ''NOT MEETING ADMISSION CRITERIA WITHIN 24 HOURS OF ADMISSION.''

**Figure 3.** *Baptist Memorial Hospital Quality Review Services patient flow management codes for levels of care*

## Reasons (Primary and Secondary) for Reported Days For Admission and Continued Stay

**Reported days fall into two categories:**

**A. Variant Days:**

1. Non-Acute Variant Days - Days when actual level of care does not equal needed level of care and needed level of care is non-acute. (Last two digits of actual do not equal last two digits of needed.)

2. Delay Variant Days - Wasted days when patient's length of stay has been extended unnecessarily. (Actual and needed level of care will be the same.)

**B. Level of Care Days Within Acute:**

3. Level of Care Days Within Acute - Days when actual level of care does not equal needed level of care, and actual and needed level of care are acute. (Last two digits of actual do not equal last two digits of needed.)

Must enter at least primary reason when reported days are noted.

Must document responsible party - M.D. (M), Internal (I), External (E)

### Lack of Bed / Services Needed

Please refer to definition #1 and #3, i.e., a discrepancy in level of care between actual and needed should be documented if you use codes 500-519.

| M.D. | Internal | External | | |
|---|---|---|---|---|
| | Y* | Y** | 500 | Appropriate (needed) bed not available (Use *8999-Hospital/Unknown BMH dept if acute care bed is needed. If A & D unit is needed, use *8036-Baptist Recovery Center. If rehab is needed, use *8028-BMH RRC or **9000 for external facility. If SNF is needed, use *8030-BMH SNF or **9000 for external facility. If ICF is needed, use **900 external facility.) |
| | | | 501-519 | TBA |

### Miscellaneous

| M.D. | Internal | External | | |
|---|---|---|---|---|
| Y | | | 520 PA | Delay or discrepancy in level of care due to current physician (Use reason code 531 for receiving physician.) |
| Y | Y | Y | 521 | Delay in diagnostic testing results |
| | Y | | 522 | Diet error resulting in delay of procedure, test, or surgery |
| Y | | | 523 | Diagnostic test / study not ordered when indicated (Use reason code 529 when test / study not performed when ordered.) |
| | Y | Y | 524 | Inadequate / incorrect prep for procedure |
| Y | Y | | 525 | Equipment malfunction |
| | | Y* | 526 PA | Due to patient/family (Use *9998-Patient or Family.) |
| Y | Y | Y | 527 | Services not provided on weekends, holidays, etc. |
| Y | Y | Y | 528 | Procedure scheduling difficulty |

PA PHYSICIAN ADVISOR
TBA TO BE ANNOUNCED

**Figure 3 (cont.).** *Baptist Memorial Hospital Quality Review Services patient flow management codes for levels of care*

### Miscellaneous continued

| M.D. | Internal | External | | |
|---|---|---|---|---|
| | Y | | **529 PA** | Due to physician's order(s) not being carried out |
| Y | Y | | **530 PA** | Quality issue causing increased length of stay (Code appropriate Concurrent Review code.) |
| Y* | Y | Y | **531 PA** | Receiving physician/facility refuses patient (*not Attending MD) |
| Y | Y | | **532 PA** | Therapy continued without measurable response |
| Y | Y* | Y | **533** | Delay due to third party payor requirements - for example, second surgical opinion (*Use 8037-Pre-Admission Quality Review Services.) |
| | Y | Y | **534** | Routine Equipment / supplies not available |
| | Y* | | **535** | Delay due to Social Work (*Use 8031-Social Work Services.) |
| Y | Y* | Y | **536 PA** | Delay in Psychological testing (*Use 8023-Psychological Services.) |
| Y | Y* | Y | **537 PA** | Delay in Psychological testing results (Use *8023-Psychological Services.) |
| Y* | Y | Y | **539** | Delay for unknown/other reasons (*If unknown MD, use 7999. If MD known, use reason code 520.) |
| Y | Y | Y | **540 PA** | Delay due to individual Psychological therapy scheduling |
| | Y* | Y** | **541** | Awaiting PRO approval of procedure (*Use 8037-Pre-Admission Quality Review Services.) (**Use 9002-Governmental agency.) |
| | | | **542-559** | TBA |

### Legal/Financial

Please refer to definition #1, i.e., a discrepancy in level of care between actual and needed should be documented if you use codes 560 - 589.

| M.D. | Internal | External | | |
|---|---|---|---|---|
| | | Y | **560** | Awaiting PAE (Medicaid) and/or mental health/mental retardation evaluation approval |
| | | Y* | **561** | Awaiting PRO approval of cease (*Use 9002-Governmental agency.) |
| | | Y* | **562** | Cease served - patient agrees to absorb costs (*Use 9998-Patient or Family.) |
| | Y* | Y | **563** | Financial obstacles to transfer/discharge (*Use 8006-Fiscal Services.) |
| Y | Y | Y | **564 PA** | Legal consequences impede transfer/discharge |
| Y* | Y** | Y | **565** | Awaiting evaluation/approval for needed level of care (*Not Attending MD) (**Use 8028-RRC-BMH or **8030-SNF-BMH or **8036-Baptist Recovery Center.) |
| Y | | Y* | **566** | Private insurance denial - attribute to each day denied (*Use 9003-Insurance.) |
| NA | NA | NA | **567** | Billed as outpatient (To be used as a secondary reason code) |
| | | | **588** | |
| Y | Y | Y | **589 PA** | Other legal/financial reason. |

PA PHYSICIAN ADVISOR
TBA TO BE ANNOUNCED

**Figure 3 (cont.).** *Baptist Memorial Hospital Quality Review Services patient flow management codes for levels of care*

**Other**

Please refer to definition #1 and #3, i.e., a discrepancy in level of care between actual and needed should be documented if you use codes 590 - 599.

| M.D. | Internal | External | Code | Description |
|---|---|---|---|---|
| | | | **590-598** | TBA |
| Y | | | **599 PA** | Variance due to practice patterns/lack of documentation/delay in discharge to appropriate level of care/placement. |

PA PHYSICIAN ADVISOR
TBA TO BE ANNOUNCED



**Figure 3 (cont.).** *Baptist Memorial Hospital Quality Review Services patient flow management codes for levels of care*

# Variance from Care Standards

Up to this point, we have been able to accomplish the monitoring and measurement of the aforementioned indicators within a clinical data base to assist with patient flow problem-solving. However, data without action are useless. Therefore, based upon the analysis of the four central monitors in the hospital-wide case management process, it would be important to identify any variance from efficient, effective, and safe management of the patient's care. If the team has set up an automated method with appropriate indicators that can be assigned either an alpha or numeric code, problem-solving activities become more meaningful because of the objective data. Once a hospital is able to organize a patient flow management monitoring system, it may be amazed to see how poorly a patient is moved through the care process. It may also be quite revealing that routine hospital operations can promote poor case management. Often, for the first time, it is realized that variant (delayed and unnecessary) days are due to inappropriate and/or insufficient levels of care and ineffective, outdated processes for delivering patient care.

Regardless of the amount of variant days found, it will be necessary for the hospital to develop several teams to problem-solve the admissions, continued stay, and discharge preparation processes. It is imperative that the medical staff be an integral part of these teams. If there is a quality improvement structure in place, the medical and hospital staff can use already established committees or teams for the problem-solving activities.

Information is the key to problem-solving, and patient flow management can provide objective, measurable data. Not only should the reason for variant days be noted, but data on who caused the wasted days should also be abstracted (see Figure 4, responsible party codes). This will enable hospital management as well as physicians to problem-solve with individuals or diagnostic/service areas. This should be done while keeping in mind possible process issues. Often inefficient systems or processes are the root cause of variant days rather than individuals. When the hospital and medical staff are able to identify from objective data that there are process issues that keep patients from receiving the best possible care, it is easy to understand the need to work together. No longer should the hospital blame the physicians—nor the physicians blame the hospital—for less than optimal patient care.

Note: When a primary reason for a variant day or concurrent review code is documented, place one of these responsible party codes in the accompanying M.D. blank.

## M.D.

Name Individual M.D. (Includes M.D.'s staff/lab procedures, etc.). Write the doctor's full name.

| | |
|---|---|
| 7900 | C.R.N.A. |
| 7901 | Medical Service Intern/Resident |
| 7902 | Surgical Service Intern/Resident |
| 7999 | Unknown M.D. |

## Internal BMH Department or Service

| | |
|---|---|
| 8000 | Anesthesia |
| 8001 | Audiology |
| 8036 | Baptist Recovery Center |
| 8002 | Bace Department |
| 8003 | Cardiac Lab |
| 8004 | Central Supply |
| 8005 | Clinical Engineering |
| 8006 | Fiscal Services (Business Office) |
| 8007 | Food and Nutrition - Dietary |
| 8008 | Food and Nutrition - Dietitian |
| 8009 | GI Lab |
| 8010 | Hemodialysis Unit |
| 8011 | Home Plus (BMH) - Use 9000 for external home health |
| 8012 | Hyperbaric (HBO) |
| 8013 | Medical Records |
| 8014 | Neurosciences (Audio, EEG, EMG, Epicare, Sleep Lab) |
| 8015 | Nursing Services |
| 8016 | Occupational Therapy (OT) |
| 8017 | Orthopedic Applicances |
| 8018 | Pathology - Lab |
| 8019 | Pathology - Tissue |
| 8020 | Pharmacy |
| 8021 | Physical Therapy |
| 8037 | Pre-Admission Quality Review Services |
| 8022 | Psychiatric Program Activities (Any group therapy) |
| 8023 | Psychological Services |
| 8024 | Radiology - MRI |
| 8025 | Radiology - Nuclear Medicine (Thal TM, Persantine TM) |
| 8026 | Radiology - Radiation Therapy |
| 8027 | Radiology - Other |
| 8028 | Regional Rehab Center (RRC-BMH) Use 9000 for external Rehab facility |
| 8029 | Respiratory Care Services |
| 8030 | Skilled Nursing Facility (SNF-BMH) Use 9000 for external SNF |
| 8031 | Social Work Services |
| 8032 | Speech Therapy |
| 8033 | Stone Treatment Center |
| 8034 | Surgery |
| 8035 | Urodynamics |
| 8038 | To be assigned |
| 8999 | Hospital / Unknown BMH Department |

## External Entities

| | | | |
|---|---|---|---|
| 9000 | External Facility | 9004 | Transportation - Between BMH facilities |
| 9001 | External M.D. | 9005 | Transportation - At discharge |
| 9002 | Governmental agency (includes PRO) | 9998 | Patient or Family |
| 9003 | Insurance | 9999 | Unknown external entity |



**Figure 4.** *Responsible party codes*

# Critical Paths

Using the tools of total quality or continuous quality improvement to solve problems identified through patient flow management data, hospitals and their medical staffs will be able to become more efficient and effective in delivering patient care. Many aspects of the hospital's health care delivery system will need to be flow charted, graphed, and analyzed using such tools such as Pareto charts, fishbone diagrams, and run charts. Once this is done, processes can be improved based upon sound recommendations. Although it is very beneficial to look at the broad scope of a hospital's process for delivering patient care, it is obvious that direct patient case management must be improved and focused upon. This brings us to the snapshot viewpoint.

Nowhere in the patient care delivery process is it more important to work together as a team than in the delivery of *direct* patient care. At this level, it is imperative that someone *manages* the care being delivered to the patient. Health care has become so complex, complicated, and diffuse that the physician can no longer direct patient care without assistance. Many case management professionals believe coordination of patient care lies squarely on the shoulders of the nurse, due to the nurse's 24-hours-per-day relationship with patients. Nurses should make sure that individuals delivering care are working together as a team to meet the needs of the patient. This can be challenging, because these needs are sometimes factual and other times perceptual in nature. Factual needs are usually related to clinical issues, whereas perceptual needs are usually related to customer satisfaction concerns. Any health care team's efforts should always be focused upon the patient's factual as well as perceptual needs.

Because of the great need to coordinate direct patient care today, guidelines were needed and thus critical paths were born. Critical paths are seen as a way to solve direct patient case management issues. These paths are a crucial part of a team's (physician, nurses, and support professionals) efforts to manage and/or coordinate the patient's care. A critical path should be developed based upon diagnoses with similar patient care needs. The critical path should then be organized to help the health care team know what intervention on any given day of a patient's hospitalization is most likely to produce the best outcomes for a given patient population. At this point, a health care team will be able to use these pathways as a map to better manage the health care delivery process and thus better meet the needs of the patient.

When a hospital is able to bring the focus of managing patient care to this level, it is often amazing how many inefficiencies can be discovered. Waste is often found because there is a lack of knowledge about what is being done for the patient, why it is being done, how it is best accomplished, and what the immediate goal is. This is usually due to a lack of working together as a team in providing care to the whole patient, not just part of the patient. Because the physician cannot always be present to direct patient care, and each individual health care worker lacks the ability to see the big picture of what is being done for the patient, there is often overutilization of treatment modalities and supplies. This is often due to repeat and/or rework because of unknown or misunderstood physician orders. One of the key causes of overutilization in hospitals is the duplication of diagnostic and/or treatment orders. This can easily happen when no one is monitoring all of the aspects of the patient care delivery process.

Even worse than overutilization or waste is the potential for the patient to get lost in an uncoordinated, piecemeal, and unmanaged health care delivery process. Patients (customers) become dissatisfied because of a lack of wisdom and understanding of how best to meet their health care needs. Critical paths are an excellent way for nurses to organize a team around an agreed-upon plan of action to meet the healing needs of the patient. With so many people involved in delivering patient care today, a critical path helps to give everyone a common vision of what should be done for a particular patient at a given point in the healing process.

# Service Lines

When a hospital has taken into account the need to improve upon hospital-wide and direct patient care delivery systems, the union of these two efforts can lead to the development of the third component of patient flow management: service lines. Service lines are developed by centering on related health care services being offered to meet the needs of groups of patients. Attempts are then made at making these services highly organized in order to meet the expectations of patients regarding the health care delivery process. Examples might be cardiac, neurologic, and/or orthopaedic services. Service lines are often used as marketing tools but should also be thought of as a way to organize patient care.

When everyone is working together for the good of the patient it is easier for hospitals to market their services. The value of each health care dollar naturally improves in a collaborative care environment because improved delivery processes lead to decreases in the waste related to medical treatment. Improved processes for patient care can have a direct or indirect impact on the patient's satisfaction and the outcomes of care. Perceptual and factual outcomes of patient care are most often influenced by the processes within which health care workers are functioning. If one is able to improve the processes, it only stands to reason that better service can be offered by health care professionals.

Service lines should go beyond the hospital walls and begin to assess the needs of the community served. Through focusing on these needs, service line management should be concerned about case management when there are health care delivery system problems that keep the hospital and its medical staff from meeting the service expectations of its customers. If a hospital's reason for existence is to serve the health care needs of its community, then it behooves the hospital to meet its customer's needs. Otherwise, dissatisfied patients will seek other hospitals that can meet their health care expectations. If this happens, it will result in a decrease in census due to a shrinking or lost patient referral base. In many ways, successful service lines are dependent upon good case management. In order to have a good product to promote, service lines must be based on the collaborative efforts of case management.

The best way to meet the needs of patients in hospitals today is to focus upon all aspects of the health care delivery process. Patient flow management must be thought of in terms of three components: hospital-wide system/process case management, critical paths, and service lines. If the progress of the patient through the hospital is correctly managed and the daily needs of the patient are met in the most effective, efficient, and safe manner possible, then it is more likely the hospital will meet the quality expectations of patients, payers and other customers. Once a hospital gains *knowledge* of how to better manage the health care delivery system, and *wisdom* about the importance of meeting the customer's quality expectations, then the *understanding* should come that the *patient* is the most important reason for an effective case management process.

# 15

# Episodic Care: A Proposed Model for Inpatient Perinatal Case Management

Lynn D. Wheeler, RN, MSN, WHCNP

*This chapter describes the events surrounding the birth process and how they relate to all four dimensions of case management. I think you will agree that this application of case management fits well with our model and is "do-able."*—R.S.H.

This chapter describes a proposed case management system for an inpatient perinatal unit. The focus is on an episodic care model with integration of case management models of self-care, primary care, and brokered care. This chapter will also identify some of the linkages required to achieve this integration.

Perinatal means "surrounding the birth process" and is used to describe the labor, birth, and immediate postpartum phases. The perinatal unit is somewhat different from most inpatient acute care units in that pregnancy and birth are wellness phenomena. Concepts of self-care form the basis for how women and their families respond to the pregnancy and work toward a healthy outcome. Most families receive primary care in the guise of prenatal care with a physician, advanced practitioner (e.g., certified nurse midwife, physician's assistant, or nurse practitioner), or lay person.

Perinatal episodic care often occurs in an institutional setting (hospital or birth center) and concentrates on the labor, birth, and immediate (one to 24-hour) recovery phase. Episodic care is also utilized for acute complications during pregnancy (such as preterm labor) or postpartum (for example, endometritis). Brokered care commonly occurs when there are non-acute (days to weeks) complications and/or teaching needs. Childbirth education could be viewed as a brokered care intervention, as well as antepartum home monitoring of contractions and postpartum mother and baby visits.

# Description of the Setting

The hospital described is located in the Pacific Northwest and is one of several hospitals within a health care corporation. The corporation also includes a visiting nurse service and extensive outpatient facilities. The bed capacity is over 500, although the hospital usually runs at 40% of capacity.

Hospital administration employs a matrix management of president, vice-presidents, and specialty program directors. Some program directors have direct management responsibility over specialized nursing departments (such as surgery), while other nursing units are included in the Department of Nursing. An illustration of the hospital administrative structure is shown in Figure 1.

The Women's Health Program director is responsible for large-scale planning and development and physician recruitment. The perinatal unit receives most its capital and operating budget from the Department of Nursing.

There are 30 active physicians on staff, the majority of whom are women. Most physicians performed their residency in the hospital and practice only at this hospital.

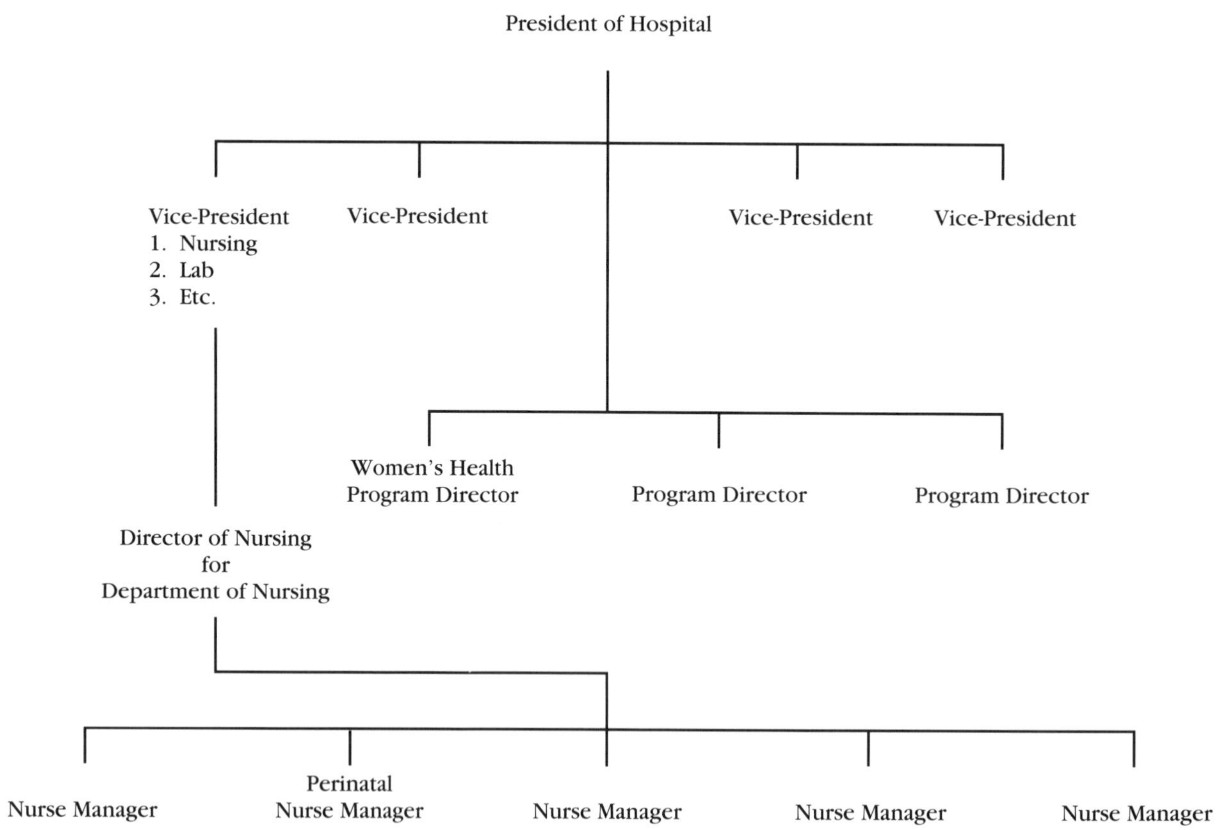


**Figure 1.** *Illustration of hospital administrative structure*

The nursing staff consists primarily of registered nurses with a long tenure (average ten years) and history of single specialty experience (i.e., labor and delivery, nursery, and postpartum) with the hospital and unit. When the decision was made by upper management to move toward single-room maternity care with a perinatal nursing staff, many of the nurses were angry about changing their existing specialty mode of care and anxious about their ability and desire to provide the high-quality care they were giving. The nurses were concerned that women and their families would not receive this new type of care as well as the current multitransfer care delivery model that used labor rooms, birthing rooms, delivery rooms, and recovery room. A cross-training program was initiated in 1990 with the goal of instituting an all-perinatal nursing staff over the coming two to three years.

The patient population for perinatal services are primarily middle- and upper-class low-risk women with health insurance. The hospital became a bloodless surgery center in September 1991, one of only four in North America. Most women attend childbirth education classes provided by the hospital. The Women's Health Program encompasses perinatal and women's health inpatient services, this including a level II nursery. Outpatient services include mammography and a women's health resource office that provides physician referral, professional and public education (including childbirth education and parenting classes), and lactation services. The Women's Resource Center is staffed by registered nurses with obstetrical expertise. Inpatient perinatal beds include a 23-bed single-room maternity care (SRMC) unit, which opened in winter of 1991, and 21 gynecology beds, which are adjacent to the perinatal unit and are also used for overflow obstetrics. Inpatient services include two operating suites on the same floor for cesarean sections and other surgeries, such as D&C and tubal ligations.

# Needs Assessment

## Patient and Family

The initial patient contact with the primary care provider may be made directly or through the Women's Resource Center. Because the registered nurses who work in the center are knowledgeable about the obstetricians, a more "customized" fit is achieved between patient and primary care provider. When making the appointment, the Women's Resource Center nurse may advise the office staff of any particular issues or problems that the woman has shared during the telephone inquiry. As of this writing, there is no systematic process to document significant issues when identified by the Women's Resource Center nurse.

During the antepartum period, a prenatal history and physical and progress notes concerning prenatal visits are sent to the perinatal unit at approximately 24 weeks gestation. An updated copy is sent at 36 weeks gestation. This prenatal record includes the estimated date of delivery, standard information such as allergies, medical, and obstetrical history, and a list of problems occuring prior to and/or with the pregnancy. This history is kept on file in the perinatal unit at the main nursing station and is filed by the unit secretary. Patient histories are not currently scanned by nursing staff, and physician offices do not routinely pre-identify patients and/or families with physical or emotional problems. At the time of this writing, it seems surprising that "at risk" patients have not and are not routinely identified prior to admission.

The period of hospitalization is, for many perinatal patients, their first hospital experience. At the time of admission during labor, there are many variables that affect the woman's perception of the event, especially her emotional state. Along with the excitement and anticipation of a new family member, most women and their family members are anxious about the safety of the mother and fetus, and fear the pain involved in the labor and delivery process (Dickason, Schult, and Silverman, 1990). The detrimental effects of the fear-tension-pain cycle are well documented in childbirth education literature (Phillips, 1987). Also documented are the beneficial effects of reducing fear and tension and, subsequently, pain by learning specific techniques or information before the event (Phillips, 1987).

Techniques of breathing, relaxation, and other exercises are often used to reduce the pain of childbirth and maintain fetal and maternal oxygenation. Most women and their partners in this population attend hospital-sponsored childbirth education classes and tour the unit. Other important sources of information include lay literature, videos, tapes/CDs, and talking with family and friends in order to gain more knowledge and be emotionally and physically prepared for the labor and delivery process.

It is also well documented that moderate to severe anxiety decreases information processing (O'Toole & Welt, 1989). Providing information using a variety of teaching methods has been found to be most effective in providing patient teaching (Redman, 1984). The depth and breadth of information available on pregnancy and birth is immense. Entire walls of bookstores are frequently devoted to pregnancy and parenting information. This signifies the importance of information on this subject to women and their families.

### Staff Nurses

The nursing staff had provided care for one of three specific patient types: labor and delivery, postpartum, and/or newborn (most newborn nurses were also proficient at level II care). A perinatal knowledge base was necessary for the nurses to grow and change from a single focus to a perinatal practice because the model of nursing care changed with the construction of a single-room maternity care unit.

A comprehensive didactic session was provided before the cross-training; however, staff still had many questions during the clinical period about "how the pieces fit into place" during the course of labor and delivery, postpartum, and with the transitioning newborn. This uncertainty is at this time not completely resolved; however, with additional clinical experience in perinatal nursing in a single-room maternity care setting, many of the questions are being answered. Questions concerning staffing levels, skill mix, number of veteran nurses in each area, etc., were high on the anxiety list in the initial cross-training phases. Questions of how often nurses needed to work with mother-baby, labor and delivery, circulate, and scrub in order to maintain or improve clinical skills were very important to the nurses.

## Process Development

### Documentation Standards

A variety of patient education materials were available, primarily addressing the postpartum period and newborn care. Intrapartum educational pamphlets included a prostaglandin gel research protocol and epidural anesthesia.

Standardized care plans were in place for the laboring patient, the postpartum patient, and the newborn. These plans listed patient problems and/or nursing diagnoses, and nursing interventions. A unit policy/procedure/protocol book addressed unit specific clinical and documentation standards and included NAACOG standards. In addition, there were Department of Nursing and hospital standards in place to cover generic patient situations.

Prior to the change to single-room maternity care, a thorough evaluation of nursing documentation was completed in June 1990 by a core group of staff nurses. The nurses' goal was to decrease the number of forms, eliminate duplicative charting, decrease total charting time, and more thoroughly document patient assessments and nursing interventions. The nursing standards coordinator who assisted with form design and content also incorporated an every-shift assessment of whether standards of care were being met. If standards were not being met, this merited a progress note. Orientation to the form emphasized exception charting.

A perinatal unit-based quality improvement committee began meeting in spring of 1991 as part of a total quality management plan. Perinatal patient teaching was identified as one of the projects needing work—discharge teaching in particular. A perinatal discharge form was developed that asked the parent(s) to circle those items they particularly wanted information about. Subjects included maternal care, infant care, and signs and symptoms of illness. Under each subject was a list of items; for example, infant care listed cord care, feeding, diapering, bathing, etc. A task force made up entirely of staff nurses developed this form.

## Critical Path Development

The Department of Nursing began work on a new patient care delivery model in 1989. As case management emerged as the model of choice, a tremendous amount of nursing energy was devoted to the development of critical paths. Critical paths for the laboring patient and family, the postpartum and postoperative patient and family, and normal newborn were written by staff nurses who were currently working in those areas in early 1991; development was guided by the women's health clinical nurse specialist who was a member of the case management committee. Physician standing orders were available to translate onto the critical path. In addition, a standardized self-medication packet was utilized for all postpartum and subsequently postoperative patients.

Unfortunately, the perinatal critical paths were developed almost exclusively by the nursing staff. Multidisciplinary communication was not ideal; unit planning and construction involved a tremendous amount of time for physicians, respiratory therapy, dietary, material services, housekeeping and pharmacy. Subsequently, case management did not assume first priority.

## Interdisciplinary Communication

Communication with other disciplines took place on an invitational basis, with nursing initiating communication. There was a variable degree of knowledge/commitment from team members outside of nursing as a result of this. The concepts and philosophy of case management were still solidifying in the minds of those nurses guiding the project and therefore more energy was spent working with nursing colleagues.

The multidisciplinary team members most frequently involved with perinatal patients and families included the obstetrician, pediatrician, neonatologist, anesthesiologist and certified registered nurse anesthesist, lactation consultants, social worker, and utilization review. Other team members involved on a less frequent or less clinical basis included pastoral services, respiratory therapy (primarily for level II newborns and the recovery area), dietary, environmental services, engineering, biomedical support, and laboratory.

The program director, perinatal nurse manager, women's health clinical nurse specialist, and neonatal nurse clinician attended obstetrical and pediatric meetings on a regular basis. In addition, a nursery team that included social work, anesthesia, respiratory therapy, neonatologist, neonatal nurse clinician, perinatal nurse manager, and women's health clinical nurse specialist met monthly to discuss level II nursery concerns and related neonatal issues. Nursing participated in hospital-wide task forces to achieve a variety of goals (examples include an epidural task force, recycling, and computerization). Formal liaisons were designated to address patient and nursing support services in the Department of Nursing.

The program director, perinatal nurse manager, director of the Women's Resource Center, women's health clinical nurse specialist, and director of nursing met bimonthly to discuss women's health issues and strategies. The unit management team met on a monthly basis to review needs and address problems. Monthly staff meetings took place, and a variety of task forces worked on specific issues involving other disciplines as needed (for example, the Pregnancy Loss Task Force involved the chaplains, laboratory/pathology, physicians, and social work).

# Implementation Plan

## Overview

The goal of perinatal case management is to anticipate significant problems and establish needed linkages so that problems can be resolved or at least planned for prior to the patient's hospitalization. It was originally thought that a case manager would be assigned only for those patients/families with problems identified by the obstetrician on the basis of prenatal history and the physical. The slant would be toward physiological diseases (such as diabetes) that put patients at risk for complications and/or extended the usual length of stay. For those patients without significant exceptions, the plan was to utilize the nursing documentation already in place and mark that the standard of care (nursing assessment and interventions on the critical path) was being met. Unfortunately, this system did not address the clinical and satisfaction outcomes.

In addition, as the unit management team consulted with other institutions, it became apparent that many patients had social issues requiring special interventions that were not identified by the obstetrician. These social issues often led to significant increases in length of stay, amount of nursing time required during hospitalization, and patient anxiety.

Copies of critical paths for the laboring woman, normal newborn, postpartum, and cesarean families will be laminated and placed on every chart back. This will serve as a guide to those newly cross-trained or those currently cross-training, as well as provide an orientation for new employees. The hope is that this would also be used as a teaching tool for families. The unit documentation task force has recently explored the use of the critical paths as a documentation tool, thus addressing the clinical and satisfaction outcomes.

It is hoped that there will be increased communication from the Women's Resource Center nurses, the office nursing staff, and obstetricians about patient/family progress throughout the pregnancy directed toward the inpatient case managers for those women identified to be "at risk". For those patients/families with identified exceptions, a critical path will be stamped with their address plate and filled out by a perinatal nurse case manager, either during the antepartum period when a problem is identified or if one develops during the inpatient stay.

## Identification of Patient Case Types

Based on the patient population, the case types identified for initial implementation are those with high-risk conditions. High-risk cases are defined as those patients having special emotional needs and/or those patients having physiological alterations that would change their critical path in a significant way. Initially, it was thought that problems identified by the physician and listed on the prenatal record problem list would be the method of targeting those patients/families with significant problems.

Examples of high-risk conditions include those patients/families with:

- Current or history of perinatal loss (at any stage of the pregnancy)
- History of emotionally difficult or traumatic labor, birth and/or postpartum period
- History of premature infant
- History of infant requiring special interventions
- Alterations in family processes related to domestic violence
- Licit or illicit drugs
- Pregnancy-induced hypertension
- Diabetes (insulin dependent)
- Clotting disorders
- Surgery during pregnancy
- Premature labor
- Bleeding during pregnancy (placenta previa or abruption)

### Future Directions

Staff education and case manager training, physician communication, and increased multidisciplinary communication/education need to take place before actual implementation occurs. Many of the nursing staff and physicians are still struggling with the transition to a new unit and new delivery of care procedures. It is a great challenge to introduce more change during this time. The linkages between the Women's Resource Center nurses, the office nurses, and inpatient nurses must be established and nurtured. Whether the critical paths remain as a guide with the documentation addressing exceptions to the identified outcomes, or whether the critical path will become the newest version of the documentation, is still undecided.

# Integration of Case Management Models

## Primary Care Aspects

The strongest link for the episodic care model is with the primary care model, in this case the obstetrician. Obstetricians and the office nursing staff could identify those patients who meet emotional and/or physiological risk criteria developed by patients/families, physicians, office nursing staff and hospital staff (including nursing staff, social work, and lactation services).

One example of this would be a woman who at the initial visit was identified as having nipple inversion that would make it difficult to breast-feed. The office nursing staff (primary care case manager) could notify lactation services so that interventions could be implemented; in addition, the hospital nursing staff could note this on the mother's problem list and provide specific interventions postpartum to ensure breast-feeding success. Another example would be that of a woman who developed pregnancy-induced hypertension (PIH) in the third trimester. This woman would be assigned a case manager to coordinate her care and provide specific teaching. Another example would be that of a family who had a previous difficult labor—either emotionally or physically. A case manager could assess specifics and plan care accordingly as well as participate in providing an extra measure of support to this family through a critical path and/or by being present.

Another method of identifying patients at risk is to scan the prenatal history and physical and problem list at 24 and 36 weeks. Those patients identified to be at risk would be assigned a case manager at that time and followed through the postpartum period, including, ideally, a home visit, but at the minimum postpartum telephone calls.

The ideal method of identifying those patients at risk prior to admission would be an antepartum contact by one of the perinatal case managers. The obstetrician and the office staff need to communicate closely with the inpatient perinatal staff. Although this sounds simplistic, at this time there is no regular communication about patients/families between the obstetrician and her/his office nursing staff and the inpatient nursing staff. Equipment that would facilitate this includes a computer with modem and fax machine. Using current information technology, a more timely prenatal record could be assimilated by the inpatient nursing staff, and if a patient was hospitalized, the obstetrician's office nursing staff could get a similar update. A collaborative group practice would be especially appropriate for those physicians who have expressed an interest in working more closely with identified members of the perinatal unit nursing staff.

## Brokered Care Aspects

With decreasing lengths of stay in the perinatal unit, an ideal brokered care service is antepartal contact and postpartal home visit(s) by perinatal unit nursing staff. The case manager would be the logical person to make antepartal contact and home visit(s), utilizing the data base provided by the woman and family, obstetrician, pediatrician, and inpatient stay. Antepartum home visits for those women unable to attend childbirth education classes due to medical illnesses would be another example of brokered care and could be performed by the episodic care case manager or primary care case manager. In the case of the mother with breast-feeding problems, the lactation consultants would continue to provide services both during the hospitalization and postpartum (some clients are seen for weeks, even months).

## Self-Care Aspects

Self-care strategies are the basis for much of the labor process and the postpartum learning that occurs. The presence of a familiar and caring support person is extremely important in how well women cope with labor. The touch, talk, and empathy of family and friends plays a major role in the perception of pregnancy, labor, birth, and the postpartum period.

Examples of these self-care behaviors in the pregnancy include:

- What and how much the pregnant woman should eat
- Exercise patterns
- Cultural traditions such as not lifting arms over the head (to prevent umbilical cord knots)
- Which doctor to see
- How to relieve discomforts of pregnancy

During labor, self-care measures include:

- Positioning
- Breathing techniques
- Use of water (whirlpool bath, shower)
- Massage
- Relaxation techniques

Encouragement provided by family and friends throughout the labor and birth are critical to the emotional energy of the laboring woman.

The postpartum period is usually where the woman and her partner receive the most advice on what to do and when. Examples include:

- How to diaper the infant
- Techniques for breast-feeding or bottle-feeding
- Amount of clothing the infant should wear
- Bathing techniques
- Maternal activity levels
- Amount the mother should eat and/or drink

The nursing staff provides information and role modeling to the family in teaching them to care for themselves and the neonate, often based on their own experiences in childbirth and parenting. In addition, the hospital gives every woman a self-medication packet with instructions on medications included and why and how to take them. This includes the pain medication ordered (usually Tylenol #3 or Darvocet N-100). The family records infant feedings and voids and stools on a flow sheet that is part of the permanent record. Patients and families identify those topics that are of concern to them on a perinatal teaching record. The patient education television channel in one hospital has videotapes on infant bathing, feeding, and other self-care measures. Patients and families also receive written information on maternal and infant care, signs and symptoms of illness, genetic testing, and follow-up visits with the obstetrician and pediatrician.

# Case Study of an Episodic Care Integrated Model

Mrs. X., a 36-year-old married woman, performs a home pregnancy test (Self-Care) on the day her period is due. She discovers it is positive and, after joyfully informing her best friend, mother, and husband, makes an appointment for prenatal care with the obstetrician/gynecologist she has been seeing for two years and who practices at the hospital where she wants to deliver. (Primary Care) Her first prenatal visit takes place at six weeks and vaginal ultrasound reveals a heartbeat and a gestational sac size consistent with a six-week intrauterine pregnancy. (Primary Care) She uses some home remedies to combat nausea which were effective when her mom was pregnant with her. (Self-Care)

Based on her obstetrician's advice and her extensive reading, she undergoes a chorionic villus sampling and alpha feto protein testing to screen for genetic anomalies and other abnormalities. (Primary Care and Self-Care) To her and her family's relief, everything is normal, and she has the added knowledge that she will have a girl. Her ultrasound at 20 weeks shows everything is progressing normally. The perinatal nurse case manager reviewing her prenatal history and physical does not flag the chart for a case manager at 24 weeks, although the nurse does make an appointment with the woman to talk to her about her needs and expectations during her pregnancy, her stay on the perinatal unit and postpartum. (Episodic Care) Based on this interview and discussion, Mrs. X. attends a community forum on how to look for child care providers, since she will continue working after the baby is born (she is a middle manager in a telecommunications firm). (Self-Care and Episodic Care) She also attends a breast-feeding class, and signs herself and her husband up for childbirth education classes. (Self-Care, Brokered Care) She takes her best friend along on one of her prenatal visits to meet the obstetrician because this friend will be with her during labor. She also signs up for a tour of the maternity unit. Her pregnancy progresses normally. The nurse reviewing her updated history and physical at 36 weeks does not flag the chart for a case manager at 36 weeks. (Episodic Care)

Two weeks before she is due, her friends give her a baby shower and her mother gives her a framed picture of her as a baby. She decides to have her mother with her during the labor. (Self-Care) Three days after her due date she begins having painful contractions and is assessed on the perinatal unit. During that time the nurse notes that her blood pressure is elevated and that she has more edema than normal. Although her cervix is only slightly dilated, the physician decides to admit her with a diagnosis of mild pregnancy-induced hypertension and to induce her labor. (Primary Care, Episodic Care) Her mother is very concerned, since she had the same condition, except they called it toxemia back then. The perinatal nurse case manager who had interviewed her previously is assigned at this point and explains in detail to the family the causes, symptoms, and possible interventions that might occur. The labor and delivery critical path is altered for induction and pregnancy-induced hypertension. The postpartum and neonatal paths are altered accordingly. Fortunately, no complications occur; she is induced the next morning with oxytocin, and receives an epidural at two centimeters dilation for pain relief. (Episodic Care) She delivers six hours later a healthy girl, to the delight of her family and friend who have been in the room with her the whole time. (Self-Care)

After the flurry of phone calls to other family members and friends, the staff nurse guides the father in infant care, including taking the baby's temperature, cord care, diapering, and first sponge bath. During her teaching the nurse also points out the infant's normal reflexes, skin color, and behavioral responses. The patient has indicated that she especially wants help and information on breast-feeding and infant signs and symptoms of illness. The infant nurses well at the first feeding and the nurse shows the patient and husband how to latch the baby on correctly and to listen for the audible swallows that are indicative of good breast-feeding. On the night shift the nurse encourages the parents to keep the infant in the room so they can practice taking care of it with help from the nursing staff. The infant sleeps most of the night, awakening several times to cry and fuss and to feed (though not well). Both parents do not rest well that night, since they are not accustomed to the infant's noises. In the morning, they watch the pediatrician's exam and learn more about signs and symptoms of illness. The obstetrician stops in in the morning and reviews the birth and admires their daughter. They send the baby back to the nursery while both take a nap. During the afternoon they watch several videos on infant care and are visited by the lactation specialist, who is able to observe a feeding session and offer more tips for success. (Episodic Care) The afternoon is filled with visting friends and admirers. That evening, the staff nurse reviews discharge instructions and reminds the parents that the perinatal nurse case manager will call them once a day for the next few days. The obstetrician plans on seeing the mother in the office in four weeks, and the infant's appointment is scheduled for two weeks. (Primary Care) Both parents will be attending a new parents' class for the next six weeks. (Brokered care)

# Vision for the Future

One goal of case management is to provide a systematic method to identify variances and to intervene to normalize the situation. To do this requires sufficient resources for getting the client back on the expected path. In the perinatal arena, this includes extensive emotional and educational resources.

In the self-care arena, the technology of an interactive holographic system such as virtual reality may offer the parents of the future a chance to practice an infant bath, diapering, or deal with vignettes involving infant illness. The Women's Resource Center could rent videotapes to offer information on physician practices, intervention rates, emotional empathy and listening skills, hospital standard compliance, and education/competency of care providers. Electronic media and equipment currently exist to provide everything from sounds conducive to relaxation (e.g., the sound of ocean waves) to mechanical stimulation (massagers) to acupressure. The sophistication of these gadgets may eventually be highly individualized according to self-described data bases or even direct input into the brain. This type of equipment could do everything from providing childbirth education to stimulating release of natural endorphins to relieving pain at childbirth and postpartum. An increasing amount of care will be provided by family members. Primary care models will utilize an increasing number of advanced practice nursing providers. Intervention services will be critically scrutinized by the primary care provider, client, and payer(s) based on the outcomes of health, cost, and customer satisfaction. More care will take place, with collaboration between the primary care provider and the client, and more so in the client's chosen environment. Computer and mechanical systems in place at the client's home or close by will take the place of many visits to the physician's office. The cost of health care will shift more to the client, though more basic services will be provided to all people. Electronic mail of standard prenatal care questions, video screen observation of the client, and recording by family member or client of fundal height measurement, weight, fetal heart tones, and urine dipstick will become standard.

Episodic care will be utilized almost exclusively for those at very high risk or in need of highly specialized technology (such as severe preeclampsia, brittle diabetics, invasive monitoring). Most diagnoses now requiring hospitalization will be done on an outpatient basis (one only needs to look at how the laparoscope has revolutionized surgery stays to get a hint of this). Episodic care dollars provided by insurance or government will be limited to a certain dollar amount, and financial penalties will exist for those clients not following self-care regimens (i.e., a heavy smoker who does not reduce the number of cigarettes she smokes per day may pay a larger co-pay when hospitalized for preterm labor and/or premature delivery). Episodic care will focus more on social and emotional factors influencing health and cost.

Brokered care will increase dramatically as the components of education and client-specific intervention previously provided by the episodic care model are replaced. Current examples of this include lactation services, home intravenous services, and antepartum home monitoring systems. Nurses and allied health personnel will be at the forefront of brokered care.

This chapter has presented an overview of a proposed case management system for an inpatient perinatal unit. The linkages required for the integration of self-care, primary care, and brokered care with an episodic care model have been detailed. As with many dynamic systems, the connection of the teams providing care, and communication consisting of careful listening and client tailored response, are the keys to achieving a perinatal case management model that works. This chapter represents a theory of how case management could work in an inpatient perinatal unit. Translating this model into practice will no doubt reveal many opportunities for modification and improvement.

## References

Dickason, E. J., Schult, M. O., and Silverman, B. L. (1990). *Maternal-infant nursing care.* (pp. 133-134). St. Louis: The C. V. Mosby Company.

O'Toole, A. W., and Welt, S. R. (Eds.). (1989). *Interpersonal theory in nursing practice.* Selected works of Hildegard E. Peplau. (pp. 270-296). New York: Springer Publishing Company.

Phillips, C. R. (1987). *Family-centered maternity/newborn care* (2nd ed.). (pp. 131-145). St. Louis: The C. V. Mosby Company.

Redman, B. K. (1984). The Process of Patient Education (5th ed.). St.Louis: The C.V. Mosby Company.

# 16

# Clinical Nurse Specialists as Case Managers

Sophia Chu Rodgers, RN, MSN

*Ms. Rodgers describes the clinical nurse specialist and case manager role as complementary. In this orthopedic practice, the patient is brought through ambulatory care to episodic care and back under the watchful eye of the case manager. The reader will appreciate how Ms. Rodgers's six roles are integrated in the "day-in-the-life" section toward the end of the chapter.*—R.S.H.

The American Nurses' Association (ANA) (1988) describes case management as "the assistance of clients in optimizing self care capability, promoting efficient use of resources, and stimulating the creation of new services." Further, ANA explains, the goals of case management are to provide quality of care along a continuum, to decrease fragmentation, to enhance patients' quality of life, and to contain costs.

Desimone (1988) defines case management as a "systematic approach identifying high-risk/high-cost patients; assessing opportunities to coordinate care; assessing and choosing treatment options; developing treatment plans to improve quality and efficacy; controlling costs; and managing a patient's total care to ensure optimal outcome."

Merrill (1985) claims that case management is often misused. It is neither preadmission screening nor utilization review. Case management is the organization and sequence of resources and services to serve a client's health care problem.

Henderson and Collard (1988) distinguish between two types of case management: medical case management and general case management. They believe medical case management focuses on the severely ill or injured who require intensive care, whereas general case management approximates second surgical opinions or utilization review. Similarly, Kerr and Birk (1988) describe case management in terms of cost containment versus client-centered care. "Cost con-

I wish to thank Keith Eckrich for his contribution to this chapter.

tainment" has little patient contact while "client-centered" case management involves direct, often hands-on, contact.

# Case Management Approaches

The approaches to case management differ depending on a health care institution's philosophy. Within episodic care, one approach uses primary caregivers as case managers, the other nonprimary caregivers. The first approach originated at New England Medical Center; the case manager is the primary nurse with expanded responsibilities for managed care. Besides providing direct hands-on care, the case manager also coordinates the total plan of care throughout the episode of illness (Salmond, 1990). Such nurses are in a collaborative practice with physicians and other health care team members. There is a sharing of plans, decision making, problem solving, goal setting, and teamwork (Weinstein, 1991).

The advantages of using this approach include empowering the bedside nurse with authority, control, and creative expression. The nurse's role is expanded to include financial decisions, allocation of resources, teaching, and patient advocacy. The patient benefits from this approach by being able to identify with the primary nurse; this allows him/her to acquire a sense of security that an advocate (the case manager) follows through the entire episode of illness even after discharge (Weinstein, 1991).

This approach, however, has its disadvantages. More time is required to specially train each primary nurse. Also, since case managers follow the patient regardless of the unit, the nurses need cross-training, which can be costly and time consuming. Additionally, expanded responsibilities can overwhelm the direct care nurse (Weinstein, 1991). Another disadvantage may be the educational preparation. Depending on the institution, a nurse can be an associate, baccalaureate, or master's-prepared. One study, funded by the W. K. Kellogg Foundation and sponsored by the Midwest Alliance in Nursing, revealed that baccalaureate-prepared nurses expressed frustration and an inability to case-manage effectively. Several reasons were cited: having to perform case management duties as well as direct patient care; the nurse's lack of confidence in his/her ability to collaborate and delegate; the feeling among some nurses that they were ill-prepared by their curricula to effect change at the systems level (Cronin and Maklebust, 1989). If the baccalaureate nurses felt this way, the same feelings may be true for associate nurses.

The second approach to case management provides the case manager with a case load. A case load ranges from 20 to 50 patients. In this approach, the case manager does not provide direct hands-on care. Instead, he/she collaborates with the bedside nurse, physician, and multidisciplinary team and is responsible for the daily planning, coordinating, and monitoring of care. The most common type of nurse used for this approach is a clinical nurse specialist (Salmond, 1990).

One advantage of this second form of case management is its ability to adapt to any type of nursing model. This is because the primary caregiver's role is not directly affected. Whether the nursing model is primary, total, or modular, this approach adapts very well. Less frustration burdens the case manager due to his/her not having to provide direct care. This allows him/her more time to concentrate on system problems. Patients benefit from this approach because two nurses work together as a team (Weinstein, 1991).

One of the drawbacks of this approach is that it could require additional staff (Cronin and Maklebust, 1989). To avoid this, though, several roles can be incorporated into that of the case manager. Case management at Lovelace Medical Center, Albuquerque, New Mexico, is an example. When the orthopedic nurse case manager position was first instituted, the position incorporated a half-time discharge planner position. Later, the case manager also assumed the role of part-time patient educator. Another pitfall with this approach may be the possibility that the case manager may interfere with the relationship between the primary caregiver and the patient. This could happen if the case manager is not sensitive to this issue. This can be avoided, however, if the case manager and bedside nurse can clearly delineate each other's responsibilities (Weinstein, 1991).

# Financial Impact of Case Management

The literature provides much information on case management's impact on reducing length of stay (LOS) and cost. At Harper Hospital, Detroit, the overall average LOS in 1987 was 10.9 days. After the 1988 implementation of case management, the LOS dropped to 10.2 days and by the end of 1989 it dropped to 9.7 days, resulting in a savings of $3,300,000 for the hospital over the two-year period (Deleon, Kuntzman, Lescamela, Schreiber, and Tessier, 1990).

Tulsa's Hillcrest Medical Center implemented a similar case management system in 1988. Eighty-four of the 190 cases of DRG (diagnosis related group) 106 (coronary bypass graft with catheterization) were case-managed. Compared to noncase-managed clients, $960,000 in billed charges and 430 patient days were eliminated.

At Tucson's Carondelet St. Mary's Hospital and Health Center, a comparison study was done for case-managed and noncase-managed total hip replacement patients. Case-managed patients had an average LOS of 8.1 days in comparison to an average LOS of 10.2 for the noncase-managed patients (Etheridge and Lamb, 1989).

Logan (Utah) Regional Hospital, a 150-bed acute-care community hospital, reported a 40% reduction in the difference between cost incurred by the patient and costs reimbursed by the prevailing payment systems on ten targeted DRGs. The administration utilized the bedside nurse as case manager as part of the answer to cost containment (Bair, Griswold, and Head, 1989).

# Models of Case Management

Some examples of structuring and organizing the models of case management are:

1. **Episodic Care Model**—As the name implies, this model falls within the acute care settings. Two components, managed care and case management, comprise this model. In an article written for *Definition*, a publication from the Center for Case Management, Inc., Zander (1990) differentiates between managed care and case management. She describes managed care as "a cyclical process organized by all related departments, managed every shift by the nursing staff." Moreover, Zander considers six elements of managed care:

   - Critical paths, or CareMaps, which are collaborative guidelines with time and sequence interventions for a particular DRG

- Shift reports utilizing critical paths as tools to give shift report
- Documentation of variance analyses which are any deviations that may occur from the critical paths
- Case consultation
- Health care team meetings
- Quality assurance

As for case management, Zander believes that this process further potentiates the effect of managed care. It allows nurses to manage patients within a specific DRG through an entire episode of illness (Zander, 1990). Case-managed patients are considered high risk and labor intensive. In all models case management attempts to coordinate parts of the health care system to form a continuum. Both components—case management and managed care—are essential (Zander, 1990). All patients should have managed care but only specific patients should be case-managed. Those would include patients who are considered high risk and labor intensive.

2. **Brokered Care Case Management**—Case managers within this model usually have minimal patient contact. Some may function as gatekeepers for the employer. These case managers may approve or broker health care services. Examples include approval for purchase or rental of durable medical equipment, second surgical opinion, diagnostic tests, or placements to extended care facilities. Other examples of case management within this model include utilization review and preadmission screening.
3. **Community-Based Case Management**—Within this model, the nurses manage the patient's care along a continuum, whether in the hospital or out in the community. As needed, the nurse case manager may provide hands-on care as well as function as a patient advocate and service broker. Moreover, the community-based case management model takes nursing beyond the hospital and allows for early assessment of potential complications and debilitation that may be associated with early discharge (Rogers, Riordan, and Swindle, 1991). Two such models are Carondelet St. Mary's in Tucson, and St. Joseph Medical Center, Wichita.

# Clinical Nurse Specialists as Case Managers

Clinical nurse specialists (CNS) are an ideal choice as case managers. Their master's level nursing preparation allows them to further expand on the concept of case management by applying one's expertise to stimulate thinking, improve the clinical and financial outcomes of the health care system, and quality of care. Furthermore, such preparation influences the future of health care through political involvement (Ralph, 1990).

Walthall (1990) describes four important components of the CNS as case manager. These roles include practitioner, consultant, educator, and researcher. As a practitioner, the case manager has a patient load for which he/she is directly responsible and accountable. Because of the advanced practice, assessing needs, implementing interventions, and evaluations are easier. The master's prepared nurse also serves as a consultant and role model for the clinical nurses. Additionally, the case manager in the CNS role continues to act as traditional educator. Research is another component of the case manager's job, and having a master's degree augments this role.

Maklebust, Corey, Viecelli, and Krzeminski (1990) state that master's prepared nurses are ideally suited to meet the economic and clinical demands of patient care in today's resource-driven environment because of their educational level. Most staff nurses have found it stimulating to share ideas with a master's prepared nurse.

In an article entitled, "The Clinical Nurse Specialist and PPS Reimbursement," Conway-Svec (1991) explains that developing comprehensive discharge planning programs and assuming responsibility for implementation are natural roles for the CNS. As more patients are discharged into the home care setting, the CNS is the ideal person to coordinate these services. Furthermore, because of his/her educational background, a CNS is expected to incorporate cost containment and time efficiency into nursing systems.

Though the role of the CNS functioning as case manager may vary, some functions are similar. These include meeting desired clinical outcomes, promoting collaborative practice, resource and human allocations needed for care, early discharge planning and detection of discharge barriers, and evaluation for cost-effective care per DRG (Cronin and Maklebust, 1989).

# Profile of a CNS Case Manager

"When you've seen one case manager, you've seen one case manager." No two case managers function identically. The case manager's roles and functions need to fit the organization, target population, and nature of the practice. My position as a case manager at Lovelace Medical Center was conceived to decrease LOS and cost and to increase patient satisfaction. The orthopedic service was chosen not because it had problems; on the contrary, it was a well-organized department in which to start.

Lovelace has 240 beds; owns its Health Maintenance Organization (HMO), which has a membership of around 138,000 members; has a high occupancy rate; and is regarded as a health care leader in the Southwest. The orthopedic department has nine physicians. Full inpatient and outpatient orthopedic services are available. Some of the most common inpatient DRGs include total hip replacements, partial hip replacements, open reduction internal fixation of fractures, total knee replacements, and laminectomy/fusion.

My six roles are clinical nurse specialist, coordinator, educator, resource person, advocate, and researcher.

As a *CNS*, I do not provide direct patient care in the traditional sense. Instead, I incorporate into my role the clinical expertise that I have acquired over the years. This means utilizing my comprehensive assessment skills, being a member of the code team, and performing advanced technical procedures such as suture removal, placement of braces, and placement of long-arm catheters. A strong clinical background allows the case manager to function also in the roles of an educator and resource person and provides credibility with the health care team. It also affords the case manager an opportunity to identify clinical issues/problems in the patient care setting and improve the clinical and financial outcomes of patient care.

As a clinician, upon a patient's admission I perform a thorough comprehensive assessment that includes the following:

1. **Physical**
2. **Psychosocial**
3. **Environmental**

a. **Social Support**
b. **Housing**
c. **Community Resources**

4. **Economic (Financial)**
5. **Functional Abilities**

With the data I develop a plan of care in collaboration with the health care team members.

As *coordinator* I work with all the members of the health care team to make sure multidisciplinary dialogue continues on a daily basis. Imagine the health care system as a spoked wheel. The nurse case manager is the hub of the wheel and all the health care team members are at the ends of the spokes. The nurse case manager (NCM) coordinates the team by taking pertinent information from one team member and channeling it to other appropriate team members. This assures timely care as the patient moves toward the established goals and outcomes.

As *resource person* I am available to answer concerns the patient and family may have while in the hospital and after discharge. For example, patients after discharge often call me to ask if something is normal, e.g., swollen knee after total knee replacement. I ask him/her a list of questions and if the knee is swollen because the patient has been up all day, I reassure him/her the swelling is normal. However, if the symptoms do not sound normal, I call the physician to consult with him/her. Patients and family feel comfortable calling me because they know me and I am accessible. If I cannot answer a question, I direct them to the right individuals or call the individuals for them. After 18 months as a NCM, I have logged over 600 phone calls.

I am also a resource for the health care team. The team consults with me because I know the orthopedic patients well through daily follow-up. Often the health care team consults with me regarding the patient's progress. This is especially true for a nurse caring for the patient for the first time, a consulting physician from another service, or an on-call orthopedist.

The role of *advocate* comes easily because rapport and trust are developed early in my relationship with the patient and his/her family. An advocate ensures that the patient's hospitalization proceeds smoothly and in a timely fashion. The patient's confidence and trust in the advocate stimulates timely problem solving.

I function as an advocate for my institution as well, through follow-up phone calls and visits with patients after discharge.

My role of *educator* expedites my providing patient and family with essential information, thus allowing them to make informed decisions. I have developed a preoperative orientation program (POP), to which patients are invited when they come in for history and physical two weeks prior to surgery. The one-hour orientation is individualized and includes showing and explaining various postoperative equipment, e.g., thigh-high sequential stockings, patient-controlled analgesia infuser, Stryker drains, incentive spirometer, etc.; discussion of daily routines, administrative policies, e.g., checkout time, visiting hours, etc.; and how to operate the room equipment. Patients who have had preoperative teaching report a decrease in anxiety. Moreover, nurses comment that such patients are more cooperative with their postoperative regimen.

In addition to the preoperative orientation, I have also developed a postoperative/home teaching program for joint replacement and back fusion patients. This teaching begins from preoperative for those who attend the POP or from day one for those who do not attend. For the first two or three postoperative days, I explain to the patient and his family the do's, dont's, and precautions associated with his/her surgical procedures. To assess comprehension, by day three to four I ask the patient and family to repeat the information back. On about the fifth day I show a video to teach joint replacement patients how to manage after discharge. After the video I give the patient an illustrated booklet that includes precautions, do's and dont's, how to manage activities of daily living, proper use of crutch or walker, examples of assistive devices, when to resume sexual activity and driving, when to call the physician, exercises, and how to prepare the home safely.

Besides being a patient educator, I also function as a staff educator. This includes providing numerous in-service programs to the nurses, nursing students, and the community.

The *researcher* role is a vital one for the case manager. Since the objectives of the case management system are to positively influence clinical and financial outcomes, studies must be done to measure this. Additionally, research findings must be shared through presentation and publication. Furthermore, as a researcher, the case manager must keep up with current research literature in order to improve patient care.

In addition to the above roles, as an orthopedic NCM, I also have four primary functions. They include: 1) promote appropriate and efficient use of resources; 2) coordinate services to decrease fragmentation of care; 3) provide quality of care along a continuum; and 4) empower patients.

Promoting appropriate and efficient use of resources is a very important function a case manager can achieve. When I first started as a case manager I noticed that many of our elderly orthopedic patients who required continued rehabilitation were transferred postoperatively to rehabilitation hospitals rather than to skilled nursing facilities (SNFs). After visiting both types of facilities, I found that patients received about three hours (1.5 hours in the morning and 1.5 hours in the afternoon) of physical therapy at the rehabilitation hospitals as compared to about 45 to 60 minutes at the SNFs. Because the average age of these patients was 75 years and up, most of them did not have the endurance to tolerate the amount of therapy provided at the rehabilitation hospitals. Besides the endurance factor, the difference in cost between the two is striking. The rehabilitation hospital room costs $600 to $1,000 per day as compared to $150 for SNF rooms. Rehabilitation hospitals are extremely valuable if patients are able to tolerate the therapy. However, if they cannot and are transferred there, then a valuable resource is misused.

Another way a nurse case manager can promote appropriate and efficient use of resources is through research and development of special projects. Being a clinical nurse specialist and having a master's degree in nursing have been an asset. It has provided the education and experience to allow me to set up research projects and special programs. One such project is the development of the long-arm catheter or peripherally inserted catheter program. I developed the procedure and protocol and co-developed the certification program to teach registered nurses how to insert and maintain these catheters. These catheters are inserted whenever patients have no peripheral venous access or may require long-term home intravenous therapy. Long-arm catheters are much more cost effective to insert than the central catheters and the risks are less. The purpose of promoting appropriate and efficient use of resources is to decrease cost.

The second function of an orthopedic nurse case manager is to coordinate services to decrease fragmentation of care. On a daily basis as a case manager, I am responsible for coordinating the multidisciplinary team to ascertain that patients are receiving the necessary care and moving toward the established and expected outcomes. When this is done efficiently, treatments and services are provided in a timely manner so the patient can be discharged early or on time and thus decrease cost and length of stay.

The third function of a nurse case manager is to provide quality of care along a continuum. Zander (1991) describes case management as going beyond the traditional geographic boundaries of the hospital and performing a linking pin function, thereby creating units without walls. For example, if an orthopedic patient is admitted to the intensive care unit, this is where the nurse case manager should initiate the assessment and develop rapport with the patient and significant other. As the patient's condition progresses and he or she is transferred to the orthopedic unit, the nurse case manager will follow the patient there. Necessary information learned about that patient can be shared and collaboratively made into a plan of care, and continuity of care can be provided. After discharge, follow-up is made by the nurse case manager, either in person or by phone, thereby completing the continuum of care. The purposes of this function are to facilitate continuity of care, promote better quality, decrease LOS, decrease cost, and increase patient satisfaction.

The fourth function of nurse case manager is to empower patients. This is perhaps the greatest contribution case managers can offer. Empowerment can be achieved by obtaining and offering information to patients and being an advocate for them so they can make informed decisions (Mullahy, 1990). An example of this may be discussion of discharge options. If an assessment is made that an elderly patient lives alone and cannot adequately care for self, then providing information regarding extended care facilities may be helpful. If the patient has family members, they should be encouraged to be involved in the decision making. A list of extended care facilities can be given to the patient and family and the decision regarding where the patient may go can be made by them. Another way to empower patients is through education,i.e., preoperative orientation and postoperative education. With appropriate and adequate information, patients can make informed decisions regarding their care. Moreover, education can also help a patient and family feel ready for discharge. Empowerment is an important function. It can increase patient satisfaction and quality of care.

When the functions and roles of the case manager are organized, a conceptual model can be illustrated as shown in Figure 1. This is the Lovelace Nurse Case Management Model.

*Preoperative orientation*—The nurse case manager provides preoperative orientation to the orthopedic patient prior to surgery. Optimally, this decreases anxiety and assists the patient in making informed postoperative decisions.

*Coordinate care through episode of illness*—The NCM assures multidisciplinary dialogue and coordination among the health care team members to ensure appropriate and timely care. The nurse case manager also functions as a practitioner, educator, resource person, researcher, and an advocate.

*Follow-up after discharge*—The nurse case manager calls the patient 24 to 48 hours after discharge for the major DRGs to see how the patient is managing and to answer questions. Patients discharged to an extended care facility are visited within seven days. Follow-up after discharge completes the continuity of care cycle and allows for assessment of any potential patient problems.

For this conceptual model, these three components are added together to potentially decrease LOS and cost and increase patient satisfaction. At Lovelace Medical Center, LOS and cost were measured in a study. The results demonstrated a decrease in LOS for partial hip replacements and open reduction internal fixation (ORIF) for hip fractures of case-managed as compared to noncase-managed patients. The findings showed that case-managed partial hip replacement patients stayed an average of 2 days less than those who were not case-managed and case-managed ORIF patients stayed an average of 3.6 days less than noncase-managed patients. Cost is another variable studied. Cost-to-charge ratios were used in this study for a true cost estimate. Cost for case-managed ORIF patients were decreased by $885.53 per patient; for case- managed partial hip replacement patients, an average cost savings of $489.81 was demonstrated. Patient satisfaction will be studied at a later time.

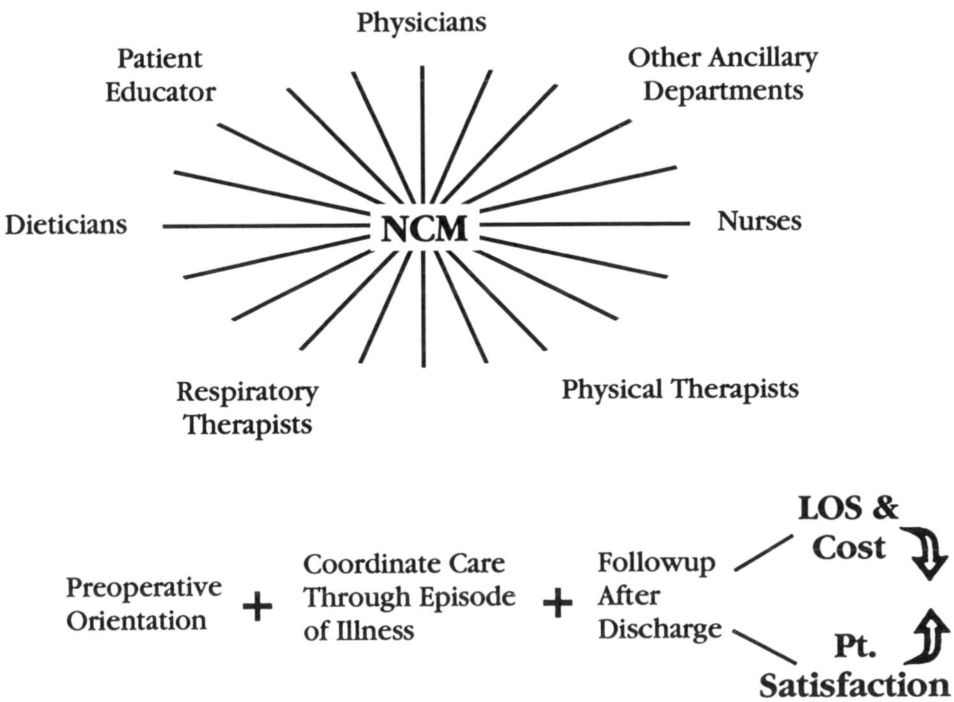


**Figure 1.** *Conceptual Model for Nurse Case Manager*

## An Orthopedic Nurse Case Manager's Day

*0700*: I check my appointment calendar. Scheduled at 1000 is a preoperative orientation with Mary Garcia, 76, scheduled for a total hip replacement next week. At 1300 is the weekly continuity of care meeting and at 1530 I am to conduct an in-service session for the nurses on the Senior Behavioral Service unit.

Upon arriving on the postoperative orthopedic unit, Joan, the day nurse, informs me that Mrs. Robinson had two bloody stools during the night. Mrs. Robinson is an 83-year-old patient who fractured her hip four days ago. She underwent a partial hip replacement. Besides her fractured hip, Mrs. Robinson has dementia, hypertension, esophageal stricture, and urinary incontinence. She lives alone in an apartment and has no family. I find out from the night nurse that the bloody stool was bright red, 30 cc for the first one and 50 cc for the second. The internal medicine physician on call was notified and a hemoglobin and hematocrit were ordered. The results were 10.5 and 32.4, which were slightly elevated from yesterday. I assess the patient. The abdomen, soft with active bowel sounds and no tenderness, appears unchanged from yesterday. Assessment of the rectal area indicates no hemorrhoids. When patient was asked if she had ever had rectal bleeding before, she said no. (Because of patient's dementia, the truth of this is difficult to assess). Her chart reveals a history of esophageal stricture but no mention of previous rectal bleeding. Since the patient has no further bleeding and appears stable, I wait until her physicians make rounds.

I check with the night charge nurse for new orthopedic admissions during the night. Georgia Simms, with a right fractured hip, was admitted to room 328. I review her chart for history. Mrs. Simms is a 78-year-old widow living alone. Approximately at 1000 yesterday, after her bath, she fell getting out of the bath tub. She lay on the bathroom floor for two hours until found by her daughter, who brings her daily lunch. An ambulance brought her to the emergency room, and a right femoral neck hip fracture was diagnosed. At approximately 1700 Mrs. Simms underwent a right hemiarthroplasty with the placement of a Biomore prosthesis. In addition to the hip fracture, she has a history of hypertension and hypothyroidism. Previous surgical history included an appendectomy over 50 years ago and a hysterectomy 23 years ago. She lost her husband one year ago due to cancer, and has in town one married daughter, her only child. Other history and physical assessments are unremarkable.

I receive brief reports from the night nurses regarding the other orthopedic patients. Nothing is remarkable except Mr. Jones, in room 320, complaining of nausea all night. He had a total knee replacement yesterday. Also, Mrs. Simms, the new patient, is very confused.

After receiving reports I assess Mrs. Simms. A woman sits at her bedside. Mrs. Simms speaks incoherently. She is restrained with a body vest. I introduce myself. The visitor is the patient's daughter, Virginia. She stayed all night because her mother became agitated and confused, which was worrisome to her. I perform a physical assessment on Mrs. Simms and then speak with Virginia over coffee in the break room. Virginia states that her mother had a zest for life and mentally she was always very alert until about one year ago. When her husband died, she became withdrawn, forgetful, and depressed. I ask if her mother had ever been evaluated psychologically since the death of her husband, and Virginia replies no. She kept hoping that her mother "would snap out of it." Virginia reports that her mother functioned fairly independently. She walked well but rarely went out. Her appetite was very poor and she seldom cooked for herself. Virginia brings her lunch and dinner daily. I ask Virginia if she has given thought about what to do with her mother after discharge; she tearfully replies no. She states that her husband was recently laid off from his job and to make ends meet, she has gone back to her teaching position at the elementary school. She cannot quit her job to care for her mother and she has not acquired enough leave time. She doesn't know what to do. I review the discharge options with her. I explain it is not safe to send Mrs. Simms home alone after the hospital. I ask if Virginia's husband can help. She replies no, because he goes out for job interviews and does odd jobs. I explore other alternatives with her. Since her mother was walking well before, it is expected that she will walk again after discharge. Physical therapy is appropriate. If her mother qualifies and Medicare approves, a short rehabilitative stay at a skilled nursing facility should be considered. Once she is physically stronger, then she perhaps can be discharged to her home. Virginia likes that option. I explore another alternative with her. Because of her mother's change in behavior in the last year since the death of her husband, it may be appropriate to have her evaluated and admitted to the Senior Behavioral Unit for a short time. This would also allow her to continue with physical therapy in addition to receiving some counseling. Virginia thinks this is a wonderful idea. I ask her to consider the options, visit the facilities, and give me an answer in a couple of days. Virginia voices relief that there are other discharge options to consider and thanks me for giving her peace of mind.

*0900*: The orthopedic physicians make their rounds. I find Mrs. Robinson's orthopedic physician, Dr. Thomas, and her internist, Dr. Lyons, in her room. They are conferring about Mrs. Robinson's rectal bleeding. Dr. Lyons, who knows the patient well, states that the patient has diverticulitis and this has happened before. Another hemoglobin and hematocrit will be done.

Dr. Thomas then sees Mr. Jones. I inform Dr. Thomas of the patient's nausea. I question if the morphine in the patient-controlled analgesia (PCA) is the cause. Dr. Thomas discontinues the PCA.

Dr. Boswick, Mrs. Simms' orthopedist, assesses the patient. I confer with the doctor about having the patient evaluated by Senior Behavioral. The physician concurs and writes the order.

*0945*: I check the laboratory values on the computer for those physicians who have not made rounds. Mrs. Quintana, a first-day postoperative total hip replacement, has a hemoglobin of 8.2 and hematocrit of 24.8. I assess her. Her heart rate and temperature are slightly elevated but blood pressure is stable. Patient informs me that she donated three units of autologous blood before surgery. Realizing that her physician, Dr. Mendelson, would normally order blood when the hematocrit is at this range but that he does not normally make rounds until lunch time, I call Dr. Mendelson to obtain an order for the blood transfusion. This ensures that Mrs. Quintana will receive her blood prior to her first physical therapy at 1400. I write the order, consult with the nurse, and the blood is hung within the hour.

*1000*: Mrs. Garcia, accompanied by her daughter, arrives for preoperative teaching. Mrs. Garcia has not been in a hospital since 15 years ago when she had a hysterectomy. She is fairly anxious about the total hip replacement. I begin the orientation by showing a video on what to expect after discharge after a total hip replacement. After the video, I ask for questions and feedback. I describe what to expect the day of surgery: admission to operating room, recovery room, and postoperative. I show them the equipment that Mrs. Garcia may have, e.g., thigh-high sequential stockings (actually placed them around her legs), wound drainage system, incentive spirometer (had her actually use it), PCA (had her push the button), Foley catheter, and IV, and explain the rationale for each. I assess the patient's comprehension of each piece of equipment. Daily routines are explained. The use of the room equipment is shown. A preoperative booklet detailing all that was discussed is given to the patient. As Mrs. Garcia and her daughter are leaving, I introduce her to some of the nurses on the unit. The entire orientation has lasted one hour. Both Mrs. Garcia and her daughter voice that it was very helpful and Mrs. Garcia states that she is less apprehensive about her surgery.

*1100*: I make rounds on several other patients. For a patient being discharged to a skilled nursing facility, I check the paperwork. A total hip replacement patient is ready for discharge and I review his understandings of hip precautions, the necessary equipment, and answer questions. For the patient who is fourth-day post-op after a total knee replacement, I show her and her husband the video on how to manage after discharge. I receive two calls from previous patients and schedule a preoperative orientation.

*1245*: After lunch I attend the Continuity of Care meeting scheduled weekly for unit charge nurses, discharge planners, social workers, dietitian, utilization review nurses, case managers, home health nurses, and speech and physical therapists. This provides a forum for presentation of high-risk and labor-intensive cases. We discuss the progress, outcomes, and plans for these patients as a multidisciplinary group.

After the meeting I make four follow-up phone calls to patients discharged 48 hours prior who are "high-risk" and "labor-intensive" cases. I query the patients regarding temperature, distance patient is ambulating, condition of wound, pain status, recall of precautions, and education. Information is recorded on a progress report with copies sent to Medical Records and the attending physician.

*1445*: I go to the Senior Behavioral Unit for the in-service program. I chance upon Rebecca, the psychiatric clinical nurse specialist, who evaluates patients for admission to the Senior Behavioral Unit. I consult with her regarding Mrs. Simms. Rebecca states that she will assess the patient in the morning.

The topic of the in-service session is hip precautions. Recently, several patients after total or partial hip replacements were sent to the unit. The nurses and technicians had requested an in-service program on patient management.

*1600*: I return to the orthopedic unit. I review the day's surgical schedule and write down the names of the postops. There were two laminectomy fusions, one total hip replacement, and one total knee replacement. I will assess them in the morning.

*1700*: I gather my paperwork and equipment and lock the office.

* * *

Health care cost has skyrocketed in the past 25 years from 6% to 12% of the country's gross domestic product, with another 5% increase projected during the 1990s. In order for health care institutions to remain financially solvent, creative and innovative approaches to cost containment must be developed. Case management is one viable approach.

Nurse case managers can be nurses with various levels of preparation. However, nurses who are master's prepared and clinical nurse specialists are ideal choices. Because of their educational preparation, they are better prepared to function in the roles of practitioner, educator, researcher, coordinator, advocate, and resource person. Additionally, they are often better prepared to deal with systems problems, collaboration, and delegation.

Having clinical nurse specialists as case managers creates an opportunity for nurses to perform in an advanced practice role. This is the reason why nursing case management is an exciting and challenging concept not only for cost containment but also for the nursing profession.

## References


American Nurses' Association. (1988). *Nursing case management.* Kansas City, MO: Author.

Applebaum, R. & Austin, C. (1990). *Long term care case management.* New York: Springer Publishing Company.

Bair, N.L., Griswold, J.T., & Head, J.L. (1989). Clinical RN involvement in bedside-centered case management. *Nursing Economics*, 7(3), 150-154.

Conway-Svec, C. (1991). The clinical nurse specialist and PPS reimbursement. *Nursing Management, 22*(5), 90.

Cronin, C.J. & Maklebust, J. (1989). Case-managed care: Capitalizing on the CNS. *Nursing Management, 20*(3), 38-47.

Deleon, E., Kuntzman, M., Lescamela, P., Schreiber, J., & Tessier, A. (1990). Case management in action. *Michigan Nurse, 63*(5), 17.

Desimone, B. (1988). The case for case management. *Continuing Care*, 17(7), 22-23.

Etheridge, P. & Lamb, G. (1989). Professional nursing case management improves quality, access, and costs. *Nursing Management, 20*(3), 30-35.

Guiliano, K.K. & Poirier, C.E. (1991). Nursing case management: Critical pathways to desirable outcomes. *Nursing Management, 22*(3), 52-55.

Henderson, M.G. & Collard, A. (1988). Measuring quality in medical case management programs. *QRB*, 33-39.

Kerr, M.H. & Birk, J.M. (1988). A client-centered case management model. *QRB*, 279-283.

Maklebust, J., Corey, R., Viecelli, R., & Krzeminski, D. (1990). Results of collaboration between case managers and staff nurses. *Michigan Nurse, 63*(5), 11.

Merrill, J.C. (1985). Defining case management. *Business and Health, 2*(8), 5-9.

Mullahy, C.M. (1990). Empowering the case manager. *Continuing Care*, 16-30.

Ralph, S.R. (1990). (Editorial). *Michigan Nurse*, 63(5), 3.

Rogers, M., Swindle, D., & Riordan, J. (1991). Community-based nursing case management pays off. *Nursing Management, 22*(3), 30-34.

Salmond, S. (1990). In-hospital case management: Responses to common questions and concerns. *Orthopaedic Nursing, 9*(1), 38-40.

Walthall, S. (1990). An enhancement of the role of clinical nurse specialist. *Michigan Nurse, 63*(5), 6,8.

Weinstein, R. (1991). Hospital case management: The path to empowering nurses. *Journal of Pediatric Nursing, 17*(3), 289-293.

Zander, K. (1990). Differentiating managed care and case management. *Definition, 5*(2), 1.

Zander, K. (1991). Case management in acute care: Making the connections. *TCM, 2*(1), 39-45.

# V

# BROKERED CARE CASE MANAGEMENT

# 17

# The Evolution Of Case Management to *Care* Management

Kathleen C. Milne, RN, BSN

*We are familiar with the assignments of worker's compensation and insurance company case managers who are employed by large corporations. These case managers typically handle large case loads and are rewarded for the savings they bring to the organization. But another trend in brokered care case management is emerging. Private organizations, sometimes consisting of just one principal (usually a nurse), that are designed to serve those in need of coordination of health care services, are springing up all over the country. This chapter focuses on one such organization that has grown to become a well-established source of brokered care.*—R.S.H.

There is significant debate about whether or not a need exists for private freestanding case management services. After all, managed care has been around since 1964 and is just now in vogue. Further, since passage of the Older Americans Act, Area Agencies on Aging exist in most every community to provide assistance to seniors. Finally, a wide variety of organizations address a range of health-related missions and goals. Why, then, would private individuals, attorneys, insurance companies, self-insured businesses, conservators, guardians, and trust departments pay for management of services that are supposedly already managed?

This chapter will address the question of why such services are needed by discussing some of the factors that have given rise to case management services and by describing in some detail an example of the brokered case management business with which I am affiliated. My preference is to describe the services in question as *care* management rather than *case* management. Use of the term *care management* portrays 1) more of a customer- or client-oriented focus, 2) a compassionate approach to problem-solving, and 3) a comprehensive view of the issues that need to be addressed. *Case Management* is broadly used, but it more typically represents a set of interventions focused on a specific issue or problem. Further, *case management* connotes that the client is managed rather than the services. Care management involves the client, emphasizes self-care, and is holistic in nature. This approach will be discussed more fully through a case study of the company mentioned above.

# Why Private Care Management Services?

Health care has become big business, accounting for over 12% of the country's GDP. Understanding the health care delivery system, keeping current with new resources and services, negotiating benefits, and evaluating care options is difficult and challenging even for those employed in the health care industry. It can be a nightmare for others. For families and individuals trying to "manage health care," the experience frequently is coupled with stress, guilt, or a sense of not having control. Finding one's way through the maze can be inefficient, time-consuming, costly, and even dangerous to one's health.

Brokered care management services have proliferated during the past decade as a response to the complexity of the health care system. For families, case management assures objective information from which to make decisions, a care plan with options and recommendations to help guide them, and a neutral party to help with the process and with the sometimes challenging dynamics. The services also assure families that prepaid health care benefits are used where possible, thus minimizing out-of-pocket expenditures. Two trends influence the need for care management services: 1) demographic trends and 2) health care system trends.

## Demographic Trends

The ratio of middle-aged adult children to elderly parents is changing rapidly. In 1970 there were 19 adult children for every nine seniors, but by 1990 there were 17 adult children for every 18 seniors (Kutza, 1991). This trend parallels the changing ratio of individuals in the work force that economically balance non-employed seniors. In 1900 there were 100 workers to seven seniors; by 1990 the ratio had increased to 100 workers per 20 seniors (U.S. Senate Special Committee on Aging, 1991). Attending such shifts is increasing stress experienced by adult children who are attempting to balance working, raising a family and, often, acting as caregiver to their aging parents. These trends also contribute to the current shortage of caregivers. Many more women are entering the work force, changing the dynamics of caregiving and managing "health care" needs. It has been reported that up to 42% of full-time employees have some degree of caregiving responsibility for an aging relative (AARP, Oct. 1988). Further, 38% of employees miss days or come to work late because of caregiving responsibilities (AARP, Oct. 1988). The population is living longer and the "boomer" generation will begin to have a significant impact on long-term care needs in 18 to 20 years.

## Health Care System Trends

Along with these demographic trends, changes are occurring in health care. Over 85% of seniors have at least one chronic disease, yet our current health care system almost exclusively emphasizes acute care (Kutza, 1991). There exists a growing need to provide services aimed at chronic diseases and self-care. This includes a need to research more of the chronic diseases that have a severe impact on quality of life and the cost of long-term care (Cassel, 1991).

Meanwhile, although many metropolitan areas have a surplus of physicians, the surplus is typically among specialty practitioners. There is no surplus of primary care physicians, and many rural areas have significant health care provider shortages. Aging in place of seniors—when individuals remain in their own home or other supported living environment through the continuum of the aging process—is occurring universally, particularly in rural areas. Clearly, there is an imbalance in the distribution of providers throughout the health care delivery systems.

Out-of-pocket health care costs for the elderly average between $1,200 and $1,500 per year. Health care is the one service the elderly spend more on in actual dollars and as a percent of total expenditures than nonelderly (U.S. Senate Special Committee on Aging, 1991). The cost of long-term care is frequently not covered by insurance or Medicare, thus out-of-pocket costs are greatly increased if such care is needed.

Another health care system change influencing the complexity for seniors is the shift toward managed care systems. It is projected that by 1996, 90% of U.S. businesses will have managed care as part of their benefit package carrying over into retirement (Frieden, 1991). Medicare saves money when managed care is used (Kahn, 1992).

In summary, changes are occurring that increase the percentage of the population in need of health services, the cost of health services, and complexity of the health care system. All of these changes increase the need for care management services.

# Profile of a Private Care Management Enterprise

The remaining portion of this chapter examines the development and array of services provided by one brokered care management business. Although the company is unique and may not represent the norm, its development and the services it provides may offer insights about the field in general. Resource Connectors, Ltd. (RCL), is located in Portland, Oregon, and most of its services are provided in the metropolitan Portland area. However, its service area extends throughout Oregon and Washington. The business was begun in January 1985 with an initial purpose of providing care management services to the trust department of a local bank. A range of personal care services were available and constituted a "social nonmedical" approach to addressing problems. A partnership was formed in the second quarter of operation between the social worker/founder and the current owner, who is a nurse. Service horizons for the company were broadened to include acute care settings and community health settings, including public health, primary care, and managed care.

During its first year of operation, the company evolved to a balanced "care management" model. Although the partnership was dissolved in 1988, the company has continued to grow and evolve, employing highly trained professionals and serving a wide variety of customers. Care management, consultation, and training form the foundation of the company's practice. Key elements include a strong nursing base with a holistic view of issues; support for a strong community network of providers and services; use of a win-win approach to problem solving; and application of self-care, preventive, and proactive interventions.

## Vision

It has been said that once a vision is achieved, the dream begins to die. Care management is an emerging field rich with unmet need and opportunity. It is vital that businesses continually examine and refine their purpose, methods, and services. In this model, management and staff of RCL have articulated a vision that includes the need to:

- Provide linkages in the health care community where there are identified gaps in service
- Develop additional tools and skills in addressing challenging client behaviors and issues
- Participate in needed research and refinement in the evolution of care management services
- Define the role of nursing (and the necessary training) in this field
- Incorporate other disciplines
- Collaborate with other health care entities in addressing long-term care needs, challenges, and possible new models of care

An exciting aspect of being a private care management business is the ability and freedom to conceptualize, develop, implement, and evaluate these expanded services or adaptations of old services in new or changed environments. Partnerships with other private and public entities are part of the future.

## Business Values and Philosophy

Key business values of the company being examined include:

- Belief in an individual's right to make health care decisions
- Belief in win-win outcomes wherever possible
- Belief in excellence, creativity, and simplicity
- Belief that nursing and care management should have an expanded role in achieving desired health outcomes, controlling costs, and managing long-term health care needs.

Because of these values, the company stresses the empowerment of clients and their options, promotion of their independence, and prevention of premature disability. Work is done with individuals and their families and with others in a win-win decision-making environment; bridges are not burned.

The philosophy of the company is to assist individuals and families in achieving their desired and/or highest attainable level of health and personal independence through the provision of effective care management and consultation services. Assessment, planning, client education, advocacy, prevention, monitoring, and evaluation are key components of the services. In addition to health care management, linkages are provided to legal and financial services related to health care and planning. Services are highly individualized, customer-centered and cost-effective wherever possible. The goals of RCL are:

- To provide a work setting that promotes excellence by enhancing the knowledge, skills, and job satisfaction of staff
- To provide customers with a comprehensive range of care management services that set the community standard and are proactive, preventive, and personalized

- To contribute to community efforts toward improving the availability, accessibility, and quality of health and social services
- To provide strong economic viability
- To provide care management services, within economic constraints, to individuals who are in need but are unable to pay for the full cost of services

## Primary Characteristics

The "model" used by the company is a bit like a chameleon. When described, it appears similar to other models of care management (self-care, primary care, episodic care, brokered care, or long-term care case management). Other care management organizations typically specialize and/or place limits on the range of conditions addressed. Parameters may be set on the presenting condition (e.g., catastrophic injury, AIDS, etc.) severity, client age, or income. Such limitations are not imposed with this model. One finds great variety in the problems presented and resolved, the players involved, and the expectations and requests made of the care manager. Staff members work with public and private providers of care, trust officers, attorneys, guardians, conservators, accountants, and many others. The depth of involvement varies—some clients and/or payers want limited consultation while others request a very intense level of involvement. A summary of services provided is shown in Table 1. Some additional characteristics are listed below.

**Community-Based—**Because of independent ownership and not being associated with any institution or service provider, all community options can be tapped when appropriate. The company participates in a number of community activities, thereby bringing a broad understanding and community perspective to its care management program.

**Client-Centered—**While the process used in providing care management is similar to other programs, the breadth and depth of issues and services requested to be "individualized" is unique. The structure supports this customized approach. Staff members are carefully selected to assure a comprehensive list of skills including 1) listening, clarifying expectations, and use of negotiation skills; 2) knowledge and research of clinical issues; 3) capacity to meet standards of care; 4) knowledge of community resources and services; and 5) understanding of the parameters for autonomous decision making. Further, the organizational structure is flattened to take advantage of those skills, giving as much independence to care managers as possible. Use of a self-managing work group is the means of accomplishing this efficiency.

The caseload for each manager is determined by severity of illness and hours projected, not by a minimum caseload "allotment." This arrangement assures that care managers are not overextended. A backup and on-call system is also in place to assure availability for the client's urgent needs.

**Staffing Depth and Versatility—**Care managers have a background in nursing as well as "expanded" practice. Experience in care management, community health, home health, counseling and crisis management, and varied clinical practices and specialties is also reflected in the team. Other disciplines also tapped to round out practice needs include master's prepared social workers, geriatric care managers, and counselors. All receive additional training in RCL care management, communication, and negotiation skills.

Care managers are assigned with consideration of the client's long-term needs whenever possible. An effective backup system assures that clients have someone familiar available. The care managers follow clients from an acute care setting to discharge planning, rehabilitation, or home care.

Requests made by customers may range from short-term consulting on long-term care options to assistance in finding a private caregiver to providing expert testimony for courts of law.

**Table 1.** *Summary of RCF Services*

**Care Management**

- Information and referral
- Assessments, including guardianship determination
- Care plan development and implementation
- Resource development, research, procurement
- Health care monitoring, anticipatory guidance, and education (includes primary care, self-care, episodic care, and long-term care)
- Caregiver procurement and supervision
- Preadmission screening and level of care determinations
- Placement and relocation
- Procurement of needed services, including legal and financial guidance
- Life care plan and cost projection
- Research, securing and coordination of benefits
- Concurrent hospital and facility review and monitoring
- Crisis intervention and problem-solving
- Involuntary transfer assessment, plan, and intervention
- Management of aging-in-place services

**Direct Services**

- Medication management
- Chronic disease monitoring
- Long-term care planning (power of attorney for health care, self determination act planning)

**Consultation**

- Individual, family, or group consultation/counseling
- Classes, training, and workshops
- Research, securing and coordination of benefits, community resources
- Expert testimony and litigation

By working in the bigger health care arena, staff members are able to provide customers with an understanding of the real day-to-day issues they face. Legal, financial, and environmental concerns are incorporated into the more common "health" care planning areas.

Another important asset of the company is the composite experience and knowledge of varied systems. In addition to traditional acute care experience, there is expertise in public health, aging services, rehabilitation, home health, mental health, community resources and services, alcohol and drug issues, and health care reform. Customers receive added value from this knowledge because it assures effective use of services and benefits when addressing individual health care needs. The talents of the care managers allow needs to be anticipated; therefore, crises can frequently be avoided or minimized.

## Clients

Clients come in all ages and present a varied range of needs. Many are frail seniors, often without families to assist them in meeting their changing needs. More often then ever before, seniors seek assistance in planning for their long-term needs before a crisis occurs. Other times it is the adult child or the "sandwich generation" who requests interventions. The services may be for themselves, their children, or their aging family members. Family dynamics are often a challenge. Having a neutral third party is an effective way of dealing with conflict that families may face. Assisting families in decision-making, helping to identify individuals' wishes, and helping to clarify expectations when needs are complex are but a few of the issues individuals and families bring.

There are seven primary sources from which clients are referred; they are as follows:

1) *Financial Managers*—These referrals most often come from such persons as trust officers, accountants, conservators, and guardians. Most often these professionals have skills and expertise in money management, yet realize there is significant unmet need that lies outside their areas of practice. Care management services are aimed at addressing unmet needs, improving quality of life, and managing benefits. Frequently, the assets are saved and out-of-pocket costs are minimized through the care management process. Assessment and monthly progress reports also provide needed accountability.

2) *Attorneys*—Referrals from attorneys may be for health care planning, guardianship assessment, family consulting and mediation, workers compensation, or medical litigation cases. This area of work is complex and exciting and is an excellent use of care management expertise and the use of win-win negotiation tools.

3) *Self-Insured Businesses*—Referrals include catastrophic illness or injury cases, Americans with Disabilities Act cases, and workers compensation or Employee Assistance Program requests. Volume of work in this area is growing and taps care management expertise effectively. Additionally, it provides businesses with alternatives to using legal services only.

4) *Private*—The source of referrals in this category is varied. Discharge planners from acute care settings, families, friends, and general word-of-mouth referrals are included. This area has great demand.

5) *Insurance and Managed Care Organizations*—Referrals include the more traditional approaches to "case" management and reflect a more medical model. Requests include "neutral" assessments for controversial or high-cost cases, information on community resources, contracting for routine services, and assessments for long-term care insurance carriers.

6) *Facilities*—Work done with facilities centers around preadmission screening, training, involuntary transfers, and managing aging-in-place services. This area contains many future needs for collaboration and testing the effectiveness of care management services of long-term care.

7) *Public*—This work includes preadmission screening, training, and specific contract work. Improved collaboration and linkages are needed in this area in order for consumer needs to be adequately met.

# Guidelines for Developing a Care Management Program

**Planning and Advisors**—The value of planning for a "new" service or business is worth noting. Planning and using the expertise available reduces the unknowns and increases the chance of meeting the planned objectives. This holds true for beginning a business, the start-up of new services, or refinement of old services. Drawing on the experience and expertise of others has many advantages. Recognizing the talents of others in the work setting and tapping on those strengths just makes good business sense.

Understanding the expectations of clients is vital in meeting specified outcomes. Many primary referral sources and most clients speak a different language because of nonhealth backgrounds. It is time those in health care listened without their "health care filters" on. What we would hear would probably surprise us. Knowing what is expected and acceptable to the market can help in determining approaches for new and old services.

**Excellence**—Strive for excellence. Care management is a relatively new area of health care and those in the lead have an ethical responsibility to set the community standard. Ethical issues abound in this work and in health care in general. A forum is needed to explore and learn from the work being done.

**Know Your Bias and Collaboration Potential**—Any organization that undertakes care management services will have a built-in bias. Understanding the bias helps in planning, defining unmet need, and identifying needed linkages. To create effective models, more collaboration and testing of models is needed; without it, we collectively support people falling through the cracks—or in some cases, floorboards.

**Define Your Target**—The unmet need in health care is significant. The importance of knowing where and how services will meet that need is equally significant. Focus on the areas you know best, and work with others in their areas of excellence to round out other needed services. Identify your market niche and payer sources, become informed about the key issues and needs and the expectations others have of your services. Planning for short-term objectives assures progress. In today's ever-changing health care arena, with its emphasis on short- and mid-range objectives, set aside time to understand how the BIG picture is shaping up.

**Define Team Responsibilities and Parameters for Action**—In any organization, clarity of purpose and expectations helps create a healthy environment. Because of the dynamic nature of health care and the fluidity of care management in particular, staff members need clear messages. It is important to allow enough time for change and to respect transition and the changes required for staff to mentally adapt to it. For example, RCF has weekly team meetings, monthly in-service sessions, and twice-yearly planning retreats and evaluation meetings. These gatherings are for the full staff; other meetings include the quality improvement committees, management team, individual care conference and supervisory review, and other one-time meetings to address special projects.

**Objectivity and Evaluation**—Develop a solid data base. It is frustrating to look at the amount of data gathered in health care and then at how little we truly know about what is effective in managing an individual's health. A common data base is needed in care management. Efforts should be undertaken to evaluate the effectiveness of different models of care management. We need to focus evaluation efforts on the success(es) of individuals achieving "their desired" health care goals and objectives. Outcomes need to be emphasized, especially individual-specific outcomes that address consumer choice. Those in health care must stop collecting and counting insignificant numbers. The process of collecting more money for providing more services needs to be evaluated against the outcomes produced. By emphasizing outcomes, we increase the likelihood that individuals will accept responsibility for their own health. This approach will lead us to more individual- and family-specific education and, it is to be hoped, distance us from legislating unenforceable or unnecessary requirements. Evaluation and reform of regulations is needed, particularily in long-term care.

# Lessons Learned from Care Management Experience

Be it a large corporation or an individual practice, there are good and bad areas to review and lessons to learn connected with providing care management services. A beginning list follows:

**Advantages of Brokered Care Management**

Meaningful work
People-oriented and client-focuses
Ability to affect many problem areas
Community-centered
Excellent knowledge of resources
Capitalizes on teachable moments
Outcome-oriented
Access to many professionals and gatekeepers
Flat organization promotes adapting to change
Excellent use of creative skills
Continuity of service
Flexibility and adaptability
Control of growth of business
True win-win outcomes
Ability to manage benefits and assets

**Frustrations of Brokered Care Management**

Inconsistent funding sources
Bias against reimbursement for nurse care management services
Public uninformed about what care management services are and how to access those services
Complex services to market, value not well understood
Lots of "semicompetitors" who have initial turf issues
Not well accepted by many doctors; seen as a potential turf issue
Some groups prefer claims or utilization review approach to care management
Few standards exist; common data base lacking
Relatively few professionals with care management experience
Financial constraints
Not enough time to study trends and develop new markets
Managing workload a challenge

**Lessons Learned**

In general, clients, families, and referral sources have been very receptive to the company's service program. Strengths most frequently mentioned include 1) the emphasis on outcomes; 2) attention to behavioral changes; 3) focus on client goals, objectives, and decision-making; 4) continuity and versatility of care managers; 5) commitment to excellence and win-win outcomes; and 6) feeling "heard".

Other lessons learned include these:

A skilled and ethical staff is important
The for-profit model is valuable for a client-centered approach
Independent legal and financial advisers should be used
Learn from mistakes
Promote safe risk-taking
Identify the problem and ownership prior to intervention or action
Health care is in major transition
Nursing can have significant impact on long-term care and health care reform
Care management is in its infancy and needs to be studied
There is no one right model
Collaboration in addressing true health care reform is important
Clients want to maintain control of their lives

## Summary

This chapter has described a customer-centered, community-based model of care management services. The hope was that through the description of this model and the sharing of ideas and insights from "the trenches," the reader would find some value or perspective that could be useful regardless of his or her discipline or outlook. Those interested in developing or refining care management programs may find the following summarized list helpful:

1. Plan before you open doors
2. Identify your community players
3. Determine your community needs
4. Recruit excellent staff (work with educators regarding needed skills and training)
5. Network
6. Determine the setting—community-based versus facility-based—and recognize the difference
7. Be open to change
8. Work toward solid funding sources
9. Work to develop a common data base and methods of evaluating outcomes

What is the future direction for the example company? We know it is effective in delivering care management services. How the concept and process can be applied has not yet been fully tapped. Exploring and developing new applications for care management services is occurring. Projects for studying outcomes are needed and will be explored. Consulting and training services have been expanded to assist others in developing "quality centers." Other areas receiving additional attention include 1) working toward a common data base and use of standards; 2) expanding the use of computers to evaluate and streamline documentation; 3) expanding client-centered services and self-help tools; 4) providing counsel regarding advance directives, health care planning, and conflict resolution; 5) expanding educational and training services; and 6) expanding linkages with current and new referral sources.

## References

American Association of Retired Persons (AARP). *The National Survey of Caregivers: Summary of Findings*. Oct. 19, 1988.

Cassel, Christine, "Money, Medicine, and Methuselah: The Allocation of Health Care Resource in an Aging Society." Third Annual Saward Award Lecture, Portland, Ore., Oct. 16, 1991.

Kutza, Elizabeth. "Population aging" lecture at Portland State University, Oct. 1991.

U.S. Senate Special Committee on Aging. *Aging America: Trends and Projections*. U.S. Department of Health and Human Services, 1991.

Kahn, Sharon. "Using Medicare to Ease the FAS No. 6 Burden." *Business and Health*, Feb. 1992, Vol. 10, No.2:38-47.

Marion Merrell Dow. *Managed Care Digest: HMO Edition*. 1991.

Frieden, Joyce. "What's Ahead for Managed Care." *Business and Health*, Dec. 1991, Vol. 9, No. 13:43-49.

# 18

# The Independent Nurse Case Manager

Susan L. Wellons, RN, BSN

*Those who have wondered if they have what it takes to become an independent nurse case manager will be especially interested in this chapter, in which Susan Wellons explores the strengths and talents needed to accomplish this daunting objective.*—R.S.H.

I would like to provide a general overview of "case management" from an independent nurse case management perspective. Most "case managers" are associated with large health care systems such as managed care organizations, health maintenance organizations, and traditional hospital systems. Most of these case managers fall into the episodic care case management and self-care case management models, which are largely driven and defined by larger organizations other than the individual case manager per se.

The independent nurse case manager from a nursing perspective is governed by respective nurse practice acts and her professional code of ethics. All of these arenas can be and very often are the various systems that the independent nurse case manager must deal with through a long continuum of care needs within an individually tailored plan.

Case management in the generic sense is a basic process with commonalities within various health disciplines and service providers. It is difficult to define case management generically since in essence all of us case manage our own lives (self-care case management). Case management can apply to any situation at any time whether it be medical case management/health care case management, social service case management, or vocational case management. Each discipline is a specialty in and of itself that directs needs in a particular area at a particular time. All of these disciplines work toward a common goal of optimal health and recovery. However, goals can vary, depending on the sponsoring institution providing the case management. These directives are often focused on the "bottom line" and quality of care considerations.

# Definition of Case Management

The National Task Force Steering Committee on Case Management, formed in February 1991, developed a definition of generic case management followed by the beginnings of a pyramid of the process utilized in case management. The definitions of case management that have arisen throughout the country have been collected by the task force to determine the commonalities between disciplines providing case management as well as to serve as resource materials for the group in its efforts to create one distinct definition that is suitable in a general generic area. This is not an easy process and is still ongoing. Another charge given to the national task force was to develop a body of knowledge and to use this to generate a consistent reference for the case management process and application.

From a nursing case manager perspective, medical case management or health care case management are the terms most often utilized. This is primarily because of the training involved with the nursing degree and professional licenser as well as the issues that arise in health care and health maintenance and health care provision and promotion. Traditionally, the RN has been the highly specialized generalist who has overseen the health care needs of the individual with illness or disability and dysfunction. This probably stems from the initial nursing role of public health nurse.

Although I am an independent nurse case manager, the team approach is central to my practice. Every team needs a coordinator, which often becomes the role of the nurse case manager. Social work has often been a partner in that role.

All components required to prevent, minimize, or optimize health care cannot be provided by any one individual. This process is tailored to an individual set of circumstances with human variable components and is a dynamic process.

One analogy is that of an orchestra and a conductor. Neither can function alone and are fragmented pieces without any connection to the other. Although these pieces are unique and specialized to create the end product for an optimal outcome, without a consistent smooth flow and timing the orchestra and the conductor fail. Another example is that of a noncooperative multidisciplinary team that can be extremely slow to proceed, losing sight of its goal of tailoring care to the individual.

Much has been written about the team approach in many multidisciplinary situations, particularly in medical settings. The team approach, however, is the exception rather than the rule. Each discipline functions within its own expertise, and interdisciplinary communication and decision making is usually extremely limited. Only in rehabilitation medicine do we see the efforts of a team approach achieved if that team is in fact cooperative.

National concern and support for case management is rapidly growing. Unfortunately, there are no guidelines, standards, or minimum qualifications established for case management. From the nursing perspective, the nursing profession has developed standards for case management primarily through various nursing groups and ultimately extending to the nurse practice acts and the professional governing body as related to licensor. Other standards and guidelines have recently been developed in the geriatric long-term care community and within the national association of rehabilitation professionals in the private sector. This, however, has not evolved until the last year or two.

The case management process and application has been a part of nursing practice for over 20 years. This can be seen through some large insurers who have historically utilized nursing services to assess the global picture of an individual's needs, not only in health care but all areas that affect recovery. These assessment skills emanate from public health and community nursing models.

My observations over the last two to three years are that the main flux of nurse case management or case management in general has caused a national pandemonium because there are no guidelines, standards, or minimum requirements for quality assurance. What has driven this case management trend is economics. Insurance and the federal government are the two main funding bodies for health care. Although there are individuals who can pay for their own care, they are extremely wealthy, and usually those individuals have extended health insurance policies and are in the minority.

The economic concern is that of eliminating wasted time and dollars with overtreatment or unnecessary or inappropriate treatment. There is also the realization that the individual is not a body part alone in relation to the injury; that the individual as a whole is affected when injury, illness or disability occur. The other difficult issues arising have been our social disincentives, with workers compensation and disability monies often seen as survival mechanisms.

Other issues are those of prevention and minimizing secondary problems and optimizing appropriate, timely treatment. Prevention has always been difficult to institute since the outcomes are not particularly observable other than maintaining health or preventing potential problems, illness, etc. Although we know various situations are harmful to us (smoking, alcohol, certain sexual practices), an epidemic proportion of disease or illness needs to occur before prevention measures are instilled. Therefore, case management is a difficult process to quantify because of this prevention and promotion orientation.

We know through time and experience that case management is an effective economic means to monitor health care dollars and utilize them to their optimal benefit. Unfortunately, we are still in our infancy with regard to the statistical gathering of proof to validate this practice.

Turf issues provide many of the reasons why case management is slow to catch on. Large organizations such as managed care organizations and hospital systems also run the risk that an assembly line case manager will be developed who is not necessarily tailoring to the individual's need but rather following a computerized program or simply authorization for this or that in relation to a benefit plan. The true global perspective is that if the job is done right in the first place and those dollars are spent appropriately, costs will be significantly reduced in the long run. It is still difficult for corporations and large organizations to see that this is of financial benefit. Although we live in a high-tech age, we are human beings, and therefore human contact often can be the most therapeutic and effective in assessment and evaluation and promotion of health and functional productivity. This is one of the roles of the independent nurse case manager.

Another problem has been developing minimum standards and qualifications appropriate for the provision of case management. This ultimately will have to be acomplished both within those professions providing nursing case management and national organizations.

Case management is pro-active, preventive, and empowering, in contrast to the reactive stance that society has normally taken regarding medical health care and social issues. The primary goal of the independent nurse case manager is to obtain the highest level of functional productivity or maintenance, to institute restorative measures if applicable, or basically enhance the individual's existence.

# Skills Needed by an Independent Case Manager

Many of the characteristics I will identify for the independent case manager are those I have observed over time working with a number of case managers in various health disciplines.

- The independent nurse case manager must be independent and autonomous—to be able to achieve the goals of providing optimal outcomes and promoting optimal health.
- The case manager must be assertive (not aggressive), understand tactful communication, and have seasoned communication skills. Often case management can assume a negative perception if demands are being made without cooperative communication or consideration of the individual.
- The case manager should be confident and not easily intimidated by any uncooperative players that may be involved. The case manager should expect some legal, medical, or large organizational resistance to the global issues that may affect recovery or maintenance.
- Case managers must be good time managers, which can sometimes mean being a delegator of tasks when those tasks are not appropriate to an individual's scope of practice and would be more efficiently performed by others.
- The case manager must be a good negotiator and understand the nature and benefit of compromise when necessary. Working within rigid and well-defined boundaries sometimes calls for creative problem solving if resources are not available.
- The case manager must be economically informed and understand the "big picture" of economics locally, on the state level, nationally, and globally.
- Business and legal savvy are also vital. As an independent nurse case manager, he/she must be legally aware of limits in the controlling nurse practice act or other regulating professional bodies.
- The nurse case manager must have good life skills and experience. Appreciation of culture and religion are a must.
- The case manager should be sensitive and a good listener, tolerant of criticism.
- Finally, the case manager must never assume he/she knows everything and can do it alone.

## Experience

An individual doing case management should have no less than three to five years in acute care experience or rehabilitation knowledge. That means knowledge of nursing principles but also an understanding of the general practices, therapies, and social services that may be necessary.

Liability risks are major considerations in an independent case management practice. Knowing the scope of practice of your specialty is a must. It is vital not to overstep the limits of your practice and knowledge and to utilize those individuals who are more knowledgeable than you in particular areas where needs are identified.

Malpractice issues and scope of practice often are associated with objective advocacy. Traditionally, advocacy of the patient has been first and foremost; however, extreme patient advocacy can also create disharmony, leading to a co-dependent relationship. Although dependence in varying degrees exists in many ways, fostering independent living to whatever degree possible is important—in other words, providing the individual with control and responsibility for his or her own life, rather than assuming control and assuming to know what is best without collaboration.

Ethical considerations are becomimg increasingly important in medical management. We are being forced to address ethical issues only because the economic impacts have now become so great that ethics in application of medicine are now being questioned. I perceive the next ten years to be an ethical turmoil in determining what is appropriate and reasonable in light of the individual's goals vs. case management plans or other system goals.

The last vital issue for the independent nurse case manager is the "business side" of the practice. In my experience, there is no substitute for a good certified public accountant if the case manager's preparaton is deficient in this area.

Other issues to consider are nonbillable time vs. billable time in a small business, and all that goes into the nonbillable time. In order to support cash flow for your business, billable time should be adequate. Nonbillable time should be spent in activities that add value to your billable time, such as improving the efficiency of your paperwork, marketing efforts, and continuing education.

## Referral Sources

Referral sources can be insurance companies with various types of policy and benefit packages, preferred provider organizations, HMOs, MCOs, state and federal government agencies, self-insured employers, legal offices with trust clients, families, primary providers, guardianships or other independent case management businesses.

## Catastrophic Case Management

In catastrophic case management or traumatic case management, the independent case manager is called at the time of injury to anticipate or determine what amount of disability may be permanent or may affect that individual over time. This form of case management is more time intensive and there are often more individuals involved, particularly in the clinical setting, and there is often crisis intervention with family or significant others. Sometimes, no family exists at all, which itself can be a crisis. There are usually multiple medical problems/complications or risks. More frequent reporting is required as well as close contact with the client contracting for case management services to keep all parties informed. This is most often a long-term process requiring months to years, and often a permanent disability is anticipated.

The independent nurse case manager functions on many levels. Although medical and nursing knowledge are important prerequisites for the role, many other kinds of knowledge need be acquired. Unfortunately, none of this other knowledge is easily learned, nor is it included in academic preparation. National task forces are just now coming to grips with a definition of the role and perhaps critieria upon which to initiate a certification process. The call is out to those of us who either aspire to be or are independent nurse case managers to contribute knowledge to our local, state, and federal organizations.

# 19

# Life Care Plan

Susan N. Riddick, RN

*For those with a catastrophic illness or injury, a life care plan is essential. Case managers who have occasion to work with such clients will benefit from this brief description of the life care plan. Ms. Riddick incorporates the various aspects of care—from self-care to episodic care—in her assessment of the situation.*—R.S.H.

## Origins of Service Coordination/ Case Management

Community service coordination, a forerunner of case management, began at the turn of the century in public health programs. Providing service coordination has always been the focus of public health nursing. Service coordination has evolved into case management, but case management as defined has expanded considerably upon the coordination of community services. Today, catastrophic injury case management often relies on the development of a life care plan, which identifies services needed to provide a continuum of care throughout an individual's lifetime.

The concept of continuum of care was used following World War II to describe the extended community services necessary to provide care for discharged psychiatric patients. The term *case management* first appeared in the early 1970s in social welfare literature, followed closely by articles in the nursing literature. The specific activities of the nurse case manager have been well described in the preceding chapters. These activities blend with the stages of the nursing process to form a framework for nurse case management activities (ANA, 1988).

In 1981, Paul M. Deutsch and Frederick Raffa first published the original format in legal literature outlining the concept of life care planning as a specific case management tool. A life care plan provides an organized, standardized and consistent, time-efficient, and comprehensive method for providing the framework of services needed during the continuum of care. The plan is designed to address quality of life issues, long-term comprehensive needs for patients and family, complications of the conditions, and nonmedical issues (Weed and Riddick, 1990).

## Key Concepts

The target population for life care planning is persons who have had catastrophic injuries and/or who have chronic disabling conditions. Diagnoses can include severe traumatic brain injury, spinal cord injury, amputation and multiple fractures, severe burns, premature birth, congenital anomalies, organ failures in transplants, cancer, AIDS, diabetes, and cardiac and pulmonary disease. These diagnoses are commonly associated with complex medical issues that will require the ongoing delivery of services from the health care system.

One of the challenges of the catastrophic injury case manager in today's health care industry is accessing and unraveling the health care delivery service system while at the same time identifying appropriate and cost-effective care within that system of services.

A life care plan for severely disabled individuals can serve as the necessary framework for successful catastrophic injury case management. Key concepts to life care planning include the following:

— individually specific, not injury-specific
— inclusive of both medical and nonmedical issues
— life-long
— dynamic (living document)
— can be viewed as a preventive rehabilitation tool

Imperative to the development of a life care plan is the establishment of a consistent, systematic approach to developing the care plan. A step-by-step approach should be developed in order to avoid overlooking any of the many complex issues related to long-term planning for a severely disabled individual. A consistent method needs to be developed to identify the problem list, determine expected outcomes for each individual problem, identify the required types of support services necessary to achieve the individual outcomes, the amount of each service to be provided, and calculation of the cost of providing the listed services.

The process of life care planning parallels very nicely with the stages of the nursing process that forms the framework of medical case management. These stages include interaction, assessment, planning, implementation, and evaluation.

# The Process of Life Care Planning

## Medical Records Review

The first step for a life care planner must be to request all medical records, consultations, depositions, school records and work records. Review of this information can provide the life care planner with an abundance of information, including not only medical diagnoses and treatment, but information pertaining to the individual's psychosocial adjustment and insight into his or her disability, support systems—either from within the family unit or from extended family and friends—and social information, including vocational and avocational interests. During the medical records review, it is useful to identify each member of the treatment team who will subsequently be involved in the life care planning process.

Key to the medical records review is the confirmation of the diagnosis. Before a life care planner can design a plan, there must be intimate knowledge and understanding of the medical aspects of the disability and the associated long-term care issues and options, as well as the functional implications of the disability and how it will affect the client's day-to-day life.

## Client/Family Interview

The client/family interview is the next step in investigating the background information necessary to the life care planning process. If at all possible, the client is interviewed in the hospital or treatment facility where he/she is residing. If the client resides at home, the interview should take place in the residence rather than in a professional setting. Family members should be included during the interview process.

During the family/client interview, the care planner obtains information that includes a medical social history, family history, socioeconomic status, employment history, school history, current treatment team, and current physical and emotional status, including limitations, current medical treatment, and long-term plans and desires. During this lengthy interview (it often takes three to five hours or longer), the care planner can begin to develop some insight into how the family has dealt with the client's disability, their experiences with rehabilitation, and their individual investment in this individual's long-term care planning. During the interview process, the care planner has an obligation to make sure that the disabled client fully understands who this professional is, his or her educational background, work background, and expertise in this particular disability. By taking the time to educate the client, the care planner is showing a degree of respect that is necessary to gain the confidence of both the client and the family.

Another part of the family/client interview includes developing an inventory of both supplies and equipment utilized by the client. Several tools have been developed by life care planners to assist in the gathering of this information. It is necessary to obtain not only the inventory of equipment but the dates of purchase and the vendor.

## Treatment Team Interview

The next phase of life care planning involves the interview of the treatment team. Although life care plans have emerged over the past ten years as a widely accepted process for cost management and economic projections, many health care professionals are still unfamiliar with the concept of life care planning. The Life Care Plan Checklist that appears at the end of this chapter can serve as a useful working document that can assist in the process of long-term planning. It is up to the life care planner to then coordinate, communicate, and clarify all information to each member of the treatment team. An example of this might be as follows: The client is a three-year-old female child with cerebral palsy. The life care planner is meeting with the therapist at the local cerebral palsy clinic. The care planner is specifically attempting to identify the long-term physical therapy needs of this child. The occupational therapist and physical therapist are both consulted in developing a recommendation. The therapists recommended that this child receive physical therapy treatments three times per week by a professional physical therapist until the age of 18. Thereafter, they recommended a home therapy program that could be administered by family members and other caretakers. The life care planner is ultimately responsible for explaining these recommendations to the other members of the care team. In this situation, the orthopedic physician caring for this child agreed with the recommendations and projections as established by the therapists. Therefore, this information was included as part of the life care plan. At this phase in the process, the care planner is beginning to develop an initial life care plan by identifying long-term care issues and options.

## Resource Investigation

The initial life care planning goes hand in hand with investigation into resources, cost, and availability of services. The process of investigating resources can be a long and arduous task involving research of community and national resources. The life care planner must become knowledgeable about appropriate facilities to treat specific disabilities. The knowledgeable expert will also be able to identify standard of care issues specific to the disability. It is suggested that life care planners take the time to tour various specialized rehabilitation programs that are available for specific injuries such as spinal cord, burn injuries, and head trauma. Professional networking can play a large part in the development of resource investigation.

## Report—The Life Care Plan

The final stage of life care planning involves compiling the life care plan information and presenting it in a form that can be thoroughly understood by the client, family, treatment team, and payer. Styles of reporting the information vary from life care planner to life care planner. The individual style for presenting information should remain consistent and thorough. The viewer should gather a clear understanding of the disability and its effect on the individual's day-to-day life, the short- and long-term needs of the individual and family, the complications of the condition, and the nonmedical issues relevant to this client. The plan should be specific in identifying resources and costs, as well as quality of life issues.

## Areas to be Covered by a Life Care Plan

Life care plans have been published in a variety of sources. The most authoritative source is *The Guide to Rehabilitation* (Deutsch and Sawyer, 1985). A general description can be found in *The Rehabilitation Consultant's Handbook* (Weed and Field, 1990).

The following is an overview of topics to be covered in a life care plan:

1. Projected Evaluations
2. Projected Therapeutic Modalities
3. Diagnostic Testing/Educational Assessment
4. Wheelchair Needs
5. Wheelchair Accessories and Maintenance
6. Orthopedic Equipment
7. Orthotics/Prosthetics
8. Aids for Independent Function
9. Home Furnishing and Accessories
10. Drug Supply Needs

11. Home Care/Facility Care
12. Future Medical Routine
13. Future Medical Care: Surgical Intervention or Aggressive Treatment
14. Transportation
15. Potential Complications
16. Architectural Renovations
17. Leisure and/or Recreational Equipment and Services

Life care plans are now being used in a variety of settings. Workers compensation agencies use life care plans to help set reserves for insurance companies, to control costs, and to effectively coordinate care. Personal injury and medical malpractice attorneys utilize life care plans to achieve settlements. Medical case managers, families and patients are using life care plans as the framework for successful, cost-effective case management.

# 20

## Community Home Visiting Services

Cecelia Capuzzi, RN, PhD

*Although most case management services are not like this one at Oregon Health Sciences University, much can be gained from examination of the process followed by the faculty of the institution in designing and implementing the program. This program anticipated and included the primary care case management dimension. Also included were interesting applications for flow charts, record-keeping forms, and data bases.*—R.S.H.

Although the Oregon Health Sciences University School of Nursing has sponsored clinical practices such as a nurse midwifery program since the late 1970s, it is only recently that faculty practices have been promoted. In 1991, the school initiated a faculty practice plan encouraging individual faculty to develop independent practices. The purpose of these practices was threefold: to provide nursing faculty the opportunity to maintain clinical expertise, to provide clinical sites for students where faculty could serve as role models, and to generate additional revenue.

Soon after the initiation of the faculty practice plan, it was seen that the university's hospital and clinics needed a home visiting service for their maternity patients. The only community resources providing home visiting services to maternity patients were the county public health agencies; and unless the situation was high risk, a referral either was denied or put on a waiting list. The School of Nursing's proposal to develop a home visiting service for maternity patients was received favorably by the hospital and clinic administrators.

I was on the faculty in the School of Nursing and taught undergraduate and graduate students in the Community Health Care Systems Department. The basis of the department's teaching, research, and practice was population-focused nursing, which included developing and managing community services. When I was approached by the department chairperson about starting a maternity home visiting service as a faculty practice, I was excited with the prospect, as I also was involved with several state policy groups advocating a comprehensive state maternity care system that included case management. This was an opportunity to implement some of my ideas.

# Development of Community Home Visiting Services

The first step in developing the faculty practice was to meet with the directors of the clinics to verify their needs and to gather information to develop a system for referral, coordination, and service delivery. Although I learned that the maternity clinics offered case management services, I decided that the home visiting program also needed a case management system that interfaced with those provided by our suppliers (i.e., the hospital and clinics).

During these meetings, I was given the names of other key individuals who were providing care to the maternity clients either in the clinics or in the hospital. In addition, I left with a tentative agreement that the hospital units and clinics would make referrals to my service once I developed the program.

Next, I met with the individuals whose names were mentioned during the meetings with the clinic directors; these included the nurse managers of the clinics and the mother-baby units, the program manager of the state's perinatal outreach program (located at the university), and the nursing discharge planners. Furthermore, I met with individuals from county public health departments; the state's Medicaid program; the state's health division, which was implementing a high-risk infant tracking system that followed developmentally disabled infants; and others I knew through my involvement with the state perinatal committees.

After collecting the initial information about the hospital and clinic needs, the current referral process, the county public health department programs, and the patient criteria for the specialized perinatal programs, I designed the faculty practice known as Community Home Visiting Services (CHVS). CHVS included two types of services: 1) a home visiting program and 2) case management. The case management service utilized a "brokered care" model where the goal was to match maternity patients with appropriate services.

Employing a systems approach, I organized the information that I had gathered in order to develop a detailed work plan to initiate the practice. I identified the *inputs, thruputs, outputs*, and *environmental factors* relating to CHVS, and further delineated each element in the model (see Figure 1).

The *suppliers* for the CHVS were the referral sources for the CHVS's customers. The major suppliers would be the university hospital (episodic care) and the clinics (primary care), although CHVS accepted customers from other referral sources (e.g., county public health clinics, community clinics, HMOs) or self-referrals. The *customers* for CHVS included both the *primary care case managers* (i.e., social workers, discharge planning nurses) and the *patients* (prenatal and postpartum women and their infants). Other inputs into the CHVS system included 1) professional staff who were the nursing faculty in the Community Health Care Systems Department, 2) *nursing students*, 3) the *support staff* (i.e., secretarial and billing personnel) and 4) *equipment and supplies*.

Five thruputs were identified. First were the *practice management* activities needed to develop and operate the practice and interact with the suppliers. These activities included marketing the faculty practice, writing contracts and policies, developing recordkeeping and data base systems, and establishing quality control measures.

Next were two categories of *customer services* thruputs: patient care services and primary care case manager services. The patient care services included intake, admission, assessment, intervention, monitoring, coordination, referral, advocacy, and case closure. The primary care case manager services included feedback and coordination of client care. The case management system provided to these clients is best illustrated as two overlapping case management systems with the client in the center (see Figure 2).

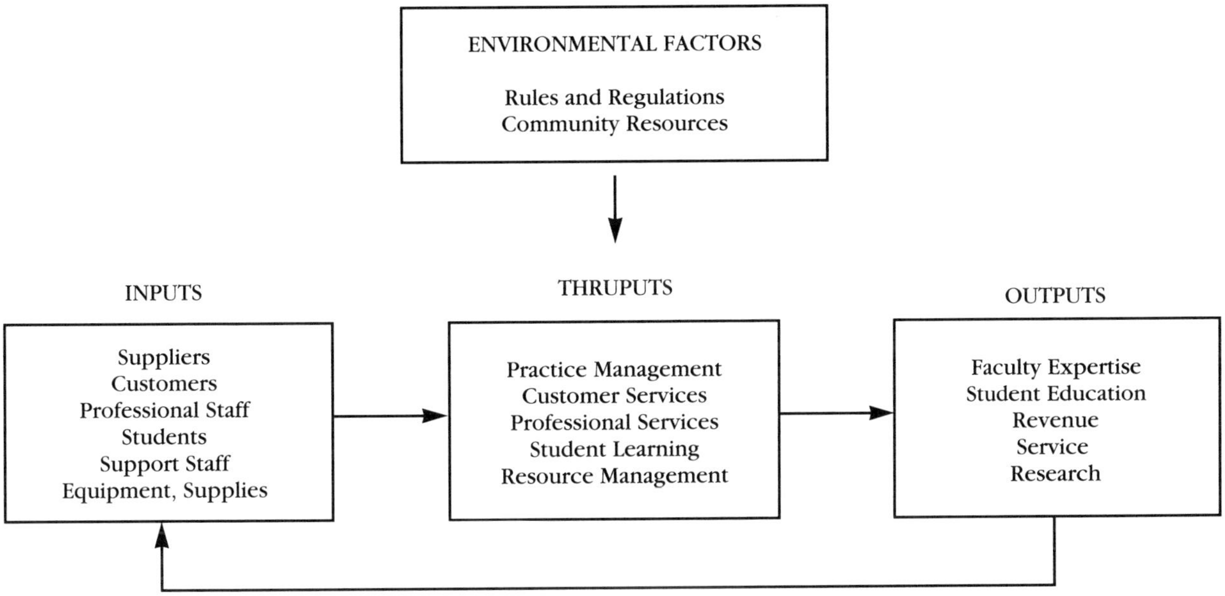


**Figure 1.** *A systems model of the Community Home Visiting Service*

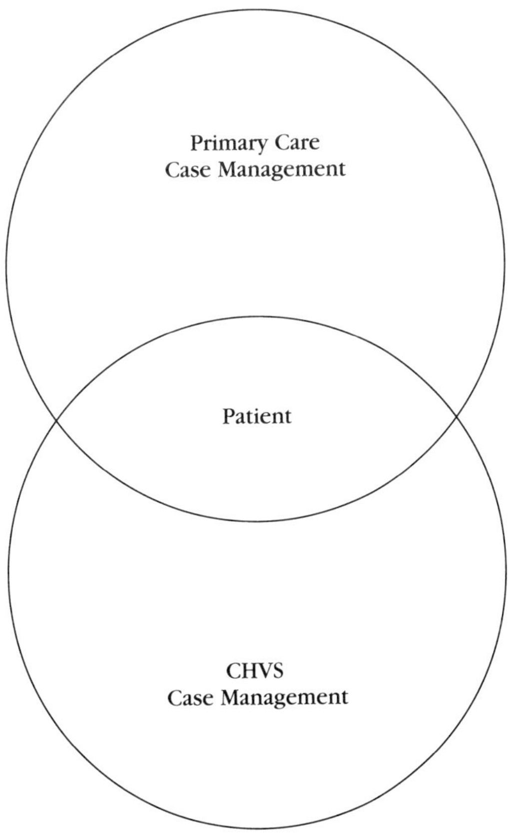


**Figure 2.** *An interaction of case management systems*

Third were the *professional staff services,* which included staff development and resource support. Educational seminars were planned and a small library of references was obtained. Furthermore, an advisory board of community and professional experts was formed to provided consultation, and a medical advisor was appointed to serve the program.

Next were the *student learning* thruputs, which involved all faculty-student interactions and activities that facilitated the student's education. The community health nursing classes guided these activities.

Last were the *resource management* activities, such as the procurement of equipment and supplies, billing procedures, management of income, and inventory accounting.

Three of the system's outputs that were identified were associated with the purposes of the faculty practice plan cited earlier—*faculty expertise, student education,* and *revenue*. A fourth output of the system was *service*—to the suppliers and to the patients. Service outcomes were to be evaluated in terms of customer satisfaction, patient satisfaction, resolution of patient problems, and increases in client health status. In the future, a fifth outcome will be *nursing research*. The faculty practice serves as a setting in which to test models of case management and client outcomes.

In the environment, there were *university, state, federal, and professional rules and regulations* that affect the operations of the CHVS. I investigated their impact on the practice's design and made the necessary adjustments. Also in the environment were other *community resources* that were similar or complimentary to the services provided by CHVS. These resources also influenced the operations of the practice.

In summary, I first conceptually designed the CHVS practice using a system. Next, it was time to test the system and begin to provide services. At this time, several tools for case management were developed.

# Case Management Tools for the CHVS

In order to administer the CHVS, including the case management component, I designed three types of tools: *flow sheets, recordkeeping forms*, and *data bases*. After meeting with key individuals involved with the current client referral processes in the hospital and clinics, I constructed a draft *referral flow sheet* illustrating CHVS's interaction with this system. The draft was sent to these individuals for review, and after several reiterations, the process for making referrals to CHVS was established. In addition, the referral flow sheet showed the process that we used after receiving the referral, including the provision for feedback to the primary care case managers (see Figure 3).

Next, I developed a *referral form* for the suppliers; the information on the referral form requested basic information about the client (e.g., name, address, date of birth, Medicaid number, reason for referral) . This information was used to process the referral and to initiate a computer *data base* for each client. The referral form also was included in the patient's record (see Figure 4).

I discovered that I needed another form to record each client's intake process. On intake, a telephone check of the patient's Medicaid eligibility was made. Medicaid guarantees that the information given about a client's eligibility status is accurate, thus a record of the call was necessary in case there were future billing problems. In addition, a check was made to verify that no other community health nurse was visiting the patient. This information was recorded on a *client intake form* (see Figure 5).

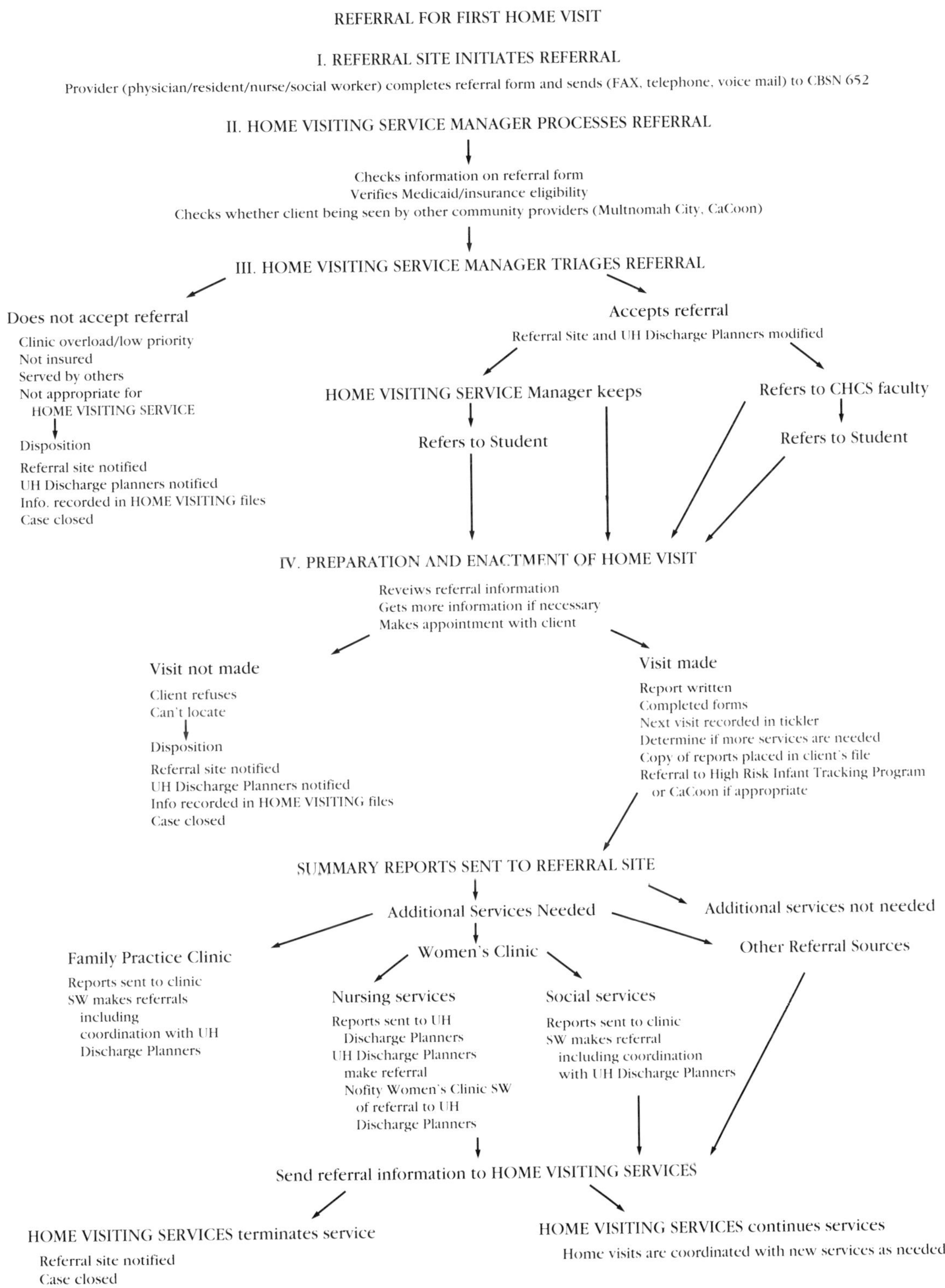


**Figure 3.** *Referral flow sheet*

COMMUNITY HEALTH CARE SYSTEMS
HOME VISITING SERVICES

REFERRAL FORM

Med Rec No.
Name
Date of Birth

SECTION A CLIENT INFORMATION

Address: ______ City/State ______ Zip ______

Home Phone: ______ Msg/Day Phone: ______ Msg Name: ______

G ____ P ____ A ____ L ____ EDC ______ Last Clinic Visit Date/Location: ______

Substance Abuse HX: ______

Visiting Services discussed? ___ Client Agreeable? ___ Primary Language: ______ Need Interpreter?: ___

REFERRAL SOURCE INFORMATION:

Prenatal Care Provider: ______ Beeper #: ____ Clinic ______ Phone #: ______

Clinic Team Nurse: ______ Social Worker: ______ SW Phone/Beeper: ______

Primary Care Provider (if different from above): ______ Agency: ______ Phone #: ______

SPECIFIC CONCERNS: (May send/fax copy of client problem list)

CURRENT MEDICATION/TREATMENTS:

EXPECTATION OF CHN:

______ Signature

______ Phone #

______ Date

**Figure 4.** *CHFS Referral Form*

Using the above information, the referral either was accepted or rejected. If the referral was accepted, contact was made with the patient to arrange a home visit; if not accepted, the referral was returned to the supplier with an explanation. Also, if the patient could not be contacted after several attempts, or refused the service, the referral was returned to the supplier. Additionally, this information was recorded on the intake form, placed in the client's chart, and entered in the patient's data base.

At the time of the first home visit, an initial assessment was made. From this assessment, a plan of care was developed and services were provided. Data about the assessments, nursing diagnoses, plan of care, services rendered, and patient's progress were recorded on separate forms

COMMUNITY HEALTH CARE SYSTEMS
HOME VISITING SERVICES

Client Intake Form

Name ______________________________ DOB ______________

Date on referral form ______________ Date referral received ______________

Medicaid Confirmation:

Medicaid ID # ______________________

_____ Recipient eligible since ______________

_____ Eligibility undetermined

_____ Recipient invalid

Name of verifier ______________________ Date ______________________

Health Department Confirmation:

_____ Health Department already following

_____ Health Department Field Services unable to follow for ______________

CHVS to follow until Health Department is able to

Health Department ______________ Person contacted ______________

Name of verifier ______________________ Date ______________________

Disposition:

_____ Referral accepted

_____ Case opened

_____ Case not opened, Reason:

_____ Referral not accepted, Reason for not accepting:

_____ HD already following or plans to follow

_____ Not appropriate for CHVS, Reason:

________________________________________________

_____ Referral not received in time to meet Medicaid guidelines

_____ Other, Reason:

________________________________________________

Date approved or denied ________________________________________

**Figure 5.** *CHVS Intake Form*

```
CHVSDATA.PFS     Enter search instructions to find the records.   , Page 1 of 2
 F1-Help  F2-Search  F3-Edit  F4-Quick Entry                        F10-Continue
ÉÉÉÉÉÉÉÉÉÉÉÉÉÉÉÉÉÉÉÉÉÉÉÉÉÉÉÉÉÉÉÉÉÉÉÉÉÉÉÉÉÉÉÉÉÉÉÉÉÉÉÉÉÉÉÉÉÉÉÉÉÉÉÉÉÉÉÉÉÉÉÉÉÉÉÉÉÉ
PT NAME:                                 DOB:        AGE:     SEX:   ETH:    MAR S:
UH #:              INS:             MC #:            EDC:              DEL DT:
ADDRESS:                            CITY:            COUNTY:                   STATE:
ZIP:             HOME #:            MSG#:            MSG NAME:
AREA:            WK#:            WK NAME:                              WK AMT:
EMERG CONT:                      EMERG #:          EMERG REL:
FA NAME:                         FA DOB:           FA AGE:    FA WITH:    FA ETH:
I#1 NAME:                        I#1 DOB:          I#1 SEX:     I#1 UH#:
I#2 NAME:                        I#2 DOB:          I#2 SEX:     I#2 UH#:
REF SOURCE:          PRIM PROV:                    PRIM AG:     PRIM #:
HV #1:               HV #2:               HV #3:                 HV #4:
PROVIDER #1:         PROVIDER #2:         PROVIDER #3:           PROVIDER #4:
CHG1:                CHG2:                CHG3:                  CHG4:
BILL #1:   NB#1:     BILL #2:   NB#2:     BILL #3:   NB#3:       BILL #4:   NB#4:
#1BY:                #2BY:                #3BY:                  #4BY:
#1TM:     #1CHT:     #2TM:      #2CHT:    #3TM:      #3CHT:      #4TM:      #4CHT:
#1TL TM:   #1MI:     #2TL TM:    #2MI:    #3TL TM:    #3MI:      #4TL TM:    #4MI:
TOTAL:           AMT PAID:         BL NPD:          AMT NB:             BALANCE:
COMMENT:                       OTHER INS:                        PYMT SOURCE:
DISP:                CLOSE DT:           ADD'L:                  ADD MI:
DUE:               FORM DT:            DATE REC'D:          DATE APP/DEN:
ºººººººººº1ººººººººº2ººººººººº3ººººººººº4ººººººººº5ººººººººº6ººººººººº7ººººººººº8

CHVSDATA.PFS     Enter search instructions to find the records.     Page 2 of 2
 F1-Help  F2-Search  F3-Edit  F4-Quick Entry                        F10-Continue
ÉÉÉÉÉÉÉÉÉÉÉÉÉÉÉÉÉÉÉÉÉÉÉÉÉÉÉÉÉÉÉÉÉÉÉÉÉÉÉÉÉÉÉÉÉÉÉÉÉÉÉÉÉÉÉÉÉÉÉÉÉÉÉÉÉÉÉÉÉÉÉÉÉÉÉÉÉÉ
DIAGNOSIS:       PLACE OF SERVICE:        PROCEDURE CODE:        DIAGNOSIS CODE:
DAYS OR UNITS:          TYPE OF SERVICE CODES:                   FACILITY #:
#HSE:     #CHILD:    #CHILD WITH:    CHILD NMS:
ICD9:                       FUNC STATUS:
NSG DX:
NSG OUTCOMES:
NSG INTERVENTIONS:
ORIGINAL ENTRY DATE:                      ENTRY DATE:
DIRECTIONS:
```

**Figure 6.** *CHVS Client Data Base*

comprising the client's record. These data are updated after each subsequent home visit. Additionally, after each home visit was completed, a summary was dictated and a copy sent to the supplier to be placed in the patient's record.

If it was determined that the patient needed additional resources after the visit, either a referral was made by us or we communicated the need to the supplier's primary care case manager. If the primary care case manager coordinated the referral, we continued to communicate with the case manager until we were assured that the services were provided.

Management data (i.e., date of home visit, provider making visit, amount of time for home visit, mileage for visit, and date of next scheduled appointment) also were entered in the patient's data base (see Figure 6). These data assisted us with the billing, client tracking, and evaluation. A weekly list of clients due for home visits or a monthly summary of referrals and home visits are two examples of reports that I created from the data base. Moreover, I was able to produce a six-month report for feedback to suppliers on the progress of the service.

The tracking of billing and reimbursements also was feasible using the client data base. Information on which home visits had been billed and payments received was entered into the data base. At the end of each month, a report of unbilled claims was generated and sent to the billing office.

In order to develop a quality control system, I first identified the information categories that were necessary. These categories were identified by looking at the Medicaid requirements for documentation; the CHVS outcomes; the standards for community health, home health and maternal-child nursing; a review of the relevant literature; and the recommended items for a nursing minimum data set. Next, I determined that we were collecting these data, and last, I created a separate *quality control data base*. The decision to have this data base separate from the client data base was for efficiency. Although I needed the quality data for evaluation, I did not need it in the day-to-day operations of the practice.

I have been operating the CHVS for ten months and we have had more than 300 referrals. With few modifications, the referral system is operating efficiently.

One important lesson that I learned was that even though the supplier had a case management system, it was necessary that I also develop the mechanisms for case management. The CHVS system interacts with those in the primary and episodic settings. Without having our own case management system, our clients would receive fragmented care.

At times, we found that the supplier had someone identified as a case manager, but the role was limited. In those cases, we expanded the patient's care. Furthermore, some case managers were comfortable in providing the social service assistance that patients needed, but were not secure in providing health assistance; in these instances, our system became prominent.

A second important lesson I learned is that a computer with a data management program is invaluable for administration of the practice that includes the case management functions of tracking and coordination. A computer allows for data storage and program revision as new needs are identified. Although there may be preprogrammed software, we found that creating our own forms and data bases met our individualized needs. After ten months of operation, we are prepared to expanded our services to serve a greater number of clients.

# Index

## D

## I



## J/K



## L



## M

## N/O



## P

## T



## U/V



## W/Z